About the Author

Kris Black has been creating interactive experiences since his junior year in high school, far back in 1993, using Apple's HyperCard program, which allowed him to create stacks of digital cards containing information, much like web pages within a website. He wasn't introduced to HTML, the code behind the web, until he took a computer science 101 course in 1998.

After graduating from the University of South Carolina, Kris began his career as a graphic designer for the South Carolina Department of Health and Environmental Control (SC DHEC) and did web design in his spare time as a hobby. After he was promoted to Art and Photography Director at SC DHEC, he decided it was time for a change. He began freelancing, building websites for clients using several different popular — and unpopular — blogging and website building tools. In 2004, after many frustrating and sleepless nights, Kris began favoring a lesser-known website building tool called Squarespace.

In 2009, Kris was offered the opportunity to work for Squarespace, Inc. as a customer support specialist. Assisting customers helped Kris gain an even deeper knowledge about using Squarespace.

In mid-2011, after leaving Squarespace, Inc. Kris continued creating and developing websites for his clients under a new business, black&hue, LLC with his business partner. He continues to use Squarespace exclusively for all site projects because he believes it offers his clients the best experience for building and maintaining their websites.

Kris and his wife live in Columbia, South Carolina. They have two creative and wonderful children who are beginning to understand what their daddy does on the computer all day.

Dedication

For Stacey, Mya, and Jaxin.

Author's Acknowledgments

I want to thank a few people who've had to make sacrifices for me to write this book.

Mom, Dad, Caroline, and Jennifer, I couldn't have chosen better parents and loving sisters.

I want to thank my kids, Mya and Jaxin. Despite your youth, you amazed me at how understanding you were when I told you I had to work instead of playing. Now that I'm done, let's have some fun.

Susan Pink, my editor, sacrificed her sanity editing this book. Susan, without you I would not have signed the contract to write this book. Thank you for taking this journey with me a second time.

To Amanda Wagasky, my day job supervisor, thank you for understanding on those mornings I texted or e-mailed you saying I needed one more hour (or four hours) to wrap up what I was working on for the book.

Stephanie J.M. Copple, we started our part-time business, black&hue, LLC, just before I accepted the contract to write this book. Thank you for your patience waiting for me to complete the book so that we can pursue our dreams of helping others.

Stacey, my wife and best friend, you stand by me through all my crazy ideas, dreams, and pursuits. Thank you for guiding me through our lives together because without you I would be lost and wandering aimlessly through life. I love you with all I am.

Publisher's Acknowledgments

We're proud of this book; please send us your comments at http://dummies.custhelp.com. For other comments, please contact our Customer Care Department within the U.S. at 877-762-2974, outside the U.S. at 317-572-3993, or fax 317-572-4002.

Some of the people who helped bring this book to market include the following:

Acquisitions and Editorial

Project Editor: Susan Pink

Acquisitions Editor: Amy Fandrei

Copy Editor: Susan Pink

Technical Editor: Michelle Krasniak

Editorial Manager: Jodi Jensen

Editorial Assistant: Annie Sullivan

Sr. Editorial Assistant: Cherie Case

Cover Photo: © iStockphoto.com/1xpert

Composition Services

Project Coordinator: Sheree Montgomery

Layout and Graphics: Jennifer Mayberry

Proofreaders: Lindsay Amones, Melissa Cossell, Christine Sabooni

Indexer: BIM Indexing & Proofreading Services

Publishing and Editorial for Technology Dummies

Richard Swadley, Vice President and Executive Group Publisher

Andy Cummings, Vice President and Publisher

Mary Bednarek, Executive Acquisitions Director

Mary C. Corder, Editorial Director

Publishing for Consumer Dummies

Kathleen Nebenhaus, Vice President and Executive Publisher

Composition Services

Debbie Stailey, Director of Composition Services

Contents at a Glance

Introduction 1

Part I: Getting Started with Squarespace 6 7

Chapter 1: What Squarespace Can Do for You 9
Chapter 2: Getting Ready to Build Your Website 17
Chapter 3: Signing Up 35
Chapter 4: Finding Your Way around Squarespace 43

Part II: Designing Your Website 61

Chapter 5: Considering Your Template Needs 63
Chapter 6: Web Design 101 71
Chapter 7: Customizing with Style Editor 79

Part III: Building Your Website 97

Chapter 8: Working with Pages and Collections 99
Chapter 9: Creating Pages in Your Site 107
Chapter 10: Building Your Pages with Items and Blocks 129

Part IV: Personalizing Your Website 149

Chapter 11: Creating Content with Content Blocks 151
Chapter 12: Adding Multimedia with Content Blocks 165
Chapter 13: Navigating with Structure Blocks 179
Chapter 14: Automating Updates with Social Blocks 187

Part V: Extending Your Website 195

Chapter 15: Configuring Site Settings 197
Chapter 16: Monitoring Site Activity 229
Chapter 17: Setting Up Shop with Commerce 241
Chapter 18: Going Out with Squarespace 267

Part VI: The Part of Tens 299

Chapter 19: Ten Features of a Good Website..301
Chapter 20: Ten Ways to Attract Attention to Your Site 311
Chapter 21: Ten Ways to Make or Save Money..321

Index 329

Table of Contents

Introduction 1

About This Book 2
Conventions Used in This Book 2
What You're Not to Read 2
Foolish Assumptions 2
How This Book Is Organized 3
    Part I: Getting Started with Squarespace 6 3
    Part II: Designing Your Website 3
    Part III: Building Your Website 3
    Part IV: Personalizing Your Website 4
    Part V: Extending Your Website 4
    Part VI: The Part of Tens 4
Icons Used in This Book 4
Where to Go from Here 5

Part 1: Getting Started with Squarespace 6 7

Chapter 1: What Squarespace Can Do for You 9

Knowing Your Options 9
    Do-it-yourself options 9
    Online versus offline 10
Building a Website with Ease 11
    Sign up in less than a minute 11
    Don't worry about hosting 11
    Get support 24/7 12
Exploiting the Versatility of Squarespace 14
    Personal site users and bloggers 15
    Business site users 15
    Website developers 15

Chapter 2: Getting Ready to Build Your Website 17

Setting Goals 17
    Defining your target audience 18
    Focusing your message 18
    Create an outline 19
    Finding a style 22
    Establishing the project's timeline 24
    Adding and updating content 24
    Maintaining your website 25

Planning Your Site's Functionality 26
    Static content 26
    Item-based content 26
    Web forms 28
    Social media integration 28
Establishing Your Website's Primary Function 28
    Blog site 29
    Portfolio site 30
    Business site 31

Chapter 3: Signing Up **35**
Signing Up for a Squarespace Account 35
Choosing the Right Squarespace Pricing Plan 38
    Standard plan 39
    Unlimited 39
    Business 40
Logging into Your Website 41
    Pressing Esc 41
    Going to Squarespace.com 41
    Going to the login page 42

Chapter 4: Finding Your Way around Squarespace **43**
Visiting the Editing Areas 43
    Preview area 44
    Content Manager area 48
    Activity area 49
    Site Settings area 50
    Commerce area 50
Using Core Features of Squarespace 51
    Uploading images to Squarespace 52
    Linking to pages, files, and other websites 53
    Editing images in Squarespace 55

Part II: Designing Your Website **61**

Chapter 5: Considering Your Template Needs **63**
Exploring the Different Templates 63
Reading the Read Me Page 64
Taking Advantage of the Blank Canvas 66
Changing Your Template 67

Chapter 6: Web Design 101 . . . . **71**
Understanding Basic Design Elements 71
Determining a Color Scheme 72
    Finding RGB and hex codes 73
    Peeking at code 74
Exploring Web-Safe Fonts and Font Styles 74

Selecting Fonts for Your Site...76
Choosing Images for Headers and Backgrounds....................76
Recognizing Appropriate Sizes and Values...........................77
    Controlling widths 78
    Setting an appropriate text size................................78

Chapter 7: Customizing with Style Editor.....................79
Locating Style Editor..79
Selecting an Element in Your Site.......................................81
Changing Your Site's Colors..82
    Choosing a color on the wheel...................................82
    Adding transparency with the slider...........................83
    Hiding an element..84
Customizing Fonts..84
    Choosing a font from the (long) list 85
    Choosing the right size...86
    Deciding on bold or italics..87
    Fine-tuning line height and letter spacing 88
    Transforming text with case changes 89
Adjusting Sizes and Values with Sliders..............................90
Modifying the Template with Other Options.........................92
Saving Your Template...92
Testing Your Template 93
Resetting Your Customizations 94
    Reverting changes before saving................................94
    Resetting all changes...95

Part III: Building Your Website 97

Chapter 8: Working with Pages and Collections 99
Defining Page Types 99
Item-Based Pages..100
    Blog page...100
    Events page..101
    Gallery page...102
    Products page 102
Pages 103
Folders 104
Links 105
Index Page 106

Chapter 9: Creating Pages in Your Site 107
Locating Content Manager 107
Determining Your Site's Navigation 108
    Positioning pages in your navigation 110
    Deleting pages from your navigation 110
    Adding pages to your navigation..............................112

Configuring Pages with Basic Settings 113
  Choosing your navigation and page titles 114
  Including a description of the page.......................................114
  Changing the URL of the page 115
  Setting a password for the page..115
  Uploading a thumbnail for the page......................................117
  Setting a page as your home page 118
  Disabling a page 118
  Enabling a page 119
Configuring the Basic Settings for a Blog Page 119
  Choosing the number of posts per page................................120
  Establishing an e-mail address for posting...........................121
  Installing the Quickpost bookmarklet...................................123
Utilizing Unlinked Pages to Add Hidden Content 123
Modifying Settings for Folders and Link Page Types 124
  Modifying folders 125
  Modifying link item settings 126

Chapter 10: Building Your Pages with Items and Blocks 129
Exploring How Pages, Items, and Blocks Work Together 129
Working with Page Items 130
  Adding an item 130
  Removing an item 132
  Setting the status of your page item......................................132
Running Through the Edit Settings 132
  Item section 133
  Options section..137
  Location section...139
  Social section...139
  Adding content to a page item 140
Working with Blocks 141
  Adding a block to your page..141
  Removing a block..143
Rearranging Blocks Using LayoutEngine 143
  Separating blocks into rows 145
  Creating columns of blocks 145
  Inserting blocks...145
  Floating blocks within content...147

Part IV: Personalizing Your Website 149

Chapter 11: Creating Content with Content Blocks 151
Understanding Content Blocks 151
Text Block...152
Markdown Block 154
Quote Block 156
Code Block..157

Form Block 158
    Customizing form elements 159
    Moving form elements 159
    Storing your form submissions 160
    Switching storage options 160
    Customizing the advanced settings of a form 160
External Link Block 161
Amazon Item Block 161
Product Block 162
Space Block 163
Horizontal Rule Block 164

Chapter 12: Adding Multimedia with Content Blocks 165
Understanding Multimedia Content Blocks 165
Image Block 166
Gallery Block 167
    Uploading images to the gallery block 168
    Pulling images from a Gallery page 169
    Choosing a display option 169
Video Block 171
Embed Block 172
Audio Block 174
Map Block 176

Chapter 13: Navigating with Structure Blocks 179
Understanding How Structure Blocks Work 179
Search Block 181
Collection Link Block 181
Calendar Block 182
Summary Block 183
Tag Cloud Block 184
Author Index Block 185
Tag, Category, and Month Index Blocks 185

Chapter 14: Automating Updates with Social Blocks 187
Understanding How Social Blocks Work 188
Connecting a Social Account to a Social Block 188
Creating Galleries from Photo-Sharing Sites 190
Streaming Your Latest Tweets 191
Checking in with Foursquare 192
Listing Your Social Accounts 193

Part V: Extending Your Website *195*

Chapter 15: Configuring Site Settings 197
Getting to Know Your Site's Settings 197
Configuring Basic Site Settings 199

Configuring General Settings...200
    Third-party services...200
    Overall site configurations 201
    Comment settings...202
Setting the Time and Geography 203
Adding Connected Accounts..203
Publishing Pages to Your Facebook Page 206
Activating Share Buttons..207
Inviting Contributors to Your Site 209
    Adding a contributor...209
    Removing a contributor...211
    Modifying a contributor's invitation 211
    Modifying a contributor's permissions...................................211
Using Your Own Domain..212
    Transferring a Squarespace-managed domain....................213
    Registering your free domain from Squarespace 214
    Pointing an existing domain to Squarespace 215
Switching Templates 216
Importing and Exporting 218
    Importing content from another website 219
    Exporting your content from Squarespace 219
Injecting Code into Your Site 220
Redirecting a URL with Advanced Settings...222
Checking Out Developer Information 223
Reviewing Your Active Sessions..224
Upgrading Your Trial Account 225
Updating Your Billing Information 226
Getting Help from Support 24/7..227

Chapter 16: Monitoring Site Activity............................229
Tracking Site Activity 230
Observing Your Traffic 230
Finding Where Visitors Come From 232
Discovering Your Popular Content 233
Finding How Visitors Search for You 234
Getting the Details of Site Visitors..234
Managing Comments on Your Site 236
    Replying to comments...236
    Deleting comments...237
    Approving comments 237
    Handling flagged comments 239

Chapter 17: Setting Up Shop with Commerce.....................241
Preparing to Set Up Shop 241
Adding Products to Your Site 242
    Adding an item to a products page 243
    Configuring a product item..245

Removing a product 250
Rearranging products...250
Configuring Your Store 250
Store settings...251
Orders 254
Inventory...257
Shipping 259
Coupons 261
Taxes 263
E-mail notifications 265

Chapter 18: Going Out with Squarespace 267

Accessing Your Site Anywhere, Anytime 267
Taking your site mobile 267
Configuring your mobile account 272
Touring the Blog Post Screen 274
Adding a blog post 275
Managing blog posts...279
Managing comments...280
Checking statistics 283
Capturing Ideas with Note 284
Connecting your Squarespace account 284
Sending a note 287
Changing Note settings 287
Modifying the account list 288
Configuring accounts to receive notes 290
Setting accounts as default destinations for your notes 291
Reviewing previous notes...292
Showing Your Work with Portfolio...293
Connecting your account..294
Viewing your images 296
Customizing Portfolio settings...297

Part VI: The Part of Tens 299

Chapter 19: Ten Features of a Good Website 301

Organized Content...301
Content Optimized for Search Engines.....................................302
About Page 303
Contact Page 305
Custom Domain 307
Custom E-Mail Address..308
Branding 308
Design Related to Content 308
Social Media Integration 309
Regular Updates and Maintenance..309

Chapter 20: Ten Ways to Attract Attention to Your Site 311

   Promote through Social Media 311
      Connecting your site to your social accounts 312
      Updating your social profiles 312
      Helping others share your content..313
   Take Advantage of E-Mail Marketing..315
   Write an Elevator Pitch..316
   Try Word of Mouth 317
   Use Stationery 317
   Include an E-Mail Signature 318
   Advertise...318
   Comment on Other Sites..319
   Write for Other Sites 319
   Use an Easy-to-Remember Custom Domain...320

Chapter 21: Ten Ways to Make or Save Money 321

   Get a Squarespace Discount 321
   Find a Coupon Code 322
   Start a Conversation...322
   Sell Out...323
   Start Shopping...323
   Sell Yourself...324
   Create a Portfolio...324
   Develop a Brochure Site 324
   Provide Exclusive Content 325
   Blog for Dollars 327

Index **329**

Introduction

. . . .

*H*ello. Welcome to *Squarespace 6 For Dummies.*

Being a Squarespace user prior to the summer of 2012 was like being a Mac user in the 1990s. It was like belonging to an elite cult of website owners, designers, and developers who understood the true importance and capability of this awesome platform.

When Squarespace 6 was released mid-2012, a paradigm shift happened for people looking to build a website in today's society of fast-paced, always on-the-go people. No longer was Squarespace just for the enlightened. Squarespace was completely overhauled, with templates built to not only look good on your desktop but be responsive and adapt to screens on mobile devices.

I've been using Squarespace since 2004, pretty much since its birth. I'm a self-taught web professional, with my first introduction to building sites on the web in 1998. Since then, I've built sites on just about every platform with every software solution. I still hand-code websites, occasionally use desktop publishing software such as Dreamweaver, and work with enterprise-level software costing tens of thousands of dollars.

What I'm better at than web design is helping others learn how to build sites. In early 2009, I was offered a job to work for Squarespace as a customer support team member. I loved that job the two years I did it, and that's when I found out how much I love helping people. I don't work for Squarespace now, but because of that job I had the opportunity to write my first book, *Squarespace For Dummies,* about Squarespace 5. And that's how we get from talking about me to helping you.

Whether you're a seasoned pro or a newbie when it comes to building websites, this book is the perfect companion to helping you create a website on Squarespace. My editors and I worked hard to make sure this book will provide you with all the essential information you'll need to build your own website.

About This Book

In this book, I cover how to use Squarespace 6 to build your own website. I describe all the major features of Squarespace and provide some tips as you discover all the wonderfully awesome ways to use Squarespace.

I wrote this book to be used as you build your site. Maybe you're building your first-ever website, or maybe you've built several websites but are new to Squarespace. Consider me as your own personal assistant you can carry around with you. Kind of creepy when I think about it, particularly if you're shoving me in your (virtual) pocket. Anyway . . .

Conventions Used in This Book

While reading the book, you'll encounter words in *italic*. Those terms, which might be new to you, are important to understanding certain aspects of what you are reading about.

Links to URLs, or places on the web, are hyperlinks. If you have the e-book version of *Squarespace 6 For Dummies*, you can click or tap a link to load the content of that particular page. Not bad, huh?

What You're Not to Read

Guess what? Like all great *For Dummies* books, you don't have to read the chapters in this book in order from beginning to end. Skim the table of contents, check out the index, or just flick through the book (my preference) until you find something you're interested in or need to know immediately.

Foolish Assumptions

The title aside, I assume that you're not a dummy (but don't tell my editors or Mr. Wiley I said that). Instead, I assume that you're a highly intelligent individual who knows how to use a computer and mobile device.

I also assume that you have an e-mail address because you need one to use Squarespace. If you don't have one, go to www.gmail.com and get one. I'll wait for you.

I'm betting that you've heard of social sharing sites such as Facebook (if you haven't, please crawl out from under your rock) and perhaps some of the cooler ones such as Twitter, Pinterest, and Instagram. If you use these or other social sharing sites, please share with your friends and followers where they can buy this book so they can be as cool as you.

I'm also going to assume that if you find this book useful, you'll send me a box of gourmet cookies. I love cookies.

How This Book Is Organized

Squarespace 6 For Dummies consists of 21 chapters, arranged as follows.

Part I: Getting Started with Squarespace 6

Chapters 1–4 provide you with the basics about Squarespace and building a website. You find out about the different pricing plans Squarespace offers, how to sign up for an account, a little Squarespace history, and what makes Squarespace so darn special. Chapter 2 talks about the process of gathering your thoughts and content for building your website.

Part II: Designing Your Website

In Chapters 5–7, I begin by helping you consider what type of template you'll need to build the kind of website you want to have, and toss in a little web design educational tips. I wrap up in Chapter 7 by showing you how to give your site a unique design by using Squarespace's easy-to-use styling controls.

Part III: Building Your Website

In Chapters 8–10, you find out how to build your site with pages and blocks. You look at the types of pages you can add to your site and how to organize your pages into different navigation areas. You then look at how to add page items, such as blog posts and gallery images and videos. To wrap up Part III, you discover how to add blocks to include content and media on your site.

Part IV: Personalizing Your Website

In Chapters 11–14, you discover how to use specific types of blocks to add content, images, and other media such as audio and video. You find out how to use structure blocks to display information on your pages such as blog posts, products, and events. Then you learn how to display content from your accounts on social media sites such as Twitter, Instagram, or Foursquare.

Part V: Extending Your Website

In Chapters 15–18, you explore the ins and outs of managing your website. Squarespace provides a detailed and robust set of features and settings for managing site contributors, analyzing your site's traffic and visitors, and managing blog posts and comments. If you are interested in creating an online store, then you're in luck as we look at setting up shop with Squarespace Commerce.

I devote Chapter 18 to using Squarespace on the go. Squarespace has the best mobile apps for maintaining a blog. You can create and edit blog posts, upload photos, moderate and respond to site comments, and view your site's traffic statistics. With specific apps for Apple devices and Android, you can work with your site from anywhere.

Part VI: The Part of Tens

All _For Dummies_ books include lists of ten, and this book is no different. You find the ten features of every good website, ten ways to attract people to your site, and ten ways to save or make money.

Icons Used in This Book

From time to time, you'll find the following graphics in the margin.

This icon highlights some important point. Paying attention to details marked by the Remember icon can help you connect the dots between different Squarespace features and aspects of building a website.

 I try to avoid geeky, technical details. Sometimes, though, I just can't help myself. This icon warns you that what I am about to discuss is an advanced coding or design technique. Feel free to skip this information.

 I provide some shortcuts and tricks to make your website building easier. You won't want to miss paragraphs with the Tip icon.

 Look out! Danger ahead. Few aspects of Squarespace can get you in trouble. Sometimes, however, you just need to be aware of how something can be affected by what you're doing or not doing in Squarespace. Be sure to read and follow the directions accompanying a Warning icon.

Where to Go from Here

If you want to find out more about the book or have a question or comment, please visit me at www.krisblack.com. For technical updates to the book, go to www.dummies.com/go/squarespace6fdupdates.

Now dive in! Give Chapter 1 a quick look to discover a little more about Squarespace and what it offers, and then head straight to your chapter of choice.

Part I
Getting Started with Squarespace 6

getting started
with

Squarespace 6

In this part . . .

- ✓ Find out what sets Squarespace apart from other solutions
- ✓ Set goals for the type of site you want to create
- ✓ Determine how you will maintain your site
- ✓ Sign up for your first Squarespace site
- ✓ Figure out the best pricing plan
- ✓ Explore the different areas and editing modes of Squarespace

Chapter 1

What Squarespace Can Do for You

. . . .

In This Chapter

▶ Understanding the ways to create a website

▶ Discovering the benefits of Squarespace

▶ Reviewing the different levels of support offered by Squarespace

▶ Building just about any website

. . . .

Squarespace is about making everything easy. If you can click a mouse or tap a trackpad, you can certainly build a website on Squarespace without knowing a lick of code.

When building your website, you'll want a solution that is easy to use, enables you to create a custom design, and provides helpful resources and support from real people. In this chapter, I show how Squarespace meets these requirements.

Knowing Your Options

You can create web pages in several ways. You can write all the code by hand, you can use desktop software such as Dreamweaver or FrontPage, or you can use an online solution such as Squarespace.

Do-it-yourself options

In the past, people coded their own websites from scratch because website builders generated messy and disorganized code, resulting in websites that loaded slowly and often didn't work correctly. Today, many good web designers still code custom HTML and CSS even if they also use the following options because they get maximum control over the details of their websites.

Online versus offline

Some people build and maintain websites using desktop applications installed on their computers such as Adobe Dreamweaver or Microsoft Expression. Those who go this route must set up and organize online data hosting and domain registration, send files to and from servers using FTP, and buy expensive software and updates, which can be used on only the one computer on which they were installed. An offline solution can offer many benefits and flexibility but can also result in unnecessary headaches and hardships, particularly if you're not comfortable transferring files to a web server, writing code, and designing a site from scratch.

Even if you find a simpler desktop software solution that offers entry-level access to building a website (such as RapidWeaver from Realmac Software), you're limited to maintaining your website on the one computer on which the software is installed. Plus, you won't be able to take advantage of using mobile devices to update your website, and you still have the responsibility of setting up web hosting on a server.

Online solutions let you create a website or a blog from your web browser. The entire experience takes place online. Ease of use, both in website setup and management, is the primary reason to choose an online solution such as Squarespace. Online solutions also free you from having to maintain offline versions of your site. Everything is hosted within the service, so you don't have to transfer pages to a web server. In addition, you can access your site from multiple computers and devices to make updates or add new content.

Reviewing the history of Squarespace

In 2003, Anthony Casalena was looking for a way to publish a website. None of the solutions he tried efficiently brought together everything he needed to publish even a basic website with static pages and a blog, so he decided to build what he needed. He spent his days attending college classes and his nights pursuing his coding hobby. Before long, he built Squarespace, which simplified the most difficult parts of building a website, whether adding content to a blog entry or designing a custom style. After sharing the software with friends, Anthony realized that he had built something that would be useful to others as well.

In the beginning, Anthony maintained the development of the Squarespace platform, responded to support inquiries, and actively promoted the company. Squarespace has now grown into a company hosting nearly 2 million websites. Bloggers, artists, businesses, and all manner of professionals have chosen Squarespace as their home on the web. To host all these sites, Squarespace has built a robust hosting infrastructure, storing website data across multiple servers to fully protect data and ensure that websites almost never go down.

Online solutions — sometimes referred to as content management systems (CMS) — enable you to not only build a website but also add, edit, and manage the pages and content on your site. Two major categories of content management systems are available. One type of CMS is manually uploaded to your own web host's servers, similar to how you transfer files when using an offline website builder such as Dreamweaver. Squarespace is one of those other types of CMS solutions, self-hosted and preinstalled on a web server for you, so you have one less setup step.

Building a Website with Ease

Gone are the days where setting up your website required painstaking hours of methodical attention to detail and dealing with techno-babble and difficult web services.

Squarespace makes the process of building your site as easy as building a tower of blocks, just like when you were a kid. To add content and features to your pages, you simply add the appropriate Squarespace block. (See Chapters 10–14 for more information about blocks.) If you want to rearrange your pages or content, just drag and drop.

In addition, Squarespace provides limitless options for the look of your site. Their professionally crafted templates enable you to get the most benefit from Squarespace features while allowing your unique style to show through. Designing your own website has never been easier. (See Chapters 6 and 7 for more information about styling your website.)

Sign up in less than a minute

Signing up for a Squarespace account takes less than a minute and requires you to provide just your name, your e-mail address, and a password.

You don't even have to worry about choosing a pricing plan from the start. You get to choose that after your free trial account.

Don't worry about hosting

If you were to create a website using ExpressionEngine or Dreamweaver, you would need to sign up for a separate service dedicated to hosting websites. Squarespace removes this task by hosting your site for you.

As you build your site on Squarespace, your files (pages, content, media, and so on) are automatically stored on the integrated website hosting system. The files are properly formatted and organized to ensure that your website is optimized for listing in search engines such as Google, Yahoo!, and Bing. In addition, Squarespace loads your site pages quickly because everything is stored on multiple web servers.

Two key benefits of Squarespace hosting your website are

- ✔ **Dependability:** No one can offer a 100 percent uptime guarantee, but Squarespace comes close with an industry-leading track record of 99.98 percent uptime (at the time of this writing). All its websites are published using multiple servers in a cloud infrastructure. If one server goes down, the rest of the servers can fill that gap until the malfunctioning server is repaired or replaced.

- ✔ **Limitless bandwidth and storage:** If you sign up for one of the two top pricing plans (see the next section for more on pricing), you get unlimited bandwidth and storage — without the delays common with other services. No more worrying about going over a set limit. You can add as many pictures and files as you like, as long as each one is less than 15MB.

Get support 24/7

Squarespace provides a number of ways for you to get help when you need it: a knowledge base, e-mail technical support, live chat, video workshops, and an online forum.

Full-featured knowledge base

Finding or figuring out answers to your questions is the best way to learn something new. The easiest way to find your answers is by using the Squarespace knowledge base at `http://help.squarespace.com`. It provides detailed information on features and functionality as well as links to how-to videos that answer the most frequently asked questions. Use the search feature to find particular words or phrases, or navigate through the sections by category.

The support team updates the knowledge base when new features are introduced and adds entries based on feedback from customers.

Fast e-mail technical support

Squarespace provides e-mail technical support by real people, 24 hours a day, seven days a week. Submit a message to the support ticket system and receive an e-mail reply in less than an hour. And if the support staff can't resolve an issue, they have direct access to a crew of engineers and developers who can clarify tough problems or report suggestions to improve the product.

If you need to contact support about an issue or a question, make sure to provide detailed information about what's happening on your site, the relevant page, and the steps to reproduce the issue.

Super-fast live chat

If you have a simple question or need something addressed instantly, send your inquiry by live chat. You can reach live chat from Monday through Friday between the hours of 11:00 a.m. and 7:00 p.m. Eastern Standard Time. The live chat window, shown in Figure 1-1, is available on all pages of the help site.

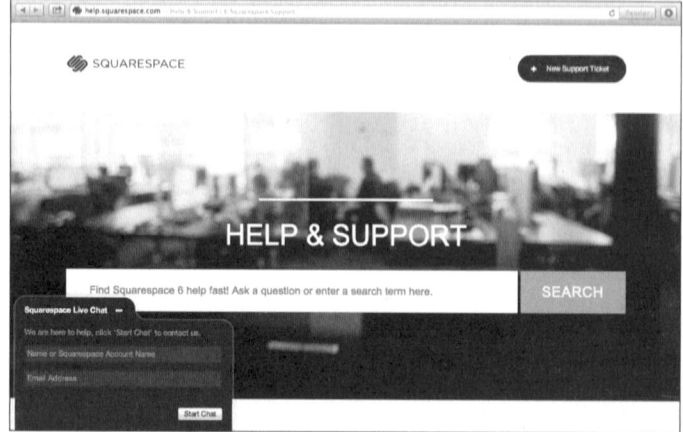

Figure 1-1:
Chatting
with
Square-
space
support.

If you have a detailed question or issue, submitting a support ticket is usually better than requesting a live chat.

Videos, workshops, and hangouts

Watching videos are a great way to learn how to do something. Squarespace has a collection of videos in the knowledge base to show you how to use and customize your site. Following is a direct link to a list of articles in the knowledge base that provide video tutorials: `http://help.squarespace.com/customer/portal/topics/172865-help-videos/articles`.

You can also participate in live workshops on Squarespace's Google+ Hangout page at `https://plus.google.com/+squarespace/posts`. If you can't make it to a live workshop, check the archive of their best videos at `http://workshops.squarespace.com`.

Community help

Do you like conversing with other users? Are you seeking help with advanced customizations and custom code? If so, Squarespace Answers is the place for you. Visit http://answers.squarespace.com and join other Squarespace users who hang out and help each other with advice on modifying and adding custom code and designs to their Squarespace sites. Heck, we might run across each other in the discussions.

Read the rules of the site before joining and asking questions. For more, visit http://answers.squarespace.com/faq/.

Squarespace developed and provides the Answers site for all users, and the company takes part in discussions. However, this doesn't guarantee that Squarespace will answer any question you ask.

Developers documentation

If you're a web professional wanting to know how to build custom designs on Squarespace, you can review documentation about their developer templates and start your own Developer trial account in the Developer Center (http://developers.squarespace.com). At the time of this writing, creating a Developer account is still in beta, but this site provides valuable insight and helpful information about developing custom templates on Squarespace.

The Developer Center and a Developer account are for folks who have an advanced understanding about web design. If you're fluent in HTML, CSS, and other web languages, you'll feel right at home and should check it out.

Exploiting the Versatility of Squarespace

Squarespace provides everything you need to create a website:

- ✔ Prebuilt features for adding pages, blogs, picture galleries, forms, and more
- ✔ Automatically built and updated navigation menus
- ✔ Website analytic features
- ✔ Social media widgets that display your latest personal updates from Twitter, Flickr, Foursquare, Instagram, 500px, and more

As described in this section, you can use Squarespace to create just about any website you can think of, such as a simple blog to share your thoughts and writing, a creative portfolio to attract potential clients, or a persuasive business site to promote your company's services.

Personal site users and bloggers

Do you want to create a blog or a personal site that you can use as the center of your online identity? The Squarespace blog page enables you to add multiple entries, much like a diary or written journal. Organize posts by date, tag, or category. Collect comments to facilitate ongoing conversations. Customize the display and style of the posts to best suit your needs — all without touching a bit of code. You can also share images and add social blocks that will pull in content from popular social sites such as Twitter, Flickr, and anyone serving up RSS feeds of your content.

If you want two blogs on your Squarespace site, one for you and another for your business partner or a loved one, simply add two blog pages. Squarespace allows you to add multiple pages of the same page type, or *collection.* (For more information about the types of page modules, see Chapter 8.) And when your blog grows in popularity, with increased traffic and comments, you can expand and add site contributors to contribute to the content and to moderate comments.

Business site users

The primary focuses of a business website are typically interacting and engaging both existing and potential customers. A successful business site will not only share information about the company's products or services but also open a dialogue with clients and prospects to communicate the company's messages and get feedback.

Some businesses favor public discussions facilitated by comments on blog entries. Other businesses prefer to communicate in a more private and controlled fashion through online surveys, contact forms, and frequently asked questions (FAQs) pages. All these options can be set up in minutes using Squarespace's form block to collect information. This information can be e-mailed to you, saved to a Google Docs spreadsheet for manipulating, or downloaded and manipulated in your spreadsheet program of choice, such as Microsoft Excel or Apple Numbers.

Website developers

Squarespace offers a true developer platform that provides you with complete control over the underlying code (HTML, CSS, and JavaScript), allowing you to build just about any type of website. If using LESS Preprocessing, Retina-ready Responsive Image Handling, Git repositories, and SFTP access get you all aflutter, a Squarespace developer account is definitely something for you.

An experienced web designer can create a fully customized website for a client, who could then easily learn to edit the website using Squarespace's built-in features. In addition, Squarespace's business-class support team can handle most of your clients' questions, keeping small web projects from morphing into long-term support nightmares.

Chapter 2

Getting Ready to Build Your Website

. . . .

In This Chapter

▶ Setting goals for your website

▶ Planning website functionality

▶ Figuring out what type of website you need

. . . .

Creating a website requires some upfront work and forethought. Think about the content you want to put on your site pages, focus that content to engage your desired target audience, and decide on the type of website you want to build. Having a plan of attack for building your site will help you think through all the important decisions you need to make to build your site quickly and efficiently.

In this chapter, you walk through all the core topics you need to think about to prepare for building your site.

Setting Goals

How do you start creating your website? Most likely, you already know the topic or topics you want to present on your site. Next, you need to do the following:

1. Define your audience

2. Focus your message

3. Create an outline

4. Find a style

5. Establish the project's timeline

6. Add (and update) your content

7. Maintain the website

Defining your target audience

Whether you're an artist creating a website to promote your work, a business owner looking to reach people across the web, or a parent wanting to show off photos of your kids, you need to choose your target audience. By defining your audience, you can focus your content appropriately, thus maximizing your site's reach.

For instance, suppose you're a photographer who specializes in weddings. You'd want to make sure that your website's content showcased photos of wedding ceremonies, brides and grooms, bridal portraits, and wedding receptions. If you also photograph high school seniors to generate additional income, your website might mention but not promote that aspect of your work.

Focusing your message

A website is more than a pretty design. Your content should have a message, an idea, or some other type of information you want to communicate to your site visitors. Too many people start to build a website without truly thinking about their message. This can be a huge hurdle in building a website that effectively targets the audience you want to reach.

By focusing your message based on your target audience, you can hone what you want to say and what you expect from your visitors as well as provide a foundation on which to build your site.

 An effective way to target your message is to summarize it in one or two sentences. Create a simple promotional pitch you could use to explain your website in a conversation.

After you have your target message, use it as the vision for everything else on your website, from the pages you create to the colors and style of your design.

Create an outline

After you have determined your target audience and target message, you need to begin to map your site's content. The information you need includes, but is not limited to, the following:

- ✔ The type of content that will be on your website
- ✔ How you want to divide the content into pages and sections
- ✔ How the pages will reference each other

For example, suppose you're starting a blog and your site has three pages: Journal, Contact, and About. The Journal page (which can also be called a Blog page) holds your blog entries, the Contact page contains a form that visitors use to send you e-mail messages, and the About page holds your bio, a brief description of your site, and links to the social sites you use. With only three page links, this site's navigation would be simple.

The process of structuring your website doesn't need to be complicated. For example, Figure 2-1 shows Squarespace's blog website, which consists of a home page with categories in the sidebar for navigation. The site has no other pages.

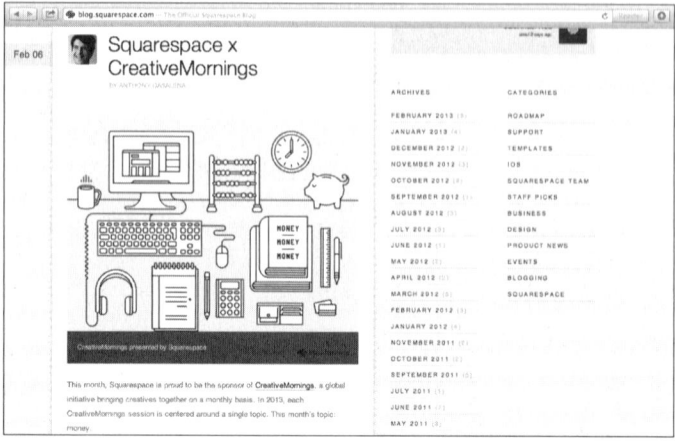

Figure 2-1:
A simple
site
structure.

Let's look at an example of a more complex site I designed. Figure 2-2 shows my website, at `www.krisblack.com`.

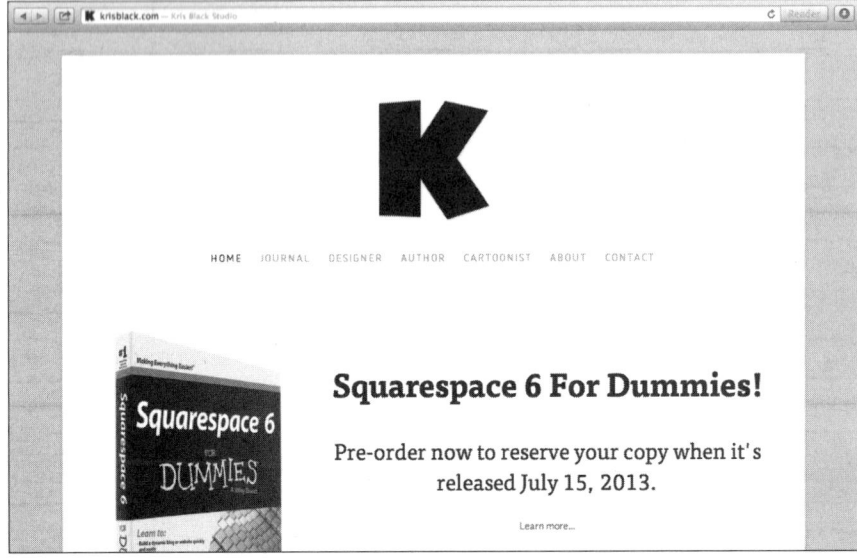

Figure 2-2:
Kris Black
Studio
website.

My previous site was a single page that featured only my blog. In my redesigned website, I wanted to showcase a range of skills and services in different industries. To help keep these diverse areas of work neatly categorized, I structured my site into three main sections: design, writing, and cartooning. (Chapter 9 shows you how to add different page types to your site; Chapter 10 provides details on structuring the content of your pages using the Squarespace LayoutEngine.)

Will your website have as many categories and areas of focus as my website? If so, you can get your site off the ground more quickly by creating an outline, also known as a *sitemap,* to show how all these elements are connected. Following is an outline of my site's pages, sections, and content:

Main Navigation

- ✔ Home
- ✔ Journal
    - • Journal Archive
- ✔ Designer
    - • Logos
    - • Websites
    - • My company, black&hue, LLC

✔ Author

- Squarespace 6 For Dummies

- My other site, Squareverse

- My comic Life's Little Hiccups

✔ Cartoonist

- Children's Books

- Comics

- Commercial

✔ About

- About me and the website

- Colophon: tools I use

- Where to send stuff to me

✔ Contact

Footer and Social Networking Links

✔ Newsletter signup

✔ Twitter

✔ Dribbble (yes, three b's)

✔ LinkedIn

✔ Flickr

✔ YouTube

✔ Google+

✔ Facebook

✔ Site credits and copyright information

If you have a larger site in mind, with many more pages, prepare an outline of all your pages and the type of content that the pages will display. Include any required functionality, such as commenting by site visitors, internal links to other pages on your site, and external links to other resources on the web. The outline serves as your driving directions to building your website on Squarespace.

If you take the time to formulate a simple outline of all the pages or sections on your site, creating the actual site will be easier.

Finding a style

Squarespace provides a diverse set of templates for you to choose from when deciding on your site's theme. These templates are categorized into three main recommended uses:

- ✔ Blogging
- ✔ Portfolios
- ✔ Business

The templates offer a variety of layouts, typography treatment, color schemes, and graphics — all professionally created by the rock-star designers and developers who work at Squarespace. And, unlike the templates in Squarespace 5, not a single template has the same features, layout, and design. Furthermore, the templates present a minimal design style to make them easy to customize.

To make your site look unique, you can customize a template style. Change colors, add a special header image or logo, switch the column layout, or move the navigation. For example, Figure 2-3 is my website, Squareverse (www.squareverse.com), and Figure 2-4 is the Dollar Bin Comics website (www.thedollarbin.net).

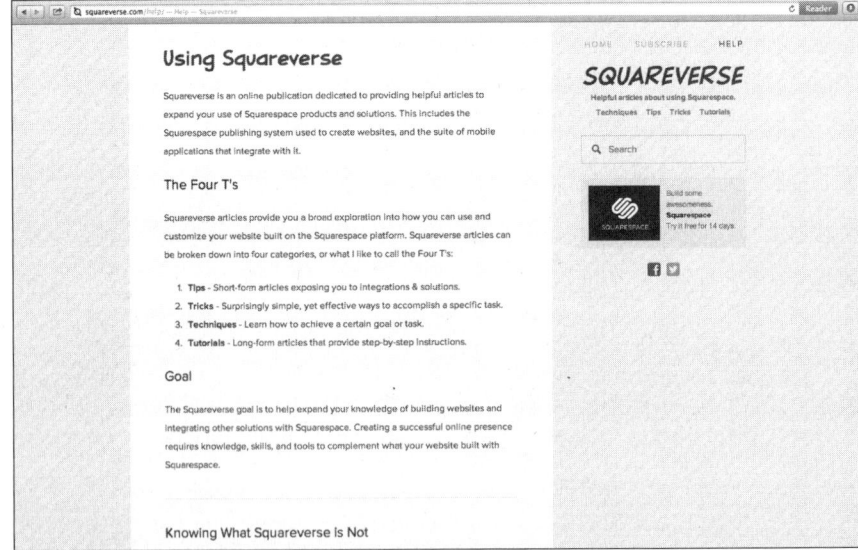

Figure 2-3:
Square-
verse web-
site based
on the Five
template.

Figure 2-4:
Dollar Bin
Comics
website
based on
the Five
template.

Each site is customized differently, but both are based on the Five template from Squarespace, shown in Figure 2-5. You can easily see how Squareverse resembles the Five template, but the Dollar Bin site has a more customized design.

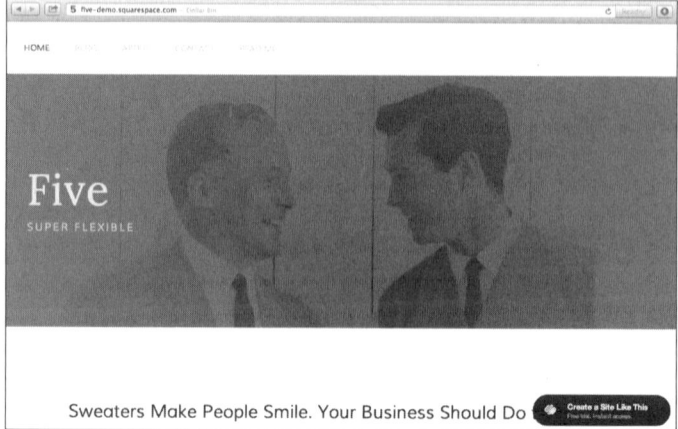

Figure 2-5:
The Square-
space Five
template
demo
website.

When customizing a template, some designers find it helpful to create a site mock-up or design style guide to use as a visual map to help make creative decisions.

Be sure to create a design style that complements your site's content and mission. The style should support and help deliver your message. If your site's content establishes a serious and professional message, using a style that conveys the opposite could confuse your visitors and perhaps make them leave your website or not trust your message.

If you're not a web designer, you may find the thought of designing a website overwhelming. Don't worry. Squarespace makes it easy to change colors, text size, and layout, as well as add graphic elements. And every change you make is instantly reflected in the site. See Chapter 7 for information on customizing your site's design in Style Editor.

Establishing the project's timeline

To stay on track when creating even a simple website, you need to have a plan of action, complete with a timeline. The first date to set on the timeline is the launch date, the day when you're ready to publicly announce your site to the world. This milestone date determines the dates of all the other tasks you need to complete to reach your goal.

After you determine the launch date, you should break down your site outline into manageable chunks and set due dates for each task, such as writing the text and finding images.

Your timeline may be as simple as setting tomorrow as the launch date for your new blog. You'd then schedule the following tasks for today: creating your Squarespace trial account, choosing a template, and writing your first blog post.

Adding and updating content

After you create a timeline, you can add your text, upload images, and apply your design to your site. Keep in mind that you want to complete your tasks on the milestone dates you set so you can successfully launch your site on time.

If you want a site that keeps people coming back for more, your content must be fresh. Sites that don't change or have the same content for a long time appear abandoned. Certain types of sites, such as blogs or news sites, require more frequent updates than other types of sites.

If you're a blogger, determine how often you want to write a new entry: every day, once a week, or once month, for example. The frequency with which you blog might depend on the type of content you write about or your target audience. If you're a wedding photographer, you're probably busiest from May to October and will find it easier to update your site during slower months. If you have a business site, you may need to update it only when you add a new service or hire a new employee.

By adding new content on a routine basis, you help to keep your site relevant and improve its ranking by search engines such as Google, Yahoo!, and Bing. This process, part of search engine optimization (SEO), is an important part of promoting your site. A great resource that I often turn to is *Search Engine Optimization For Dummies,* 5th Edition by Peter Kent (Wiley).

Whatever timetable you decide to use for site updates, follow through on your commitment. Being consistent makes your site more appealing and keeps loyal visitors happy. In addition, a site consistently updated with quality content has a better chance of ranking higher in search engines than a site that isn't updated.

Maintaining your website

Every website needs basic long-term care to keep the site up and running. This maintenance doesn't necessarily entail a ton of work on your part but does require that you keep active with your site.

Following are some simple site elements that you might need to address on an on-going basis:

- ✔ **Comments:** If you allow commenting on your blog posts, you should moderate the comments and conversations. You'll want to check that people aren't doing something that you don't allow, such as promoting another site's service, using profanity, or instigating arguments with other commenters.

- ✔ **Form submissions:** If you use a form block to collect data or information from your site visitors, you can receive this data by e-mail, in a Google Docs spreadsheet, or in an e-mail subscriber list in your MailChimp account. (See Chapter 11 for more information about using form blocks.) If you receive form block submissions by e-mail, for example, you'll communicate with site visitors through e-mail, which may not require you to log in and maintain anything on the site.

- ✔ **Statistics:** Check your site's statistics routinely so you'll be aware of what information on your site interests people. You may be surprised to find which pages are the most popular.

The more you interact with your visitors or see what parts of your site interest them, the more you will be able to engage them.

Planning Your Site's Functionality

In the old days, websites were designed like print media — that is, like electronic pieces of paper, with content that didn't change. Now, however, people are accustomed to sites that offer functionality in addition to static pages. When planning your site, think about how it will interact and connect with the audience to deliver your message.

Static content

Generally, static website pages are the easiest pages to create. The content on these pages rarely changes. Following are examples of static pages:

- An About page, which might provide a brief or detailed bio, a description of your work, and a summary of what your site provides
- A pricing page that describes your services and fees
- A privacy policy or terms of service page

The only functionality of a static page is to enable your visitor to read the content and possibly click a link to view more information.

Item-based content

Item-based content refers to a section of your site that organizes multiple pieces of content. Squarespace provides the following four types of item-based content:

- Articles in a blog
- Gallery of images
- Portfolio of work
- Products for sale

Following are examples of these four popular types of item-based content.

Blog

If you write a blog, it might be a simple online journal or a source of information on a news site. The content is in the form of a blog entry, with the publish date and perhaps an associated category. More modern and robust blogging systems also offer a secondary form of categorization called *tagging*, which links a keyword in your entry to other journal entries with related or similar content. Generally, most people use the tagging feature as a keyword list of important information within the blog entry.

You can use a blog to create any type of page that is routinely updated with new information. Typically, the information is formatted for a consistent look and style. For example, headers within articles have the same font size and color and images sport the same border styling and are possibly the same width and height.

A blog is the perfect type of page to use for anything that you can collect and categorize — for example, articles, photos, or even comics, such as my web-comic Life's Little Hiccups (www.hiccupscomics.com/).

Image gallery

When you want a collection of images on your website, an *image gallery* is the way to go because it simplifies the tasks of uploading and displaying.

Some image galleries display images directly in a web page, with text or thumbnail navigation to move from image to image. Other galleries offer a more theatrical experience in which the images are displayed full screen, with the site obscured in the background.

Portfolio

Showing off your body of work as a creative professional helps to secure more work from new clients. Some of the best portfolios I've seen combine the features of an image gallery and written descriptions about each piece in the portfolio.

Providing context about the body of work offers more insight and in-depth analysis of the scope of the project. As your portfolio grows, you may find it helpful to organize it into groups of similar projects.

Store

What better way to make money than to offer real, tangible goods to sell on your website? Even selling digital goods, such as e-books, can be a great way to supplement your site's earning potential.

As you add more items to your store, you may find that you want to organize your items into categories. For example, if you're an artist, you might separate lower-cost prints from original paintings to help customers who are searching for more affordable items.

Web forms

Web forms enable you to collect information from your site visitors. These forms can range from simple ones for receiving e-mail messages from site visitors to advanced forms that collect data for you to compile and analyze. The Standard pricing plan limits you to just 4 form fields, but the unlimited and business plans allow you to create an unlimited number of form fields from all 16 form field types. All Squarespace accounts have access to form blocks.

Social media integration

Millions of people use social media sites such as Facebook, Flickr, Google+, LinkedIn, Pinterest, Reddit, and Twitter. Adding ways for your site visitors to connect with their social media sites can attract more visitors to your site.

You may even want to pull some of your updates on these social media sites back onto your website to provide up-to-date content. For example, why not place your Twitter updates on your site? You can update your Twitter status from any mobile phone, countless third-party apps, and the Twitter site itself.

Remember to consider your message, content, and target audience when deciding what types of social media integration you want to add to your site. Perhaps your audience prefers pinning — sharing your blog articles on Pinterest — versus Tweeting about them on Twitter. If so, you may decide to make the Pinterest button more prominent.

Establishing Your Website's Primary Function

After you sign up for your Squarespace account (in Chapter 3), you need to choose a template from the many that Squarespace offers. But how do you know which template is right for you? The decision isn't difficult after you understand the three basic types of sites most people create.

Even huge, robust websites can be broken down into three types of sites:

- **Blog:** A blog can be as simple as an online journal you keep only for yourself or as complex as a news site where you, or a team of contributors, publish articles on a routine basis.

- ✔ **Portfolio:** Whether you bake cakes or design installations, you probably want to show off your hard work. Having a website to use as a portfolio lets people see what you can do.

- ✔ **Business:** Managing a business is hard work, so why not take advantage of having a website to showcase your business and potentially drum up new customers?

These categories are oversimplified, but keeping this simple will help you figure out which type of site you need.

Don't think that your site has to fit neatly into one of these three categories. Instead, your site might be a combination of two or all three. What's important is figuring out which one of these types of sites best describes your primary goal.

Blog site

Blogs, which make up a large portion of websites today, are nothing more than online journals where people post entries for others to read. One of the main goals of a blog is to start a conversation with your site visitors.

Blogs are a great way to attract new readers to your website.

The basic function of a blog is to enable you to post entries that are organized into topics and sorted in chronological or alphabetical order. Squarespace has a great set of blog features you can add to your website.

A blog website is one of the simplest websites you can create. Squarespace does all the heavy lifting to connect all the entries into an organized collection.

The Dollar Bin Comics website, at www.thedollarbin.com, is a great example of a blog site (refer to Figure 2-4). My buddy, Adam Daughhetee, has been organizing this site for years using Squarespace. With the recent move to Squarespace 6, Adam is taking advantage of all the structure blocks to help visitors move around the site to discover new content.

Are you thinking of creating a portfolio or business site? Consider adding a blog to your site as well — even if the last thing on your mind is writing content for your website. An actively maintained blog can generally help establish a site higher in search results from search engines such as Google, Yahoo!, and Bing. So even if your site's main goal is to let people know where you are located downtown for a quick bite to eat or to promote your craft through a portfolio, having a blog can help connect you to visitors and establish a relationship to increase your brand awareness.

Portfolio site

As a professional designer, I understand the need and desire to show off the work one creates — to promote past work to get more work from new or existing clients, or to freely share my work with others. Having a portfolio website is one of the best ways to help other people discover you and your work.

Putting images of your work in an easy-to-browse slideshow or in organized site pages can help visitors see what you are capable of creating. For instance, my client and friend Nikole Nelson is a designer with a focus on "creating unique, conceptual environments focused on brand identity," as seen on the about page of her website, at www.nikolenelson.com/about/. She has a powerful portfolio of work, with international clients such as New Balance, Coach, and Urban Outfitters. Showcasing her work on a website is just a natural step in her creative journey.

One of Squarespace's most successful markets is the creative professional, due to its impressive set of features for handling and manipulating images:

- ✔ Automatically scaled images for viewing on high-definition devices such as the iPhone or iPad
- ✔ Interactive slideshows with plenty of customization options
- ✔ Grid-based display of images on your pages
- ✔ Specialized templates optimized for portfolio sites
- ✔ Advanced image editing

I'm going to step out on a limb and say that creating a portfolio site is what Squarespace does best.

While a portfolio site can have a blog and contact page as described above, what sets a portfolio site apart is that it displays a gallery of images. This can be as simple as one gallery of a few images or multiple pages of galleries displaying images across a wide range of topics.

Squarespace has a powerful Gallery Block that allows you to display a gallery of images with a highly customizable set of features. See Chapter 12 for more information about adding images to your site using the Gallery Block.

Some of the templates Squarespace offers are optimized for using as a portfolio site. During the sign-up process or in your Squarespace site (under the Site Manager➪Settings heading), you can see which templates are optimized for a portfolio site by choosing to sort the templates by the portfolio category.

While you can create a simple page with a single gallery, you might want to consider using a Blog page to organize single images or small sets of images into different categories. The advantage of this would be to allow your images to be commented on by site visitors (see Chapter 16 for managing blog comments), or to take advantage of a blog page's integration with social media sites as seen in Chapter 15.

Business site

Running a business is the most difficult thing I've ever done. I never have enough time in the day, and it seems as though someone always needs something from me. Does that sound like your life too? Building a website is the last thing you want to do, but you know you need to do it.

Maybe you run a local eatery, like my friend Rob Reed's Immaculate Consumption business (www.immaculate-consumption.com), here in Columbia, South Carolina. He works in the kitchen every day, crafting delicious sandwiches and serving up some of the best coffee in town. His goals were to create an online presence for his business, showcase his menu, and provide ways for people to connect with his business. His website features his complete menu, contact information, and location — everything customers need, as shown in Figure 2-6.

Figure 2-6:
The
Immaculate
Consump-
tion
website.

Building a business website is not like building a blog or portfolio site. Business websites generally offer information and utilize calls to action, messages to help engage potential customers to contact you or buy what you're selling. Getting customers to contact you can be done through a form on your site, or maybe by providing location information and a map to find your business in town.

A business site might provide information divided into pages that provide more in-depth content such as:

✓ Services the business provides

✓ Historical information about the business

✓ Short biographies of people involved in the business

✓ Testimonials from customers

✓ Forms for collecting specific information from site visitors

Most of these pages are simple and only need to use a single page on the site to display the information.

Use LayoutEngine to arrange your content in horizontal rows of information, such as the layout on the service page of my business website, black&hue (www.blackandhue.com), shown in Figure 2-7. (See Chapter 10 to find out how to use LayoutEngine to arrange blocks on your pages.)

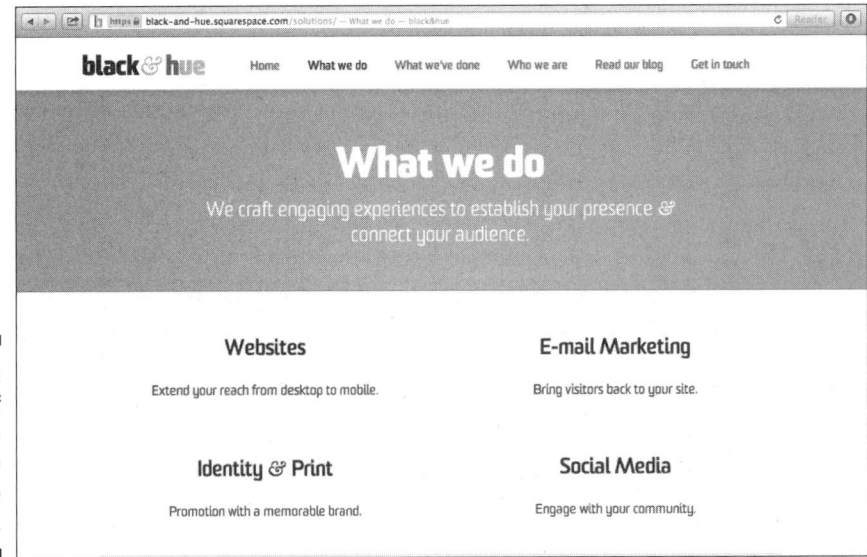

Figure 2-7:
Example of
a service
page on the
black&hue
website.

Creating an advanced form for collecting specific information from your site visitors can help you jump-start conversations with potential clients or provide support for current customers.

Any website can incorporate any of the pages and Squarespace features mentioned in this chapter. A business site can have a blog, and a portfolio site can have a services page if you take commission work. If you are struggling to figure out what should go on your site, check out Chapter 1 for help in establishing your website goals.

Chapter 3

Signing Up

. . . .

In This Chapter

▶ Signing up for an account

▶ Choosing a pricing plan

▶ Logging in to your account

▶ Deciding on a Developer account

. . . .

Squarespace has been referred to as the Apple of the website builder industry for its beautiful interfaces and attention to detail. Other platforms boast thousands of widgets and features, but many of these are buggy and not properly supported or updated. At Squarespace, platform changes and new features are built, tested, and debugged internally to ensure the quality of the product.

Signing Up for a Squarespace Account

Signing up for your Squarespace account is easy. You don't need to worry about purchasing your account up front because you can create a trial account for free. Simply choose a template, provide your first and last name, use a valid e-mail address, enter a password, and — voila — you have a website ready for customization.

Signing up is so quick and easy that I don't mind waiting for you to do it right now. Here's how:

1. **Visit** www.squarespace.com.

   You arrive at the Squarespace home page, as shown in Figure 3-1.

2. **Click the Get Started button to display the template selection page, shown in Figure 3-2.**

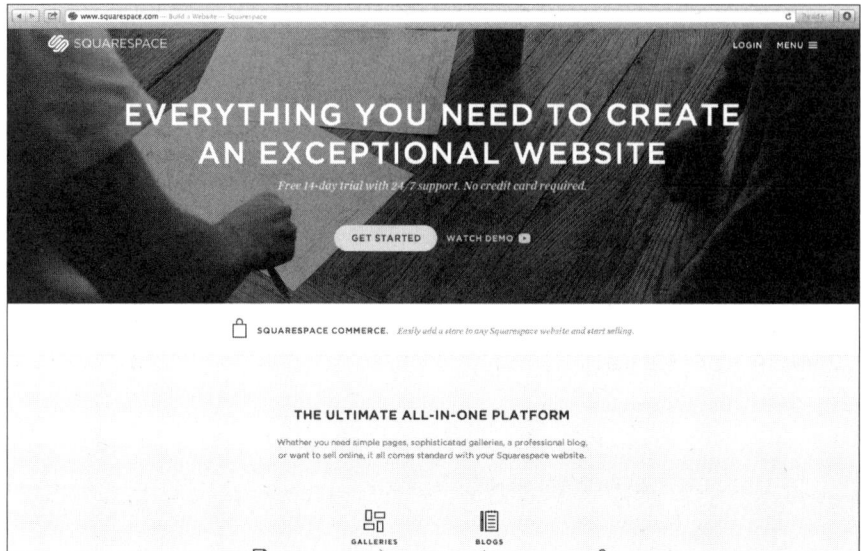

Figure 3-1:
The home
page of
Square-
space.

View templates by recommended categories

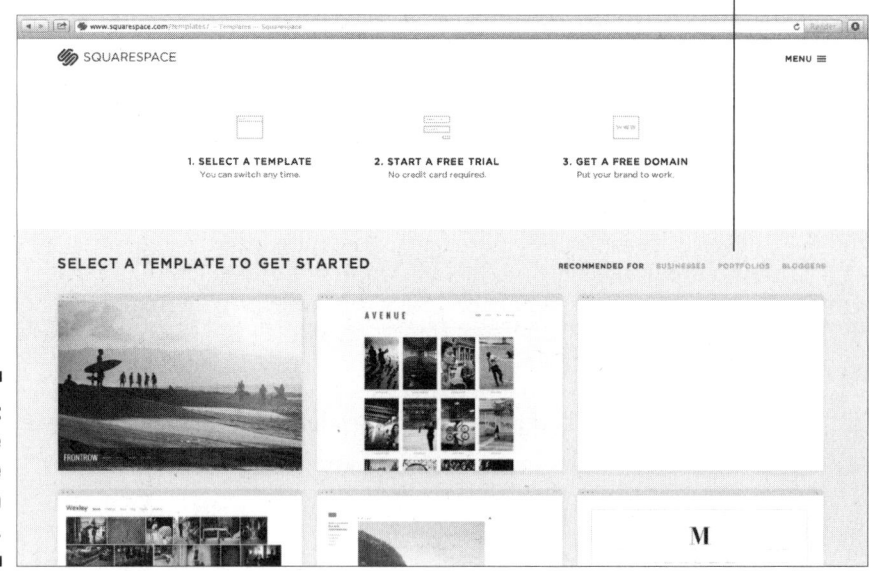

Figure 3-2:
The
template
selection
page.

3. **Choose a template.**

   The template selection page shows you all the templates Squarespace offers, organized into three main categories: business, portfolios, and blogging. You can choose to scroll through all the templates, or you can narrow your search to one of the preceding categories. Then:

   a. **Hover your mouse over a template.**

   b. **Click the template to display further information and to see some examples of customer sites using that template.**

   For details on the different types of templates, see Chapter 5.

   Don't get too caught up or flustered with choosing your template. You can easily change your template after you have signed up for the free trial account. (See Chapter 5 for details.)

   c. **When you find a template you like, click the Start with This Design button.**

   The Create Your Website signup screen appears.

4. **In the Name fields, type your first and last names.**

   Your first and last names are used to create your Squarespace account name, which in turn is added to the beginning of your website's unique URL.

   If you want to use John Smith as your account name, for example, type John in the First Name field and Smith in the Last Name field.

   If you want to create a custom domain, without `squarespace.com` (for example, `www.johnsmith.com`), see Chapter 15.

   If you're creating an account for your business or brand, you can use your business or brand name in the first and last name fields. For instance, I created my account for the brand Squareverse, my website where I publish helpful tips and tricks for Squarespace sites and apps. In the first name field I used *Square,* and in the last name field I added *Verse.*

   Squarespace account names must begin with a letter and must be 3–25 characters. You can use letters, numbers, and hyphens in the account name.

5. **Provide a valid e-mail address.**

   Make sure that the e-mail address is one you use routinely because Squarespace uses that address to send important notifications about your account.

If you're creating your second, third, or fortieth website with Squarespace, you can use the same e-mail address you used for another Squarespace account. You will have one less bit of login information to remember, and you will also be able to switch to another one of your Squarespace accounts by clicking the Squarespace logo in Site Manager. Also, make sure to use the same password you used with the other Squarespace accounts, which leads us to Step 6.

6. **In the Password field, type a secure password.**

   When creating a password, don't use obvious options such as your account name or the words *square* or *space.* And don't share your password.

Choosing a secure password is important. You can find many online articles on how to create a secure password. The best passwords are ones that are a combination of real words and numbers assembled in a phrase that is neither predictable nor discernable. To check your password's security, check out the How Secure Is My Password? site at `http://howsecureismypassword.net`.

7. **Click the Create Your Website button.**

That's all there is to it! You have an official Squarespace account, and a website that's ready for you to customize and fill with content.

Choosing the Right Squarespace Pricing Plan

Squarespace has three pricing plans, based on the type of website you want to build: Standard, Unlimited, and Business. I discuss the details here, but you can also visit `www.squarespace.com/pricing` for more information.

If you visit the pricing page, the monthly price shown requires that you pay for one year in advance. Squarespace offers a 20 percent discount to those who pay for a year upfront. If you decide to continue using Squarespace after you create a trial account, you can toggle the payments in your site's Account Center to see the monthly cost without the discount, with a 20 percent discount (for one year in advance) and with a 25 percent discount (for two years in advance). Note that you don't have to decide on a plan right now. Simply sign up for the free trial account. Then return to this section after the trial period, when you've evaluated the product and figured out which features you need for your site.

Standard plan

The Standard plan is Squarespace's most cost-efficient plan. Although it doesn't provide all the features found in the Unlimited plan, you do get Squarespace's core features. Listing all the features would double the size of this book, but the highlights follow:

✔ Point-and-click editing to change your site design (see Chapter 7)

✔ Use of LayoutEngine to build your pages (see Chapter 10)

✔ Analytic graphs and reports (see Chapter 16)

✔ Ample storage space for images and other media files you upload (see Chapter 12)

✔ Free custom domain if you pay yearly (see Chapter 15)

✔ All the page types and the base set of building blocks (see Chapters 8–14)

The Standard plan provides enough pages, bandwidth, and storage space for a basic website or blog: 20 pages, 2GB (gigabytes, 1GB equals 1000MB) of storage and 500GB of bandwidth.

The one feature that might seem confining is the 20-page limit. However, 20 pages in Squarespace is not necessarily the same as 20 pages on the web. Some types of pages, such as a blog page, can display content in multiple views, allowing you to determine how the content will be presented to your site visitors. So although you can have just a single Squarespace blog page, it can display multiple web pages with different content. See Chapter 10 for more information about using the blog page collection.

Unlimited

The Unlimited plan provides you with access to everything in the Standard plan, with the following extras:

✔ Unlimited bandwidth and storage space

✔ Unlimited contributors

✔ Advanced form blocks to collect more detailed information from site visitors

✔ Integration of form blocks with Google Docs and MailChimp

✔ Capability to publish site updates to a Facebook page

Form blocks under the Standard plan enable you to create a form to receive e-mails from site visitors. Under the Unlimited plan, you can use the advanced features of form blocks to create custom forms.

In addition, you can connect form blocks to MailChimp, thus providing you with an opportunity to collect e-mail addresses for use in marketing efforts. You can also connect form blocks to a Google Docs spreadsheet. You can, for example, collect answers from many people and compare the answers. The submissions from the form block are entered into a new row in the spreadsheet. Download the spreadsheet and open it in your favorite spreadsheet editor to manipulate the data. See Chapter 11 for more information about using form blocks.

If you have a Facebook page for your brand or business, you may want to automate the process of publishing to the page. Or you may want to display on your Facebook page the contents of a website page. See Chapter 15 to find out how to do this.

Business

The Business plan provides you with access to everything in the other two plans and adds the capability to create an online store using the fully integrated e-commerce features:

- ✔ Unlimited physical and digital products
- ✔ Mobile store
- ✔ Inventory tracking
- ✔ Product configuration with multiple variations and SKUs
- ✔ Tax, shipping, and coupon controls

Squarespace Commerce integrates with Stripe, a payment-processing service that charges a fee of 2.9 percent plus $0.30 for all successful transactions. Squarespace does not impose additional fees or charges to your transactions.

If you already have a store with another service, you may be able to import it to your Squarespace site. At the time of this writing, Squarespace supports importing from Big Cartel and Shopify. All of your images and available data in those e-commerce solutions will be imported. See Chapter 17 for more information about Squarespace e-commerce.

Logging into Your Website

To begin customizing your site, you need to be able to gain access to it as the site owner. You can do so in three ways. In this section, I describe all three, from easiest to most difficult.

Pressing Esc

The easiest way to log in to your website is to press the Esc (Escape) key on your keyboard when you go to your website in your browser. Visit your site at your Squarespace URL (`http://your-account.squarespace.com` or your custom domain) and press the Esc key. When the login prompt appears, enter your e-mail address and password to get into your website.

Using the Esc key has some drawbacks. For instance, if you add custom code to your site that uses the Esc key to exit out of a full-screen experience, you can't press the Esc key to log into your site. A couple of examples are watching a video or a slideshow in full-screen.

You can disable the Esc key functionality for logging into your site by going to Site Manager➪Settings. See Chapter 15 for more information.

Going to Squarespace.com

Another way to log in is to visit the main Squarespace website at `www.squarespace.com` and click the Login link at the top right of the website. When you see the login prompt screen, enter the e-mail address and password for your site. This method is handy if you forget the Squarespace URL or account name for your website

If you manage more than one Squarespace account with the same e-mail address and password, you will be logged into the last website you logged into.

To switch to another Squarespace website you manage or to which you contribute, go to Site Manager and click the Squarespace logo in the lower-left corner of your browser. From the pop-up menu that appears, select the other Squarespace site.

Going to the login page

To log in directly to your website, you can bookmark your site or type your site's login address (http://*your-account*.squarespace.com/config) in your browser's URL field. You will be taken directly to the login screen, where you can enter your e-mail address and password to log in to your website.

If you forget your password to log in to your website, click the Forget Password? link under the far right of the password field, and type the e-mail address you use to log in to your site. You will receive an e-mail message with a link to click to reset your password.

Chapter 4

Finding Your Way around Squarespace

In This Chapter

▶ Understanding the different editing areas

▶ Knowing where to go to perform a task

▶ Discovering where you go to style your website

▶ Finding out where to add content that appears on multiple pages

▶ Uploading images

▶ Creating links to pages, files, and other websites

▶ Editing images

*Y*ou signed up for your brand-spankin' new Squarespace account and logged in to your site. What do all those icons mean? Where do you go to add a new page? Where do you change the color of the site title? How do you upload images? Can you link to other pages in your site? Can you link to another website?

If you're asking these or similar questions or want a high-level overview of Squarespace, this chapter is for you. Here, you review the different areas in Site Manager and modes in Preview so you'll know how to get around your Squarespace site with ease. You also look at common features you'll encounter throughout the entire Squarespace interface.

Visiting the Editing Areas

The previous version of Squarespace, Squarespace 5, had the following four editing modes:

 ✔ **Content:** Add text and media to your site.

 ✔ **Structure:** Create content containers in the form of pages and widgets.

✔ **Style:** Apply a design to your site.

✔ **Website management:** Configure and administer site settings.

Squarespace 6 no longer has these editing modes. Instead, editing tasks are split between Site Manager, which is your site's administration area, and a floating toolbar in Preview.

Site Manager has the following five editing areas:

✔ **Preview:** Modify your site's design in Style mode using Style Editor. You also have access to a Content mode for managing content and blocks in your site's layout structure.

✔ **Content Manager:** Add pages to your site's navigation (see Chapter 9). You can also add content to your pages using an extensive selection of blocks, and arrange those blocks on the page with the help of LayoutEngine. (Check out Chapter 11 for all the juicy information on LayoutEngine and blocks.)

✔ **Activity:** Study how people visit your site to find out what content is the most — and least — popular. Also catch up on conversations in the comments of a blog post.

✔ **Site Settings:** Control your site's settings and configuration.

✔ **Commerce:** Manage your site's store orders, inventory, shipping, coupons, taxes, and other e-commerce settings.

In Figure 4-1, you see the Content Manager screen and the icons that represent the different editing modes of Squarespace.

Now let's look at the five editing areas of Site Manager in a little more detail. The first area takes you to the front of your site, which your site visitors will see.

Preview area

In the Preview area, you can see how your site will look to site visitors — without having to log out from managing your website. While you're previewing your site, a floating toolbar appears in the lower right of your website, as shown in Figure 4-2, the home page of Immaculate Consumption. The first two icons on the toolbar — Content and Style — are the Preview editing modes. The final icon, the gear icon, takes you to Site Manager.

Preview

Content Manager

Activity

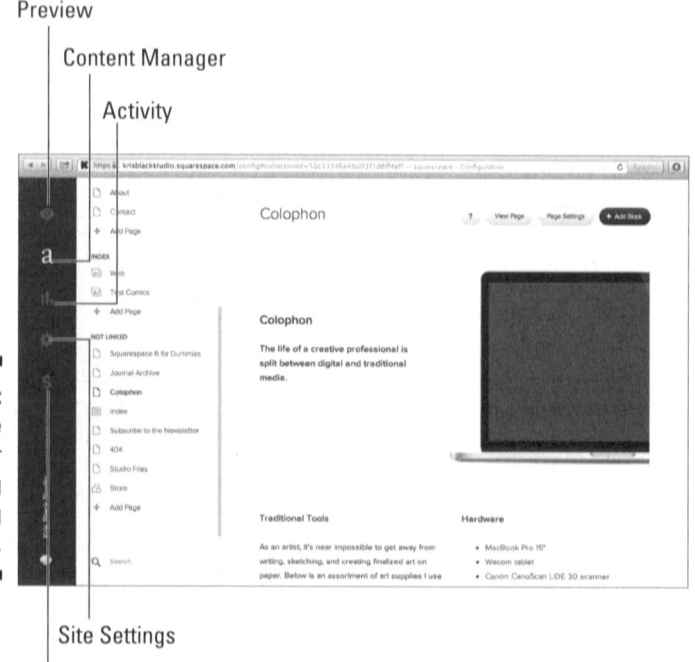

Figure 4-1:
Site
Manager
showing
all editing
areas.

Site Settings

Commerce

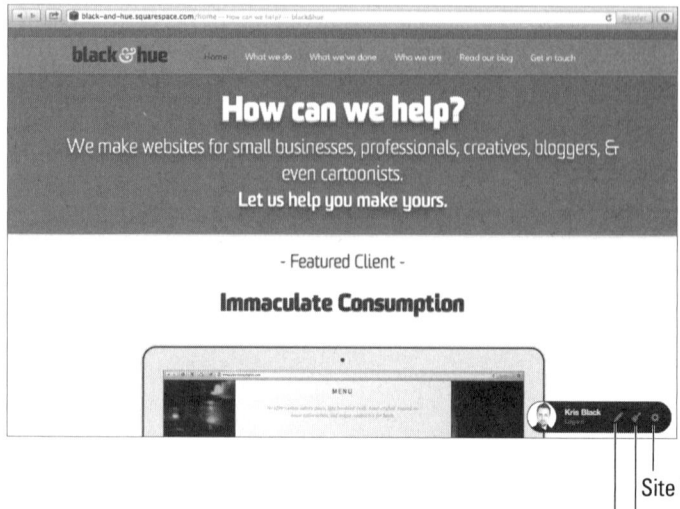

Figure 4-2:
Preview and
the floating
toolbar.

Site Manager

Style editing mode

Content editing mode

Content mode

Selecting the pencil icon while in Preview switches the screen to Content mode. In Content mode, you can use some of the same features in Content Manager, described next.

In Chapter 10, you find out how to use blocks to add content to your pages. Some templates enable you to also add blocks in certain areas in the layout of your site just like you add blocks to pages in Content Manager. These layout areas, which are indicated by a dotted outline, are not accessible from Content Manager and can be edited only in Content mode. Use the plus sign button in the lower-right corner of an editable area to add a block.

For example, depending on your template, you may be able to add blocks to your site's footer, a sidebar, or to the top of your page. Figure 4-3 shows Content mode and a couple of areas — a sidebar and the top of the page — where blocks can be added.

Figure 4-3: Content mode showing examples of where to add blocks in the layout.

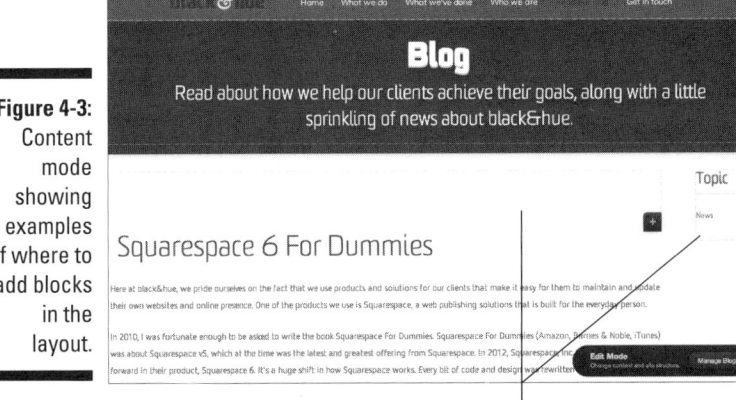

Editable areas of Content mode where you can add blocks

If you want to modify the content of a page, you need to switch to Content Manager. Simply click the Manage Page button in the Preview toolbar while in Content mode, and you will immediately exit Content mode and go to Content Manager within Site Manager.

Site Manager is an area of your site hidden from site visitors where you can administer site settings and configurations. In Site Manager, you can

- Add content to your pages
- Manage your blog's content

✔ Update a gallery page

✔ Check your site traffic statistics

✔ Configure sitewide settings

✔ Manage your store

Is the Preview toolbar covering something you want to see on your site while in Content mode? You can move the toolbar by simply dragging it.

To exit Style mode or Content mode while still viewing your website, click the x in the Preview toolbar. To get to Site Manager, click the gear icon in the Preview toolbar. And Site Manager will lead you to our next topic of discussion, Content Manager.

Style mode

To modify your site's template, select the paintbrush icon to switch to Style mode. Style Editor slides into view on the left side of your site (as shown in Figure 4-4), allowing you to use an intuitive set of controls to modify select elements determined by the current template. See Chapter 7 for details about styling your site using Style Editor.

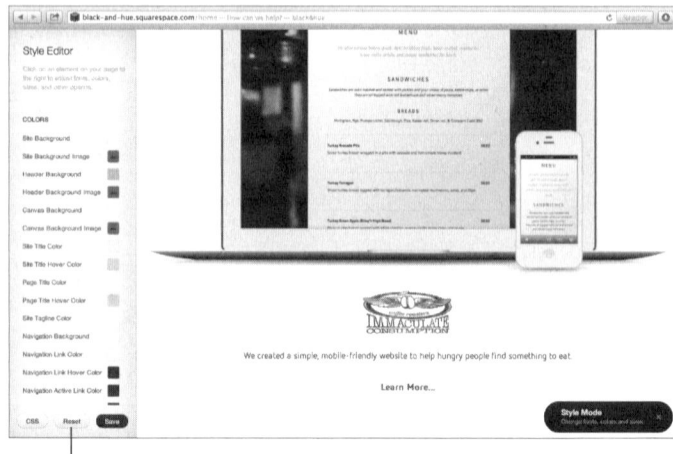

Figure 4-4:
Editing your site with Style Editor.

Style Editor

You can add CSS code in Style Editor and see how that code renders your site in real time.

Content Manager area

You add pages to your site's navigation, configure your pages' settings, and add content to your pages in Content Manager. Content Manager contains one of Squarespace's most powerful features, LayoutEngine, which you use to structure the content of your pages.

In Content Manager, as in Content mode in Preview, you add content to your pages using blocks, which are available in three categories:

✔ **Content:** Add content such as text, images, and videos to your pages.

✔ **Structure:** Display content from your blog, gallery, and products pages such as category or tag listings; previews of blog posts, gallery media, and products; and dates when you post content.

✔ **Social:** Display activity and updates from your social networks, including Twitter, Flickr, and Foursquare.

You can add as many blocks to your pages as you like, and you can arrange them in just about any way you can imagine. Chapters 11–14 go into detail about the types of blocks and how you use them to add your content to your site.

Figure 4-5 shows my website, `www.krisblack.com`, in Content Manager. The icons representing the other areas in Site Manager are on the left, the navigation column is in the middle, and the LayoutEngine area, where you add your content in blocks, is on the right.

Areas in Site Manager

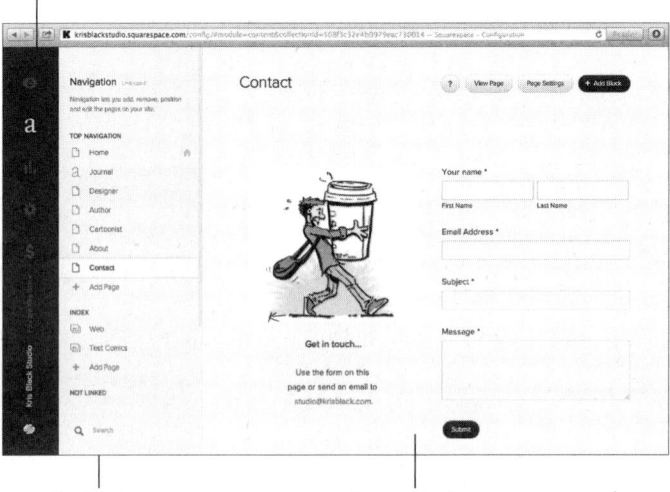

Figure 4-5:
Content
Manager
in Site
Manager.

Navigation   LayoutEngine

Managing multiple Squarespace sites

If you're managing more than one Squarespace site, you'll want to be able to move between sites quickly and easily. In Site Manager, click the Squarespace logo in the lower-left corner. A pop-up list appears, displaying all the Squarespace sites to which you have access

with the same login and password in use for the current website. The figure shows the pop-up list when I'm logged into my black&hue website. The list displays my black&hue account, as well as two client sites I'm working on with my business partner.

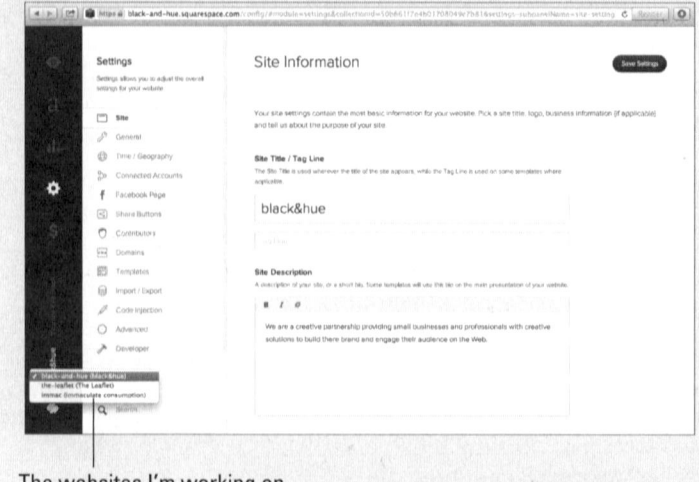

The websites I'm working on

Activity area

Knowing what content on your site is popular can help you adjust that content to increase the activity of your visitors and your audience. The Activity area of Site Manager gives you a good overview of the following site statistics:

- **Traffic Overview:** Check out general information, such as page views, the number of unique visitors to your site, and how many search engines index your pages.

- **Referrers:** See which websites on the Internet are referring people to your website.

- **Popular Content:** Use this set of metrics to find out which pages on your site are the most popular.

- ✔ **Search Queries:** Find out what keywords and search engines were used to search for your site.

- ✔ **Detailed Activity:** If you need to satisfy your inner geek, check out the useful information in Detailed Activity, such as a visitor's IP address, the type of browser used to access your site, where the visitor is from, and how the visitor got to your site.

If your site has a blog page and people comment on your blog posts, you will need to manage those comments. The Activity area enables you to respond, approve, and delete comments as well as mark comments as spam. See Chapter 16 for more information about managing comments.

Site Settings area

The Site Settings area is where you maintain the configuration of many site features that aren't necessarily visible to your site visitors or that apply to all or most pages in your site. These features include adding a site title, adding and managing contributors, importing content from your old site, and managing the social sharing of your site's content.

These settings are important to the overall functionality and configuration of your site and should not be ignored. At the least, evaluate each feature to determine whether it is something you could use to your advantage. To help you decide which features you should use, check out Chapter 15, where I describe the Site Settings area in depth.

The Site Settings area contains advanced features, such as creating URL redirects and adding custom code to your site's HTML <head> area. Although not everyone will find these features useful, they do give you more control over your site.

Commerce area

If you have a Business plan (see Chapter 3 for information on the different pricing plans), you can use the Commerce area to sell physical items such as t-shirts, crafts, and artwork, or digital items such as music, e-books, and fonts in a store on your website. You can configure and maintain your store as you would the rest of your website.

Squarespace provides you with a helpful four-step guide to get you started with Commerce, as shown in Figure 4-6.

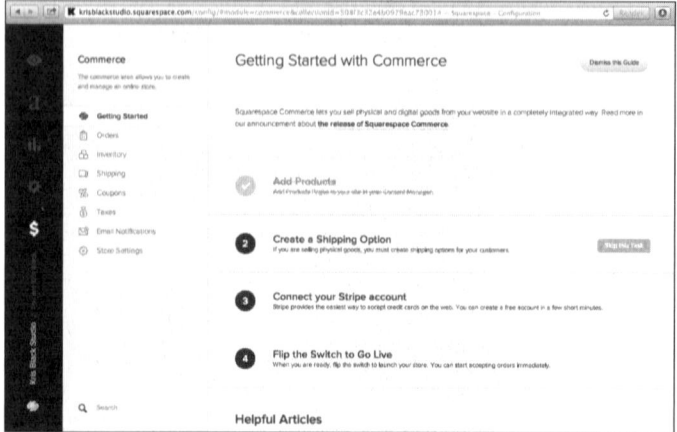

Figure 4-6:
Getting
started with
Commerce.

In the Commerce area, you can

✔ View your orders

✔ Add products and track inventory

✔ Create shipping methods

✔ Manage promotions with promo codes

✔ Set tax requirements for in-state customers

✔ Configure custom e-mail notifications

✔ Set your store's return policy, terms of service, and privacy policy

Chapter 17 goes into all the wonderful details about configuring your store and selling your stuff on your Squarespace site.

Using Core Features of Squarespace

As you add content and configure settings, you'll encounter two core features that make interacting with Squarespace easy:

✔ Adding images

✔ Linking to pages, files, and other websites

Because you'll encounter these features in numerous areas of Squarespace, I thought it would be beneficial to describe them in one place instead of repeating myself numerous times.

Uploading images to Squarespace

You can get an image on your website in three ways:

- Drag and drop the image
- Select and upload the image
- Find the image on another website

The first two methods involve uploading from your computer. In the third method, you pull an image from another website. Anytime you add an image, you will see the box shown in Figure 4-7.

Click to upload or drag and drop an image

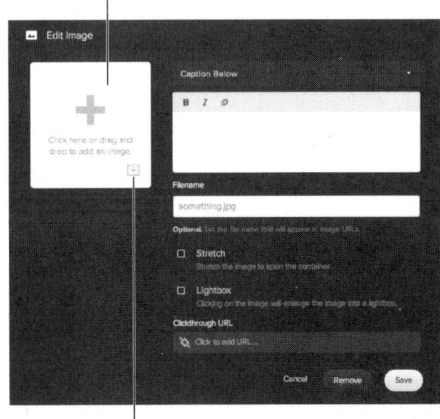

Figure 4-7:
Upload your
image here.

Click to pull image from another site

Clicking the box will open a system dialog box where you can navigate to a folder on your computer, select an image, and upload it. If that seems too cumbersome for you, you can simply drag an image file from your computer and drop it over the image box. Either action will upload the image to your site.

In some areas of your site, such as a gallery page or a gallery block, you can drag and drop multiple images. Now that's a huge time-saver.

If you want to upload an image from a website, see if the image box has an icon in the lower-right corner (refer to Figure 4-7). If it does, click that icon and type a web address in the dialog box that appears. Then click the Find

Images button, and Squarespace will locate any available images at the web address you provided and display them for you to select. Click the image you want to use and Squarespace will pull that image into your website.

Linking to pages, files, and other websites

The heart of any website is its content, particularly the words you write, the images you display, and the descriptions you add for your site and individual pages. When adding content, you may have the option to turn content into a link to a page or a file on your site or on an external website.

You will encounter two link settings in multiple areas on your Squarespace website:

✓ **Link icon:** In areas where you can type text, you can select a word or group of words and click the link icon shown in Figure 4-8 to turn the selection into a link. Here are a few examples of where you'll see the Link icon:

- Text in content blocks

- Descriptions in image and video blocks

- Page descriptions

- Site description

Link icon

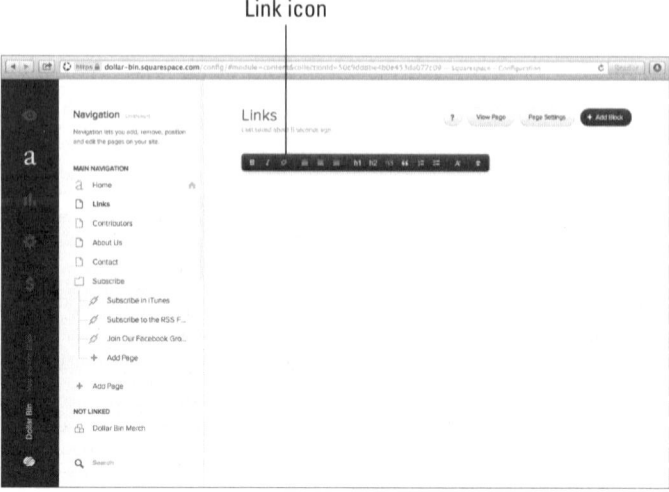

Figure 4-8:
Click the
Link icon
to make
your text
clickable.

✔ **Clickthrough URL:** In page items and blocks (see Chapter 10), you might find the Clickthrough URL setting, which turns the page item or content you're adding in a block into a link. You might see a Clickthrough URL setting in

- Image blocks

- Images in a gallery block

- Images and videos in a gallery page

With either of these settings, the process of adding a link is the same. A small pop-up dialog box will appear, as shown in Figure 4-9, with the following options for adding a link:

✔ **External:** Type the URL of the external website. If you want the URL to open in a new window, select the New Window option. See Figure 4-9, left.

✔ **Files:** You can upload a new file or link to an existing file, as shown in Figure 4-9, middle. You upload a new file in the same way you upload an image. You can drag and drop the file. Or you can click anywhere in the white area to open a system dialog box and find and select a file on your computer. If you've already uploaded a file to your site, click the Existing File icon and then select the file in the list.

✔ **Content:** Select a page on your site from the list that appears, as shown in Figure 4-9, right. The pages will be sorted into

- Blogs

- Galleries

- Pages

- Products

- Template pages

Figure 4-9:
Adding a
link to an
external
web page,
a file, or
another
page on
your site.

 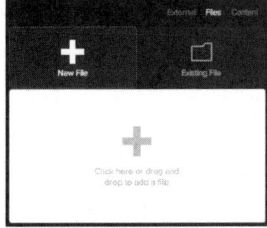 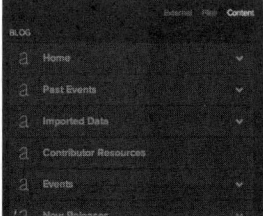

Adding links to your site is such a common task that it's handy the process is so easy.

Now that you know how to get around your Squarespace site and use some of the most common features, it's time to begin creating your website.

Editing images in Squarespace

After you've added an image to an image box, as described in the preceding section, you will have three options for editing the image:

- ✔ **Set the focus of the image:** Set the focal point of the image for use in other areas of your site that might display a cropped view of the image.

- ✔ **Remove the image:** Hover your cursor over the thumbnail of the image in the image box. Click the trash can icon that appears at the top of the image to remove the image.

- ✔ **Edit and manipulate the image:** Use the built-in image editor, Aviary photo editor, to modify and enhance the image.

These settings will not appear until you hover your cursor over the image in the image box. Let's look at each of these options in more detail.

Removing an image

If you need to add a new image to an image box, you must delete the current image in the image box. Do the following:

1. **Hover your cursor over the image in the image box.**

   A pencil icon and a trash can icon appear at the top of the image box.

2. **Click the trash can icon.**

   The image is immediately deleted from the image box.

Be certain that you want to remove the image because you will not see a confirmation message. After the image is removed, you can't recover it from your site.

Focusing on an image with the focus ring

Some Squarespace features that display images pulled from other areas of your site automatically crop those images. For example:

- ✔ Gallery pages may crop your images depending on the template you're using and the settings configured in Style Editor.

- ✔ Gallery blocks may crop images if you have set the block to Auto Crop the images it shows. (See Chapter 12 for more on adding a gallery block to your site.)

- ✔ Summary blocks display cropped thumbnail images you add to the Options settings of a blog post. (See Chapter 10 for details on adding blog posts.)

When you upload an image to your site, you can set the focus point of the image, which determines which areas won't be cropped. You set the focus by repositioning the focus ring over the image in the image box.

1. Hover your cursor over the image in the image box.

A translucent circle called the *focus ring* appears, as shown in Figure 4-10.

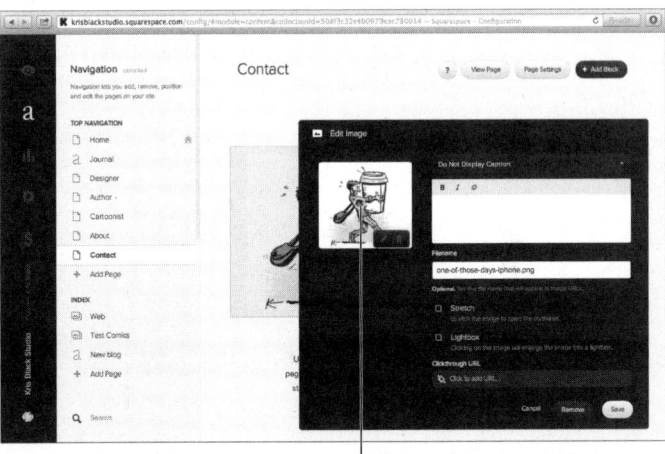

Figure 4-10:
The focus ring over an image in an image box.

Focus ring

2. Drag the focus ring to reposition it.

Position the focus ring over an area of the image that should be the focal point if the image is cropped.

Repositioning the focus ring will ensure that images used in other areas of your site are displayed as you intended.

Editing an image with the Aviary photo editor

You may already be familiar with Aviary, the powerful, built-in photo editor in Squarespace. Aviary is used by plenty of other web services and mobile apps for your smartphone or tablet.

You will probably find yourself relying less on your favorite photo editor and more on Aviary as you become familiar with its features. You can do the following with the Aviary photo editor:

- Adjust the image orientation by rotating the image or flipping it horizontally or vertically
- Crop the image with predefined size ratios or free-form cropping
- Resize the image
- Add text in different font styles and colors
- Automatically adjust an image's color, brightness, and contrast
- Adjust the saturation and sharpness
- Add special effects
- Remove blemishes, whiten specific areas, and draw using different size brushes

By using Aviary to edit your images, you can stay on your website when adding content instead of jumping back and forth from Squarespace to a photo-editing app on your computer. That way, you can spend more time adding content.

To use Aviary, do the following:

1. **Hover your cursor over the image in the image box.**

   The pencil and trash can icons appear at the top of the image box.

2. **Click the pencil icon.**

   The Aviary photo editor window opens and displays your image, as shown in Figure 4-11.

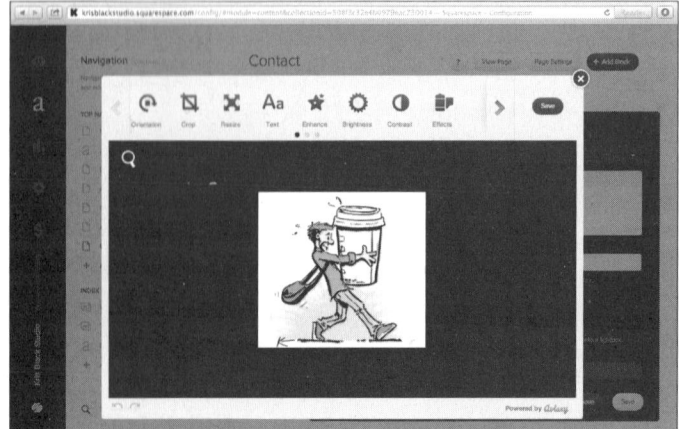

Figure 4-11:
An image
opened in
the Aviary
photo editor.

3. **Click an editing icon to choose a setting to adjust your image.**

   At the top of the Aviary editing window, you will see a row of icons with names representing the settings and features you can use to edit your image. Arrows to the left and right of the icons enable you to shift the row of icons to reveal more icons.

4. **Edit your image.**

   When you click an editing icon in the Aviary window, the row of icons is replaced with the editing controls for the icon you clicked, as shown in Figure 4-12. You can then edit your image and click the Apply button to apply the changes to your image or click the Cancel button to disregard your changes. Clicking either button returns you to the row of editing icons. You can then select another editing icon and repeat this step.

Editing controls

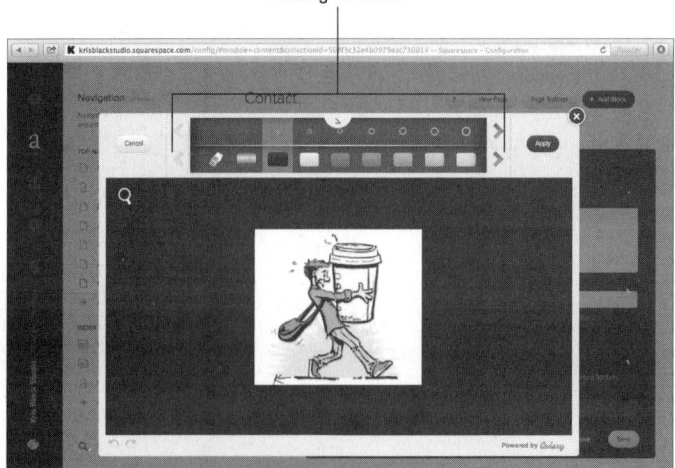

Figure 4-12:
Adjusting
a setting in
the Aviary
photo editor.

5. **Save your changes.**

   When you have finished editing your image, click the Save button to the right of the row of editing icons. The Aviary window will close and you will see the changes to your image on your site.

You can stop editing your image at any time by clicking the x in the upper-right corner of the Aviary window. A dialog box appears with the following options:

✔ **Resume:** Return to editing your image in the Aviary window.

✔ **Close:** Close the Aviary window without saving any changes.

✔ **Save:** Save any changes you have made and close the Aviary window to see the changes to your image on your site.

Using the Aviary photo editor to edit your images is fast and easy. It's a great addition to Squarespace and one that I've used a lot for simple editing and adjustments.

If you want to edit images on your mobile device, search your device's app store or marketplace to download the Aviary mobile app. After editing the image in the Aviary app, you can use the Squarespace app to upload your image to your site. See Chapter 18 about using the Squarespace app to update your site.

Part II
Designing Your Website

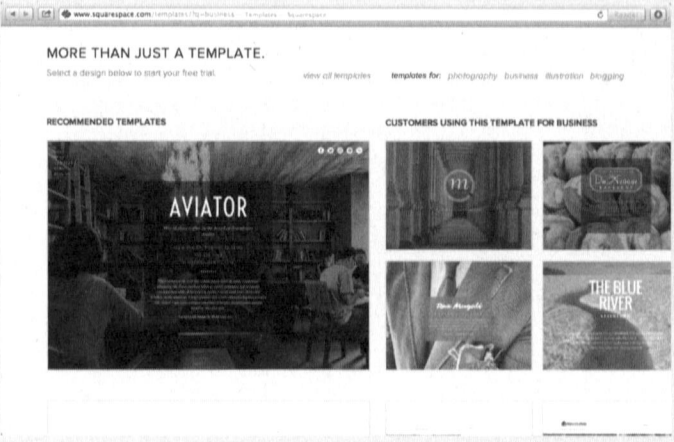

In this part . . .

- ✔ Select and modify a template
- ✔ Preview templates on your site
- ✔ Get schooled in web design basics
- ✔ Customize your site's design

Chapter 5

Considering Your Template Needs

. . . .

In This Chapter

▶ Checking out the templates in Squarespace

▶ Exploring the Template previews

▶ Changing your site's template

. . . .

A template is the foundation of your site, so choosing the right template is critical. However, Squarespace has so many templates that finding one that provides you with the necessary features and layout can be overwhelming. To make your decision easier, they have created helpful previews and demo websites to showcase each template. In this chapter, we explore the types of templates Squarespace offers.

Exploring the Different Templates

Squarespace offers templates in several categories, which can be sorted to help you find the template that might best fit your site needs. The categories are

✔ Blogging

✔ Business

✔ Portfolios

Each template offers a unique layout, and some offer unique features. For example, the Avenue template uses the index feature in Content Manager to automatically create an overview of pages contained in the index. You could then use this overview with thumbnail images that link to each page.

All templates have a corresponding example site you can view. Squarespace's designers have gone to great lengths to use real (or what appears to be real) businesses, artists, and professionals to craft these websites. In this way, you see how a real website is constructed from a particular template.

Time to launch a demo. Simply do the following:

1. **Go to the Squarespace Template Page.**

   On the home page, click the Template link in the main navigation, which takes you to `www.squarespace.com/templates/`.

2. **Select a template.**

3. **Click the Live Preview link.**

   The preview site opens as an in-page viewer, as shown in Figure 5-1.

4. **(Optional) If you want to view a larger preview site, click the preview site URL, which is next to the Start With This Design button.**

   The preview site opens in a new browser window.

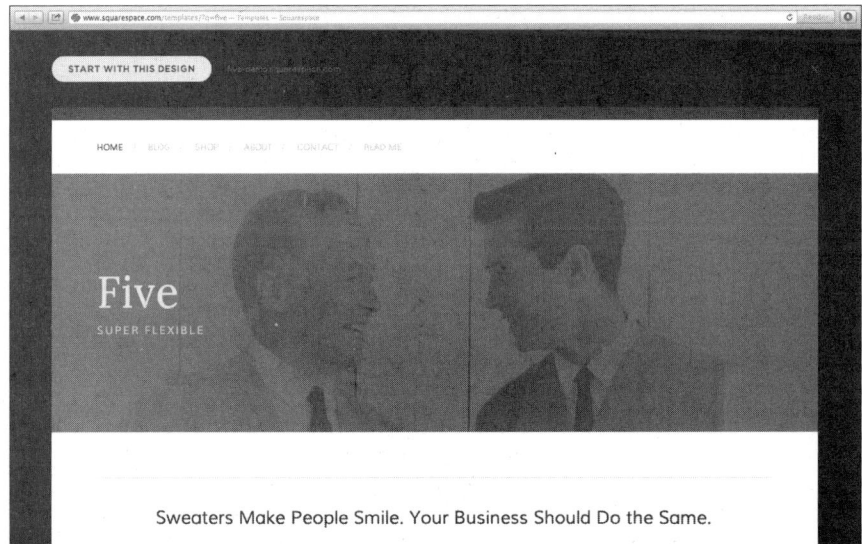

Figure 5-1:
An example
of a
template
preview
site.

Reading the Read Me Page

While checking out template previews in the preceding section, you probably noticed the ReadMe tab. Select that tab to find out the special features each template provides. For example, the Read Me page for the Five template (`http://five-demo.squarespace.com`) begins by explaining how to position sidebars on your site pages. The visual representations of the different sidebar options make this task simple, as shown in Figure 5-2.

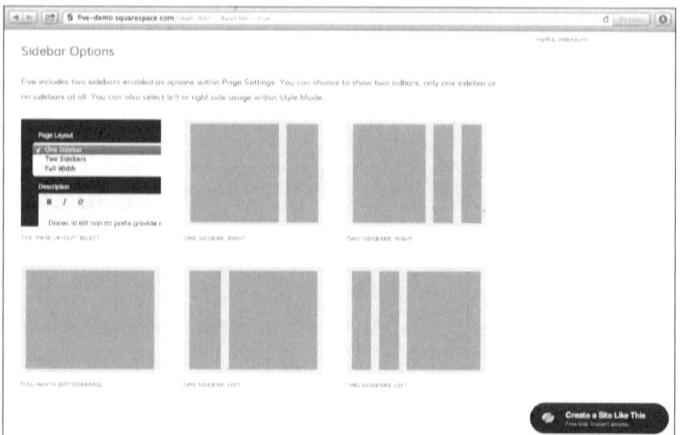

Figure 5-2:
The Read
Me page
for the Five
template.

The Five template is one of my favorite templates because it's one of the most versatile. The sidebar options and the navigational positioning options enable you to easily adapt this template for just about any type of site.

As another example, the Read Me page for the Native template (`http://native-demo.squarespace.com`) provides an overview of the different types of media files you can upload. The template is designed to reformat your site based on the type of device (smartphone, tablet, or desktop computer) your site visitor is using. Figure 5-3 shows screenshots of the Native template on a desktop browser (left) and an iPhone 4S (right).

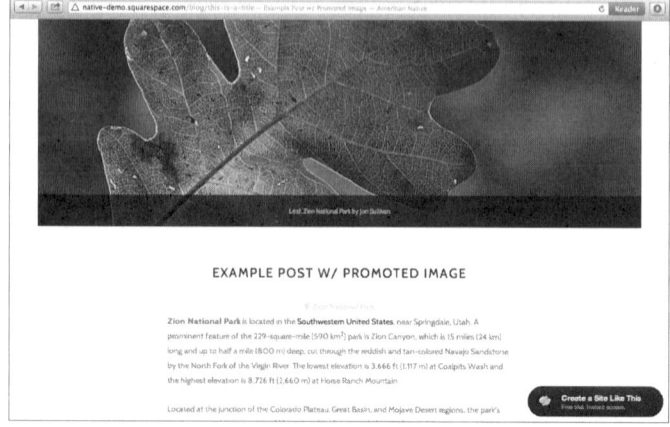

Figure 5-3:
The Native
template on
two differ-
ent devices.

While reviewing a preview template, you can select it for your trial account. Simply click the Create a Site Like This button, in the lower-right corner. Then follow the sign-up process as described in Chapter 3.

Taking Advantage of the Blank Canvas

The Templates page is a colorful place, with all the different templates you can peruse. After checking out a few demo sites, however, you may be wondering, "Where is the color?" That is a darn good question, and one that I had when I started using Squarespace 6. However, when I began building my own site and sites for my clients, I soon discovered why the templates themselves (without the images) are so stark.

The lack of color is not by mistake — these templates are meant to be a blank canvas to which you can add your own content, images, and colors. The result is a site that represents your brand — not one that looks like you modified a template from a website hosting service. Whereas other services provide you with templates with predetermined color schemes, flashy features, and many bells and whistles, Squarespace provides an infinite number of possibilities. All you need to bring to the virtual table is your imagination and your content.

To see this versatility in action, go to the Templates section of the main Squarespace site (www.squarespace.com/templates/) and click a link to display a particular category of template. For example, if you click the Business link, you see all templates in the Business category. In addition, though, click any template and you'll see Squarespace customer sites using that template to build their site, as shown in Figure 5-4.

Figure 5-4:
Examples of sites built by customers using the Momentum template.

Squarespace template   Customer sites

Although the customer sites have the same general structure and layout, they look unique due to the addition of personal content and the use of Style Editor to customize the design.

Changing Your Template

In Chapter 3, you walk through the process of choosing a template to sign up for your trial account. As you begin designing your site by adjusting settings in Style Editor and adding content, you may find that you need a different template.

Squarespace enables you to change your template anytime. All the text and media files you add as content to your pages remain intact. Your page layouts created using LayoutEngine will remain the same. You can feel secure about your content not being modified when you switch templates.

However, selecting a new template can affect a few aspects of your site:

✔ **Style:** The settings in Style Editor will change based on the different style options offered by the other template. The templates do not provide the same style features, so the fonts, sizes, and colors in your site may change.

✔ **Layout:** Part of the design of a template is the positioning of features and elements on a page. You can expect the navigation, the page widths, and the location of certain content to shift. Watch out for templates that don't offer sidebars if your current template does offer sidebars.

✔ **Navigation:** Not all templates have the same navigation structure and areas where you can add pages. For example, if you utilize a secondary navigation area in your current template and switch to a template that doesn't provide this area, all pages in the secondary area will be moved to the Not Linked navigation area.

✔ **Special features:** If your template offers a special feature, such as page-specific header images, it may not be available in another template. Explore the Read Me page of the new template to compare it to your current template.

To preview how another template will look on your Squarespace site, follow these steps:

1. **Log in to your website.**

   Content Manager is automatically loaded. If you were already logged in to your site and in Preview mode, click the gear icon in the Preview toolbar to go to Content Manager.

2. **Click the Settings (gear) icon, which is in the upper left.**

   The Settings area appears on your screen.

3. **In the Settings list, click Templates.**

   The template you are currently using on your site appears in the upper left of the template thumbnail list, as shown in Figure 5-5.

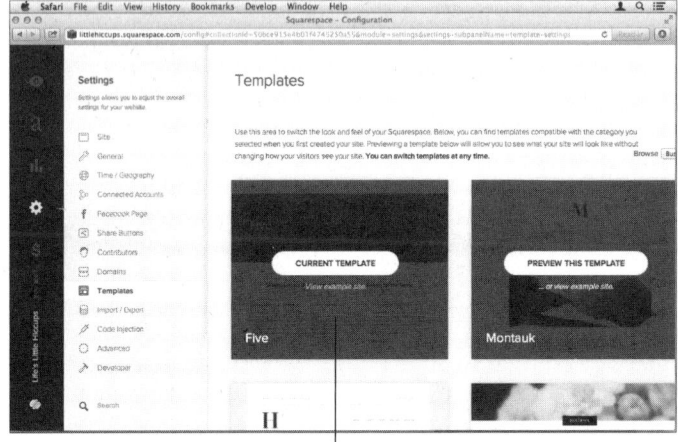

Figure 5-5:
You can preview other templates.

Your current template

4. **Preview another template.**

   Hover your mouse cursor over another template and click the Preview This Template button that appears. The screen switches to preview mode so you can see how your site appears with the new template.

5. **Click around your site to see how the template switch affects your pages.**

   You'll more than likely notice that all the fonts and some colors are different, and the navigation is located in a different area of your pages. To alter the style settings of any of these elements, simply open Style Editor while previewing the template.

   The box in the lower-left corner of your site displays the name of the template you're previewing.

6. **Return to the list of templates or enable this template by selecting one of the following in the box in the lower-left corner:**

   • **Cancel:** Stop previewing the template you are considering, and return to Templates in Site Manager's Settings.

   • **Enable template:** Switch your site to the new template, reloading the page you're viewing. (You will be asked to confirm your decision.)

While you are viewing the list of templates (refer to Figure 4-5), you can view a template's example site. Click the View Example Site link, which appears below the Preview This Template button when you hover your mouse over a template. The demo site opens in a new window.

Any changes you make to a template you've previewed won't affect your active template. Feel free to fully explore the template you're previewing to see if it will provide the style and layout features you need.

If your current template has an index navigation area and an index page and you switch to a template without these elements, any gallery pages in your index navigation area will be moved to the Not Linked navigation area, and the index page will be removed from your site. The index navigation area and index page are major features of templates categorized as portfolio templates. If your site depends on these elements, make sure you use one of the following templates:

- ✔ Avenue
- ✔ Flatiron
- ✔ Hudson
- ✔ Jenson
- ✔ Jirick
- ✔ Minsk
- ✔ Montauk
- ✔ Qubert

So how do you style your website and customize the template you've chosen to use as your site's foundation? Read Chapter 6 to discover the site elements you can modify, and then check out Chapter 7 to see how you can use Style Editor to customize the look of your site.

Chapter 6

Web Design 101

. . . .

In This Chapter

▶ Understanding basic web design

▶ Choosing your site's colors

▶ Using web-safe fonts

▶ Setting the mood with fonts

▶ Selecting background images

▶ Calculating the correct size

. . . .

*D*esign is subjective. A design that I may find appealing, you may find repellent. To oversimplify the topic of what is good design, I'm going to state for the purposes of this chapter that good design communicates a message or an idea effectively. The trick is being able to recognize good design — and knowing why it is good.

People, myself included, go to school to learn this stuff. How can I teach you about design in a few pages? I don't have to — the Squarespace templates already provide you with a solid foundation. You need to apply only simple design changes to make their website template your own. In this chapter, you discover some basic elements of designing a website and find out what you need to focus on to customize your Squarespace website.

Understanding Basic Design Elements

Before you begin customizing your site's template, let's look at what types of elements on your site you can customize. As pointed out in Chapter 5, each Squarespace template is structurally different from the others, with its own features and settings that you can customize. However, all Squarespace templates offer a set of basic features that can be modified.

In any template, you can make the following changes:

✔ Add color to major site features

✔ Adjust the size and styling of text

✔ Control the width of your site

✔ Show or hide site features

✔ Add images to the background and to other elements

When you find a template you are interested in, be sure to check out the preview site's Read Me page. The Read Me page won't tell you everything about the template, but it will highlight all its important features.

Determining a Color Scheme

When figuring out a color scheme for your site, you can quickly become lost in the process of matching colors, adjusting color values (darker versus lighter), and deciding where to include color.

When I set forth to choose a color scheme for a site, I find at least three colors that work well together. Then I choose one of those colors as my primary color, the color that will stand out the most on the site. The other two colors become supporting colors used in minor elements and features of the site, such as text links and divider lines, or for styling text.

Creating a mood board

I like to put together a mood board when I'm trying to come up with a design for a website. A *mood board* is a collection of design elements such as images, fonts, patterns, textures, color, and anything else that visually represents the feeling and emotion you want to convey. Mood boards can be digital boards you create in applications on your computer or mobile device or physical collections of things you find in the real world. Check out the following resources for collecting the elements of a digital mood board:

✔ Evernote at www.evernote.com

✔ Pinterest at www.pinterest.com

Finding RGB and hex codes

After you've chosen the colors you want to use on your site, you need to find the specific color names in one of two color methods used in Squarespace:

- ✔ **RGB** (red, green, blue) is the color method used to display colors on a backlit screen such as that found on a computer monitor, an iPhone, or a TV. The range of each color is measured from 0 through 255. If all three colors are set to 0, the color presented is black. If all three are set to 255, the color is white. By varying the values of the numbers, you can create a near unlimited supply of color.

  In addition, when the RGB color method includes transparency, it's called RGBa. The *a* represents the alpha channel, which controls the color's transparency on a scale from 0 (completely transparent) to 1 (completely opaque).

- ✔ **Hexadecimal,** or hex, color is a simplified form of RGB commonly used in web design.

Although you can certainly just eyeball the color in the color wheel setting (see Chapter 7 for details on using the color wheel), sometimes it's nice to know the exact color you want to use. To find out more about web color, read the thorough Wikipedia article at http://en.wikipedia.org/wiki/Web_colors.

So how do you find the color you want to use? It's fairly easy if you have the right tools on your computer or know where to look. Following is a list of *color pickers,* applications you can use to find the exact color displayed on your computer screen:

- ✔ **ColorZilla** (www.colorzilla.com/firefox/) is a free browser plug-in for Firefox or Chrome.

- ✔ **ColorSchemerColorPix** (www.colorschemer.com/colorpix_info.php) is a free Windows application.

- ✔ **xScope** (http://iconfactory.com/software/xscope) is a paid-for Mac application popular with web designers. It has other features in addition to a color picker that you may find useful if you want more designer features.

- ✔ **ColorSchemer** (www.colorschemer.com) is a robust color picking and designing application available for Mac, Windows, iPhone, and iPod touch. This application is not free but it does offer expanded capabilities to help you explore color harmonies, and it can even suggest color schemes for you. If you have an iPhone or iPod touch, check out the ColorSchemer app, because it's pretty nifty.

Peeking at code

If you're a web professional or someone who doesn't shy away from a little digging in a site's code, you can peek at the color code on a site by inspecting the site's source code. Follow these general instructions:

1. **Right-click the element containing the color you're interested in.**

2. **Select the option in the pop-up menu to inspect the element.**

    The browser displays the underlying code.

Because each browser's source code inspection works differently, following are the basic instructions for inspecting elements in the four browsers Squarespace supports for editing your site:

- ✔ **Safari:** Enable the Developer menu bar in Safari's preferences by choosing Advanced⇨Show the Developer Menu Bar.

- ✔ **Chrome:** Unlike Safari, Chrome already has its inspect element feature enabled, so no configuring is necessary.

- ✔ **Firefox:** Firefox, like Chrome, has a basic inspect element. For more advanced code-viewing features, you need to install Firebug.

- ✔ **Internet Explorer:** Press F12 on your keyboard to open the Developer Tools included in your site. If pressing F12 doesn't work, choose Tools⇨Developer Tools.

Code peeking works only for colors rendered by the browser, such as text color and the background colors of site elements. To determine the color in an image, you will need to use one of the color pickers mentioned previously.

Exploring Web-Safe Fonts and Font Styles

Fonts on the web have been a long-time limitation for anyone building a website. Traditionally, web browsers render the text on a website using the fonts installed on the computer the website visitor is using. If you want your text to be the same across all computers, you would need to use a font everyone has on their computers. For years, the only fonts consistently available on the majority of computers were

- ✔ Arial
- ✔ Courier New

✔ Comic Sans

✔ Georgia

✔ Impact

✔ Times New Roman

✔ Trebuchet

✔ Webdings

✔ Verdana

As technology matured for the web, a few more fonts became more common. In addition to the preceding list, Squarespace recognizes the following fonts:

✔ Courier

✔ Helvetica

✔ Helvetica Neue

✔ Lucida Console

✔ Lucida Sans Unicode

✔ Palatino Linotype

And the fun doesn't stop there, because Squarespace also gives you access to a wide selection of fonts provided by Google web fonts (`www.google.com/webfonts`) and Adobe Typekit (`www.typekit.com`).

Google web fonts and Typekit host fonts on their servers, and you add code to your site to apply a particular font. It's similar to how YouTube hosts a video on its site (and servers), but you can add code to your site to watch the video there.

Both services offer fonts in a variety of font families. Google web fonts are free to use, and more than 600 font families are available on the Google site. Squarespace has curated a smaller (but still long) selection of some of the best fonts Google offers to be directly available in its Style Editor.

Typekit is a paid-for service that offers access to a large selection of premium fonts by leading font foundries. However, Squarespace struck a deal with Typekit, so you can add a select list of fonts to your site for free. If you have a paid Typekit account, see Chapter 17 for information on how to add one of your Typekit Kit IDs to your site to use any Typekit font.

Selecting Fonts for Your Site

Fonts can not only help style your site but also set the tone and mood of your design. If you want to create a Goth-style site, for example, you may want to use a Blackletter font to style your headings. For a playful, kid-friendly style, you might choose a cartoonish font. The art of choosing a font, styling your text, and creating an appropriate reading experience is a part of design called *typography.*

Choosing fonts for your site can be hard with so many options. Generally, a good rule to follow when deciding on the typography for your website is to choose at least two fonts that complement each other. Use one font for headlines and titles, and use the other for your body text.

The body font you choose should be easy to read, particularly if you plan on putting long passages of text on your site. Don't choose a font with a lot of fancy swirls or overly dramatic features. If you aren't sure where to start, try a simple sans-serif font such as Arial or Helvetica or a simple serif font such as Times New Roman or Georgia. (Serifs are those little lines that extend from the end points of letters and symbols. A serif font has those extensions; a san-serif font does not.)

You can be more liberal with the font you choose for headlines and titles. These elements are typically only one or two lines long, a few words at most, and larger in size than the body text.

 Tommi Kaikkonen created a useful interactive guide that can help you easily learn more about web typography. Visit www.kaikkonendesign.fi/typography/ and walk through all the important aspects of styling fonts, spacing them, and making subtle changes, such as using dark gray instead of solid black. He has a little something for everyone, newbies and hardcore typographers alike.

Choosing Images for Headers and Backgrounds

After you've chosen your colors and decided on a few fonts, you may want to add a header image and maybe a little texture or pattern to the site's background. That's great, but how do you decide which images to use? Keeping things simple is the best way to go when designing a website.

Before choosing an image to use at the top of your site in your header, answer the following questions:

✔ **Are you going to use a logo instead of your site's title?** If so, make sure your header image will work well with the logo. I suggest that you add your logo to the site first, and then add a header image behind it.

✔ **Will the header image need to seamlessly blend with the background?** Blending an image with the background can be hard work and may require more advanced knowledge of a design application such as Adobe Photoshop. Some Squarespace templates don't allow you to add a background image. Other templates let you add a large header image that stretches to the edges of your site.

If you want to add a background image to your site, adding a texture or pattern that can seamlessly repeat is your best option. You can make one in an application such as Adobe Photoshop or Illustrator, or you can find a pattern or texture online to use (search for *repeating background patterns* or *website patterns*).

My favorite resource for finding patterns and textures is Subtle Patterns, at `http://subtlepatterns.com/`. Their patterns complement Squarespace templates well.

Recognizing Appropriate Sizes and Values

When it comes to setting the width of your website and the size of text and images within it, you might feel as though you have an unlimited canvas to work on. Although this is true in some aspects, Squarespace does a good job of setting your website's boundaries with default sizes and values.

The sizes and values you have control over differ from template to template but generally fall in two categories:

✔ **Element width:** Examples of elements whose width you can resize are your website, the sidebars, and your logo.

✔ **Text size:** The text you can modify are sitewide elements such as the site title, page titles, the author of a blog post, and text in a sidebar.

Controlling widths

Squarespace gives you plenty of options and settings for controlling the width of your site and major site elements such as the header, navigation, logo, and footer. Some templates even offer you finer control over the width of particular elements within the site. For instance, the Hudson template gives you separate spacing options for both blog posts and regular pages. The Qubert template offers a similar approach but focuses on allowing you to adjust the project width, project detail width, and page width for nonproject pages.

Setting an appropriate text size

Keep in mind that text sizes appropriate for a printed document are not necessarily appropriate for the web. For instance, suppose you're adding your restaurant's menu to your website. You might want to match the size of your printed menu, but that size on the web may be too small. Experiment, and don't be afraid of increasing your font sizes.

I can hear you asking, "But Kris, what about iPads and iPhones? Setting a large font size for a computer might make the text too big on these types of devices." That's a valid concern, but Squarespace has you covered. The templates are optimized, with the size and value of elements and text resizing on these devices.

Now that you have a general understanding of design and how to apply it to styling your website, it's time to dig in and start customizing your site. The next chapter takes you to Style Editor and shows you how to adjust settings, upload your own images, and apply color themes to express your own unique style.

Chapter 7

Customizing with Style Editor

- -

In This Chapter

▶ Finding Style Editor

▶ Adding color to your site

▶ Using images in your design

▶ Changing your site's fonts

▶ Adding custom CSS code

▶ Testing your design on multiple devices

- -

*O*ne of the biggest advantages of using Squarespace to build your site is Style Editor. As mentioned in Chapter 1, other methods of designing websites require you to write your styling code and then refresh your web page to see how it affects your design and content. Style Editor, however, enables you to customize your site's design by adjusting simple settings while seeing how those changes affect your site in real time. Even if you write custom styling code in the CSS window, the changes are instantly reflected in your site without refreshing the page.

As you know by now, each Squarespace template is unique, but they all share certain common elements and features. I can't go over every possible element and feature (the book would top out at 1,000 pages), but in this chapter I provide you with the core knowledge you'll need to become a world-class Squarespace champion, able to design your own site with confidence.

Locating Style Editor

You use Style Editor any time you need to modify the design of your site or specific elements in your site. Style Editor is a part of Style mode, which you access in the Preview area. Follow these steps to load Style Editor in your browser:

1. Log in to your website.

You are taken to Site Manager.

2. **Click the Preview (eye) icon, at the upper left of the screen.**

Preview Editor appears on the screen, as shown in Figure 7-1

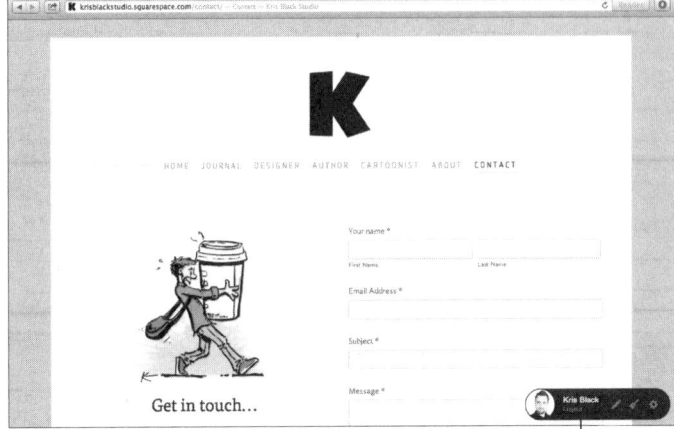

Figure 7-1:
Preview
Editor float-
ing in the
lower right
of your
screen.

Preview Editor toolbar

3. **Click the paintbrush icon in the Preview Editor toolbar, at the lower right of the screen.**

Style Editor slides into view on the left side of your browser window, pushing your site over to the right, as shown in Figure 7-2. The Preview Editor toolbar is replaced by the Style Mode button, indicating that you are in Style mode.

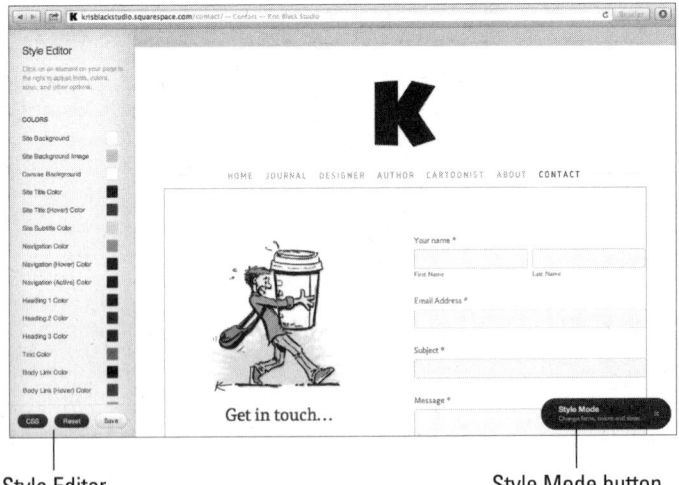

Figure 7-2:
Style mode,
with the
Style Editor
sidebar on
the left.

Style Editor   Style Mode button

When you have finished customizing your site with Style Editor and want to exit Style mode, follow these steps:

1. **Click the Save button, at the bottom of Style Editor.**

   Any changes you've made in Style Editor are saved.

2. **Click the x in the Style Mode button.**

   Style Editor slides out of view, and the Style Mode button changes back to the Preview Editor toolbar.

Style Editor is divided into five main sections:

- ✓ **Colors:** Choose new colors for text, links, borders, and the site background. You can also add background images in this section.

- ✓ **Typography:** Adjust the text on your site by changing the font family, the font size, and the line height; add bold or italics; and more.

- ✓ **Sizes and Values:** Adjust the width and spacing of elements on your site.

- ✓ **Options:** Configure template-specific settings, such as page header heights or sidebar position on your blog page.

- ✓ **Custom CSS:** Add custom CSS code to apply advanced styling. Click the CSS button at the bottom of the Style Editor to open the CSS dialog box and add your custom code.

To see all the sections just mentioned, you need to scroll through the Style Editor list. Style Editor doesn't display a scrollbar in some browsers, but it does scroll if you use your mouse's scrolling mechanism or your touchpad device.

Next, you look at how to select site elements that you want to modify.

Selecting an Element in Your Site

Before you can style an element, you have to select it in Style Editor. You can do so in two ways:

- ✓ **Click the element name.** If you're familiar with the different elements of your site and what they are called in Style Editor, you can simply scroll through the list of elements in Style Editor and choose the one you want to modify.

- ✓ **Click the element in your site while in Style mode.** A nifty little aspect of Style mode is that it disables links on your site. When you click an

element, the Style Editor list is filtered and displays only the element names that can be used to style the element you selected.

If you select the wrong element or want to modify another element, click the Show All link at the top of Style Editor to display all the options in the list and start over.

Changing Your Site's Colors

If you're accustomed to how design applications let you select colors in a color wheel, you'll feel right at home with selecting colors in Style Editor. But if you've never encountered a color wheel, don't worry, because it's easy to use.

Choosing a color on the wheel

To change the color of an element on your site, do the following.

1. **In the Colors section of Style Editor, click the element name.**

   The pop-up color wheel shown in Figure 7-3 appears.

Color indicator

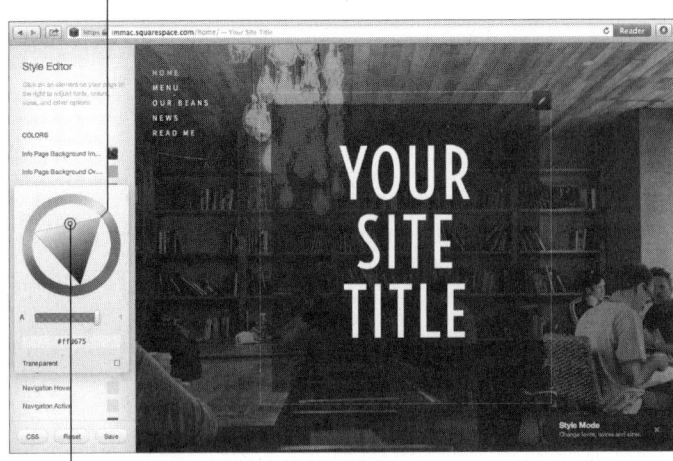

Figure 7-3:
The color wheel in Style Editor.

Value selector

2. **Change the color in the color wheel.**

   The inner triangle is pointing to a dark indicator line in the color wheel. Click and drag that line to select a color. You can also click anywhere in the color wheel to jump the indicator line to that point.

3. Modify the value of the color.

A color's *value* is the darkness or lightness of the color. To change the value of the selected color, drag the value selector disc (labeled in Figure 7-3) anywhere in the triangle. Each corner of the triangle displays the selected color in the color wheel, or black, or white. As you move away from the corners, the values start to blend.

If you want to select a gray color, just move the value selector disc along the edge of the triangle between the white and black corners. The color selected in the color wheel will not matter as long as you keep the disc next to the edge between the black and white corners.

Adding transparency with the slider

To make the selected color transparent, so that a background image can show through, use the slider below the color wheel. Just click and drag the slider to the left. The farther left you drag, the more transparent the color becomes. Dragging the slider all the way to the left makes the color completely transparent.

In Chapter 6, you can read about the two web color methods, RGB and hexadecimal. When you drag the slider to the left, the color method changes from hexadecimal (with the preceding # symbol) to RGBa, as shown in Figure 7-4.

Figure 7-4:
The color changes from the hex color method to RGB.

Color method

Changing the channel

When you move the slider in the color wheel, Squarespace uses the RGBa, not the RGB, color method. The RGB color method code is written in two ways. For example, 50 percent gray, halfway between white and black, is written as `rgb(128,128,128)`. This tells the browser to make each RGB color (red, green, and blue), or channel, 50 percent of its value.

However, if you want the color also to be transparent, you use the second method, RGBa. The

a represents the alpha channel, which controls the color's transparency on a scale from 0 (completely transparent) to 1 (completely opaque).

To get a transparent 50 percent gray, you set the alpha channel to 0.5 using the color black. Black in RGB is written as zeros for each color channel, so the code would be written as `rgba(0,0,0,0.5)`. The last number (0.5) is the alpha channel.

Understanding how transparency works in a browser can help you create some stylish effects on your site. For example, make your content's background color transparent to allow the background image of your site to show through. For more on transparency, see the nearby sidebar, "Changing the channel."

Hiding an element

Suppose you have an element on your site that you want to hide. In other words, you want the element to be 100 percent transparent. Simply select the Transparent option at the bottom of the color wheel dialog box. The element will become transparent instantly.

Customizing Fonts

When you're writing content for your site (for example, in a text block), you can style individual words or groups of words. In Style Editor, however, you don't style individual words on your site. Instead, you style the text elements that your site contains, such as your site title or blog post titles. Style Editor enables you to control how these elements should be displayed across the entire site.

All Squarespace templates are unique, so they don't display the same styling options. Therefore, the following styling options may or may not be available for your typography elements:

- ✔ **Font-family:** Change the font
- ✔ **Font style:** Make the text bold or italic
- ✔ **Font size:** Change the text size
- ✔ **Line height:** Alter the height of each line of text
- ✔ **Text transform:** Change the case (uppercase, lowercase, capitalized)
- ✔ **Text decoration:** Underline, overline, or strike through the text
- ✔ **Letter spacing:** Control the amount of space between individual characters (known as *kerning*)

Choosing a font from the (long) list

In Chapter 6, you discover that Squarespace provides access to a long list of fonts from Google web fonts and Adobe Typekit. To find out what fonts are available, click an element in the Typography section of Style Editor. A pop-up font window appears, as shown in Figure 7-5. At the top of the window, you see the font used for that element. To select another font, click the font and then click a font in the list that appears.

Figure 7-5: An element's font window in Style Editor.

Font window

Fortunately, each font name in the list is displayed in that font, making the list a preview of what the fonts look like. But to see how all letters and numbers look in a particular font, you must select it. The font list remains open, and the selected element in your site is updated with the new font. If you don't like what you see, keep selecting fonts in the list until you find one you like.

If you forget which font you are using as you scroll through the font list, look to the left side of the list; the currently active font will be indicated by a colored bar, as shown in Figure 7-6.

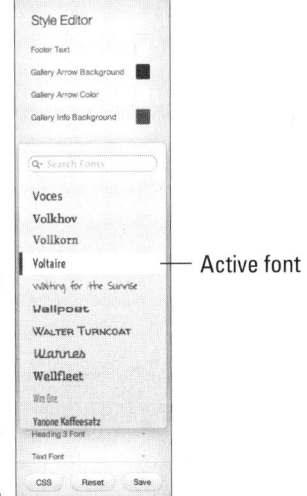

— Active font

Figure 7-6:
The cur-
rently active
font for a
typography
element.

Choosing the right size

Setting the size of your text is straightforward. If you want the text for the selected element to be larger or smaller, you just need to adjust the default size accordingly, which can be done in one of two ways:

- ✔ **In the pop-up font window (refer to Figure 7-5), hover your cursor over the Font Size option to reveal a slider you can drag to adjust the size of the font.** As you drag the slider left or right, the font size's numerical value is updated, and the text on your site changes.

- ✔ **Double-click the font size's numerical value and type a new value.** If you want to set the font size to a specific value, typing it is easier than adjusting the value with the slider.

Some templates will display font size settings for specific elements in the Sizes and Values settings area of Style Editor.

Deciding on bold or italics

Some fonts have a bold setting, or an italic setting, or both. Other fonts are designed with varying levels of bold or italic.

If a font you select has a bold or an italic setting, it will appear in the text styling window, as shown in Figure 7-7. Simply click the check box next to either bold or italic to set your font with that style.

— Bold and italic

Figure 7-7:
Bold and
italic
options.

Speaking of style, if the font has varying levels of bold, you will see another option in place of Bold and Italic called Style. The Style option has a pop-up list of numbers, called *weights,* which increase in increments of 100. The higher the number, the bolder the font. Generally, a value of 400 (shown in Figure 7-8) is considered the same as a regular font (one that is not bold and is a normal weight).

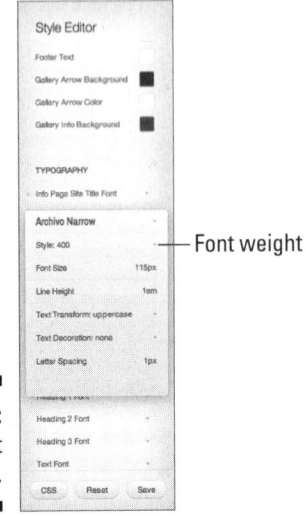

— Font weight

Figure 7-8:
Font weight
set to 400.

Fine-tuning line height and letter spacing

It's always a good idea to make sure your text is spacious enough so that visitors can easily read your site. Squarespace offers you a couple of ways to make your text more legible:

✔ **Line height:** The line height value is calculated in em units. One em is equal to the pixel value of your font size. So if your font size is 12 pixels (px), setting the line height to 1em is equal to a line height of 12px, and setting the line height to 2em equals a line height of 24px. What would 1.5em equal if your font size were still 12px? That's right, 18px. (Half of 12 is 6, and 12 plus 6 pixels equals 18. Whew. I bet you never thought math would come in handy for designing a website.)

When setting line height, I suggest never going below 1.2em to allow for a little bit of space for letters with descenders (such as g, j, and p).

✔ **Letter spacing:** Letter spacing, also known as kerning, is the spacing between individual characters. Letter spacing is best used on titles and headers, not for body text. When measuring letter spacing in Squarespace, the units are in pixels. You can add a negative value to bring your letters closer together.

To modify the line height or the line spacing, you use the slider that appears when you hover the cursor over either option, as shown in Figure 7-9.

Figure 7-9:
The slider
control for
adjusting
the line
height.

— Line height slider

Transforming text with case changes

You may want to display headers and titles as all capital letters or all lower-case letters, despite how you type them in your site. Or maybe you want the first letter of each word in a title capitalized. You can do this by choosing the appropriate option for the Text transformation setting.

In a Typography element's font window (refer to Figure 7-5), click the Text Transform option to reveal a pop-up menu with your choices: None, Capitalize (cap the first letter), Uppercase (cap all letters), and Lowercase (lowercase all letters).

For blog post titles, I always leave the Text Transform feature set to None. Why? Styling your text using the Text Transform feature is absolute and does not take into account words such as iPhone and terms you usually lowercase in headings, such as prepositions. Read the sidebar "Search engines read text but don't see it" for more considerations about using the Text Transform feature.

Search engines read text but don't see it

When you're deciding on whether or not to use the Text Transform feature to style your text in all uppercase, all lowercase, or headline style (capitalizing the first letter of each "important" word), you need to take into consideration how search engines see your site. No matter how you type text on your site, these style modifications are seen only when people view the text on your site. When a search engine indexes your site's content, the text will be indexed as it was typed on your site, disregarding how you styled your text.

If you become complacent and start typing your blog titles in all lowercase letters because you set your blog title element in Style Editor to style the first letter of each word as a capital letter, a search engine won't know that your site's style is doing this. For example, if you titled a blog post *squarespace for dummies is awesome so you should buy it*, your site would display it as

> *Squarespace 6 For Dummies Is Awesome So You Should Buy It*

A search engine such as Google would index only what you typed in your content. Therefore, if your blog post showed up in search results, it would appear like this:

> *squarespace 6 for dummies is awesome so you should buy it*

The lesson here is that no matter how you style your text to be displayed on your site, you still need to make sure to type your text how you want it to be displayed when your style can't be applied to it.

Adjusting Sizes and Values with Sliders

The Sizes and Values section of Style Editor is where you can adjust the widths (and sometimes heights) of site elements, the spacing between elements, and some other values for elements specific to the template you are modifying.

To adjust any sizes or values, do the following:

1. **In the Style Editor list, hover your cursor over the element you want to adjust.**

   The slider appears.

2. **Drag the slider.**

   Move the slider left and right until you find the value you want. The element in your site changes as you move the slider.

The elements you will find in the Sizes and Values section of Style Editor differ from template to template. However, you generally find the following elements:

- ✔ **Site width:** This setting adjusts the width of the overall container for your site.

- ✔ **Page and blog widths:** Some templates allow you to modify the blog width separate from normal page widths.

- ✔ **Site logo:** If you upload a logo to replace your site title (see Chapter 15), you can adjust the size of your logo as you style your site.

- ✔ **Social icons:** If you add your social accounts to your site settings (see Chapter 15), you may want to display icon links to them on your site. You can modify the size of the icons with this setting.

- ✔ **Thumbnails:** Controlling the size of the thumbnails on your site will allow you to display more or fewer thumbnails per row.

You can also adjust the *padding* (the space around the inner parameter) of many elements. Some of the common site elements that offer this adjustment follow:

- ✔ **Canvas:** The *canvas* is the area of your site where all your content resides. You can adjust the spacing along the edges of the canvas.

- ✔ **Blog posts:** When more than one blog post appears on a page, you typically adjust the spacing above or below the post to give it some space.

- ✔ **Pages:** Adjust the spacing around the content of your pages.

- ✔ **Footer:** Adjust the spacing above your footer to push it farther away from your site's content.

- ✔ **Navigation:** Adjust the spacing above and below your navigation or between individual page links.

- ✔ **Thumbnails:** Add space between your thumbnails to make a more spacious grid of images.

Adjusting sizes and spacing on your site can create more room for your content if you need a denser website, or space things apart if you don't want a lot of content on your site.

Modifying the Template with Other Options

At the bottom of Style Editor is the Options section, which contains settings specific to each template. In general, the Options section enables you to do the following:

- ✔ **Hide or reveal elements:** Some elements on your site may be hidden or revealed, if they're not shown by default.

- ✔ **Move or reposition elements:** You can choose to reposition some elements on your site. For example, a sidebar may be moved to the left or right side of your site, or the social media icons may be moved from the bottom to the top of your site.

- ✔ **Change alignment:** Change the alignment of elements, such as your navigation, to align to the right, left, or center of your site.

- ✔ **Make mobile-specific settings:** Some templates enable you to dictate certain settings when your site is viewed on mobile devices.

- ✔ **Select a different style for social icons:** Some templates let you choose to display your social media icons as round or square.

Most of these settings are configured by either clicking a check box to activate or deactivate the setting or selecting an option from a pop-up list.

Saving Your Template

Unlike LayoutEngine, which autosaves your changes as you work (see Chapter 10), Style Editor requires you to save your changes manually.

To save your changes to Style Editor, simply click the Save button, which is located at the bottom of Style Editor, as shown in Figure 7-10.

That's it; simple as pie. However, what if you forget to save your changes and click the x in the Style Editor toolbar to exit? No worries — a warning dialog box will appear, asking you to review your changes. Your options are

- ✔ **Save:** Save your changes and continue exiting Style Editor.

- ✔ **Discard:** Do not save your changes but do continue exiting Style Editor.

- ✔ **Cancel:** Stop your attempt to exit and resume editing in Style Editor.

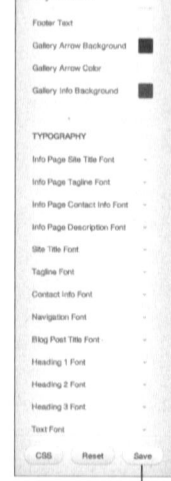

Figure 7-10:
Save your
changes in
Style Editor.

Click Save to save your changes

If you close your browser window or tab without saving your changes, you will not see the warning dialog box, and your changes will not be saved to your site.

Testing Your Template

When adjusting styles, you should test your site on different devices such as an iPhone, an Android phone, an iPad, and a Kindle Fire or other tablet, particularly if you add your own custom CSS code.

Squarespace templates are designed to work on mobile devices, so you won't be testing to see whether your site is working. Instead, you may find that some adjustments you made in Style Editor, or custom CSS you added, have undesirable results you don't prefer on mobile devices.

As professional web designers will attest, designing a website to work on multiple devices with varying screen sizes is not easy. Designing a template with customizable features for thousands of customers to use, as Squarespace has done, and making that template successfully work at different screen sizes, is even harder work. Some settings and features need to be generalized to work for the widest possible customer base. Chapter 18 has more information about Squarespace on mobile devices.

To test your site, and any template changes you made in Style Editor, do the following:

1. **Open your device's web browser.**

   If you have more than one device, check your website on all of them, particularly if you have an Apple device and another manufacturer's device such as an Android-powered tablet or phone.

2. **Type your website's URL in your browser's URL field.**

   You can check your site with your Squarespace URL (`http://your account.squarespace.com`) or a custom domain (`http://www.yourdomain.com`) if you've mapped one to your account (see Chapter 15).

If you're still using a trial account, viewing your website without logging into your site will display the Squarespace Trial warning. This warning will state that your site is not yet visible to the public. You will need to enter an access code to view the site on your mobile device. I suggest entering your website as a visitor, not as the owner, because you will not be editing your site on your mobile device.

Resetting Your Customizations

What if you don't like a modification you made to an element but forgot what the settings were before you made your adjustments? Worse yet, what if you made several modifications to your template, saved your changes, and then decided that you wanted to erase everything you did and start over? Fortunately, Squarespace has you covered and provides solutions for both situations.

Reverting changes before saving

As you make adjustments in Style Editor, each changed element in the style lists sports a small dot to its left, as shown in Figure 7-11. This dot indicates that the element has had an adjustment or change made to it since you entered Style mode or last saved your changes to Style Editor.

To revert changes to an element, do the following:

1. **Hover your mouse cursor over the dot.**

   The dot changes to an x.

2. **Click the x to remove any changes.**

   Because you've removed the changes you made to the element, the dot next to the element disappears.

The dots are hard to see

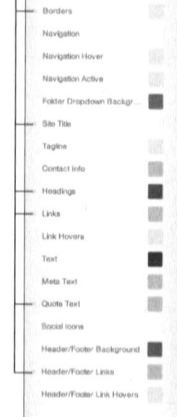

Figure 7-11:
A dot
appears
next to a
changed
element.

After you save your template changes by clicking the Save button at the bottom of Style Editor, any dots next to elements you modified are removed, and you can't revert individual elements to a previous state. However, you can still revert everything to a previous state. Read on.

Resetting all changes

If you want to undo everything you have ever done to your template — reverting it to how the template looked before you customized anything — follow these steps:

1. **Click the Reset button, which appears at the bottom of Style Editor.**

2. **Confirm or cancel resetting your template.**

   This is your last chance to change your mind about removing all changes you made to your template. Confirming to reset the template is permanent and cannot be undone, even by Squarespace Support. If you are having second thoughts or do not want to proceed, click the Cancel button.

Part III
Building Your Website

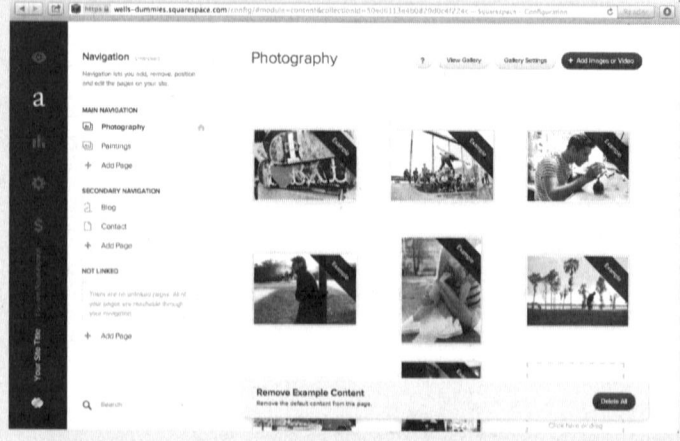

Create an event listing section on your site using the Events page feature at
www.dummies.com/extras/squarespace6.

In this part . . .

- ✔ Discover the different types of pages you can add to your site
- ✔ Add pages to your site for collecting your content
- ✔ Use LayoutEngine to create unique content arrangements on your pages
- ✔ Add blog posts
- ✔ Create a gallery of images
- ✔ Find out about blocks and how to use them to add content to your site

Chapter 8

Working with Pages and Collections

In This Chapter

▶ Adding collection type pages: blog pages, events pages, gallery pages, and product pages

▶ Corralling pages into folders

▶ Understanding the pages page

▶ Adding links

▶ Using an index page

*E*ach template creates its own set of pages on your site. You can choose to keep these pages or remove them. But before you get to any of that, this chapter explains the types of pages you can add to your site.

Defining Page Types

Squarespace 6 has a new, commonsense approach to pages, also called *collections,* which are used to contain items you add to your site. If you were a user of Squarespace 5, you may remember that you could add to your site many different types of page modules. Squarespace 6 has considerably fewer page types because you add any specialized content to *blocks,* a new type of module (see Chapter 10).

Because specialized content is put in blocks, Squarespace requires only a handful of page types:

> ✔ **Page:** The page page type (yup, it's a bit confusing) is displayed as a single page on your site. You use blocks (see Chapter 10) to add content to a page.

✔ **Blog, events, gallery, and products:** Before you can add content in blocks to these pages, you must first create items — blog posts, events, gallery media (images and videos), and products — where you add your blocks. These items are then sorted and displayed as determined by page settings (see later in this chapter) and sometimes by style options in Style Editor (see Chapter 7). The individual items on these pages can have their own unique page in your site.

You can also add to your site two other collections that are not exactly pages but allow you to extend the functionality of your site navigation:

✔ **Folder:** A folder is a collection of other page collections in a grouped list, usually displayed as a pop-up menu, in your navigation.

✔ **Link:** A link enables you to create a text link in your navigation to another website, a file you uploaded to your site, or a page within your site.

All these terms can seem confusing at first, so let's look at this collection of types in more detail.

Item-Based Pages

The most robust pages you can add to your site are blog, gallery, and products pages. These page types help you organize content. You may want to organize articles into a journal, add several products to a store section, or collect videos or images into a portfolio.

Blog page

A *blog page* is a versatile page collection that you can use on your site for more than just a blog. (See Chapter 2 for more on the different types of websites you can create.) You might use a blog page, for example, to organize your articles into categories such as site news, events, and reviews.

A blog's content is organized into *items,* which are more commonly known as blog posts or entries (like entries in a journal or diary). You can organize blog posts by the following attributes:

✔ **Title:** Text that describes the content of the blog post

✔ **Categories:** Blog posts collected under similar topics

✔ **Tags:** Blog posts connected with similar keywords

✔ **Publish date:** Date when a blog post goes live

✔ **Author:** Person accredited with writing a blog post

Refer to Chapter 13 to find out how to add structural blocks to your site that can filter and display posts from a blog based on some of these attributes.

Blog pages provide you with the opportunity to allow site visitors to comment on what you post on your site. Chapter 16 discusses how to manage commenting on your site if you're using the Squarespace commenting feature. If you will be using Disqus, a more advanced third-party commenting feature, see Chapter 15.

You can use a blog page in many different ways. Here are a few possibilities:

✔ **Multiple blogs:** Add multiple blog pages to your site to create a more robust organization of site content, such as for a news site.

✔ **Journal or diary:** Record your daily activities in a private, password-protected blog only you or special loved ones can access.

✔ **Comic book, comic strip, or graphic novel:** Post a comic book, a comic strip, or other sequential art on your site.

✔ **Video or photo:** Create a daily photo journal or video series.

Events page

You can add multiple events to an *events page*. You can use an events page to create a listing of upcoming appearances at conventions in your particular industry, special sales events, or performance dates for your band.

You can choose to display events in one of the following layout formats:

✔ **List:** Events are displayed in a list showing the event title, a description, and a thumbnail if added.

✔ **Calendar:** Events are displayed in a traditional calendar view.

If you have only a handful of events to list, the list view would be your best option for displaying the events on your site. If you're displaying lots of events, you may want to display the events in a calendar view.

When you click the event title in either layout format, the event's listing page appears. Individual events pages contain the following information:

- ✔ **Title:** The name of the event or text that describes the event
- ✔ **Dates:** The date and time when the event takes place
- ✔ **Description:** Information about the event
- ✔ **Location:** The address where the event occurs
- ✔ **Subscription links:** Links to add the event to your calendar application
- ✔ **Categories:** Events collected under similar topics
- ✔ **Tags:** Events connected with similar keywords

Gallery page

A *gallery page* is similar to a blog page in that it holds more than one item, in this case images and videos. Like the blog page, the gallery page can hold multiple items. When you add an item, you choose whether the item will be an image or a video.

A gallery page's layout is configured by the template you use for your site. You can't modify that layout unless the template allows you to do so. See Chapter 7 for details on modifying your template with Style Editor.

Gallery pages can be added in a special navigational section called an index, as explained later in this chapter. The following people are a small example of those who might use gallery pages to create a collection of images or videos showcasing their work:

- ✔ Photographers
- ✔ Illustrators
- ✔ Designers
- ✔ Animators
- ✔ Tradesmen
- ✔ Product designers

Products page

A *products page,* like the gallery and blog pages, enables you to add items. In this case, the items you add are things you want to sell. Squarespace commerce functionality is fully explored in Chapter 17.

On a product page, you can set the price of your item, add variants (such as color, size, style, material), track inventory, and add multiple images of your product, creating an automatic gallery view on the item's sale page. You can also calculate shipping costs based on an item's weight or provide a flat-rate shipping cost. In addition, you can sell digital items; your site can send the customer a download link via e-mail after the sale.

You can use the products page to sell all sorts of things, such as

- ✔ Original artwork or prints
- ✔ Digital files of your work
- ✔ Carryout or delivery orders for your restaurant
- ✔ Homemade clothing or crafts
- ✔ Old equipment for sale
- ✔ Memberships to a password-protected page (see Chapter 21)

A products page will display all the products you add to it. However, you do not have to display your products page if you would prefer to have more control over where your products are displayed on your site. To not display the products page, move it to the Not Linked navigation section (see Chapter 9). Then you can use the products block to add individual items to a specific location in your site. See Chapter 10 for information on adding blocks to your site.

Pages

Pages don't allow you to add items; instead, you add all your content and functionality to blocks directly on the page. See Chapter 10 about adding blocks to your pages and items.

You use pages to create individual, single pages of your site. These pages might contain a simple form block (see Chapter 11) for creating a contact form so that people can send you an e-mail. Or a page might use social blocks (see Chapter 14) to display updates from your different social accounts such as Facebook or Twitter.

In Chapter 10 you find out how to use LayoutEngine to arrange multiple blocks on a single page to create dynamic content. Single pages work great for creating the following types of site pages:

- ✔ **Home:** Present introductory information and a call-to-action to promote your business and motivate people to click through to other pages of your site.
- ✔ **About:** Provide information about you, your company, or blog contributors.

✔ **Services:** Display the services your business offers or the types of products you sell at your store.

✔ **Menu:** Put your cafe's menu on your site, such as the Immaculate Consumption menu shown in Figure 8-1.

Figure 8-1:
The
Immaculate
Consump-
tion menu
using a
single page
type.

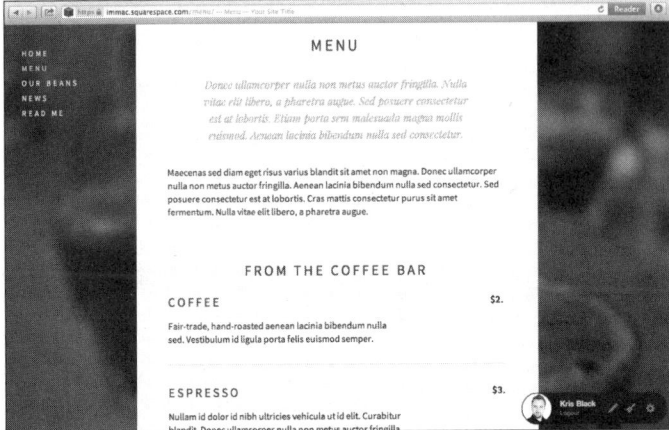

Folders

Folders do not have a page view on your site but instead collect multiple pages into a list. When you add a folder to your site, it creates a pop-up list in your navigation. Some templates may offer additional configurations in which the folder content creates a secondary navigation.

You can use folders to keep your navigation organized into sections. Then, when a site visitor hovers a cursor over the folder name in the site's navigation, the pages in that folder are revealed, as shown in the upper right in Figure 8-2.

Consider organizing pages into folders when you want to

✔ Shorten the amount of pages initially displayed in your navigation

✔ Collect similar pages under a single list

✔ Hide less important pages

Pages in folder

Folder name

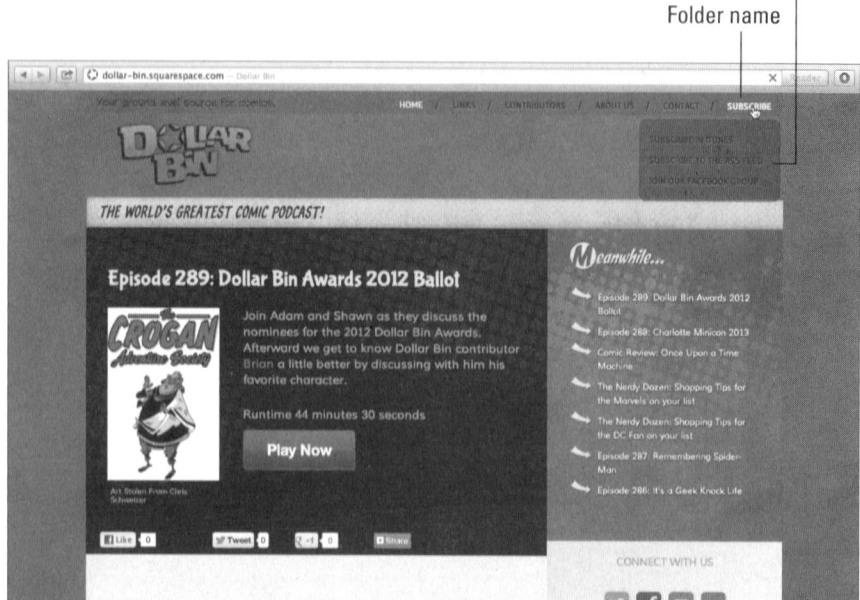

Figure 8-2:
A folder
containing
pages in a
pop-up list.

Links

Links are not pages but a simple way to add a link in your site's navigation. For example, if you want a link to your Facebook group or page, you would use the links page, such as the one shown in Figure 8-3.

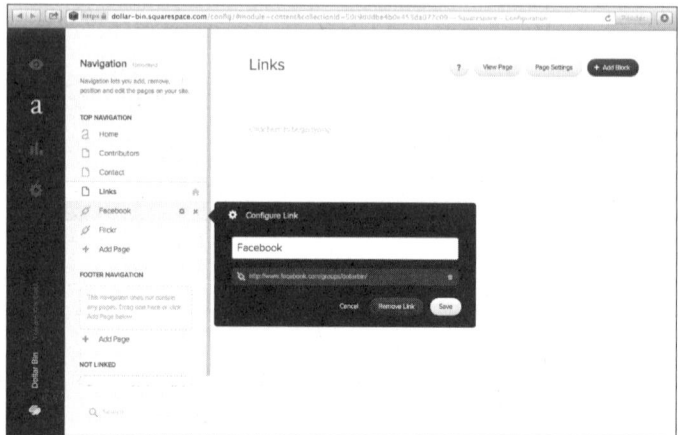

Figure 8-3:
The Dollar
Bin uses a
links page to
link to their
Facebook
group.

Some other uses for a links page follow:

- ✔ Link to hidden pages added in the Not Linked navigational area (see the next section)
- ✔ Link to a specific blog category
- ✔ Allow site visitors to directly download files from your site
- ✔ Link to another site

Index Page

Some Squarespace templates provide you with an index page accompanied by an index navigation area. The *index page* displays the content or page thumbnail of another page in the index navigation area. (See how to add a page thumbnail in Chapter 9.)

You can't add an index page if the template you selected doesn't include this feature. The look and functionality of the index page differ from template to template. The following templates provide the index page feature:

- ✔ Avenue
- ✔ Flatiron
- ✔ Hudson
- ✔ Jenson
- ✔ Jirick
- ✔ Minsk
- ✔ Montauk
- ✔ Qubert

As seen from this short list, the majority of the templates on Squarespace do not provide an index page.

If your site's template has an index page and you switch to a template without an index page, your index page and the index navigation area are removed, and any pages in the index navigation area are moved to the Not Linked area. You can, however, get the index page back by switching to a template that supports index pages.

"What are the navigation areas?" you ask. Well, I'm happy to tell you about them next, in Chapter 9.

Chapter 9

Creating Pages in Your Site

. . . .

In This Chapter

▶ Moving pages in your navigation

▶ Configuring page settings

▶ Customizing advanced page settings

. . . .

*W*hen you create your Squarespace trial account, you select a template for your site. That template has a certain selection of pages added to it by default. You can keep, remove, or rearrange these pages. You can add new pages and customize your pages. What you decide to do will depend on what content you want to add to your website.

In this chapter, you explore the different navigation areas you can use to add, remove, and modify pages; adjust page settings; and configure page settings.

Locating Content Manager

You work with the content in your pages and manage those pages using Content Manager. Here's how you find Content Manager:

1. **Log in to your website.**

   See Chapter 3 for details on logging in. The screen displays Site Manager.

2. **Click the Content Manager (a) icon, in the upper left.**

   Typically, when you log in to your site, Content Manager is automatically loaded into view for you.

Content Manager contains three main areas, as shown in Figure 9-1. On the far left are the editing mode icons. To the right of the icons is the Navigation area, which contains a list of all the pages on your site divided into navigational areas. On the right side of the screen is the LayoutEngine preview of the currently selected page in the Navigation column.

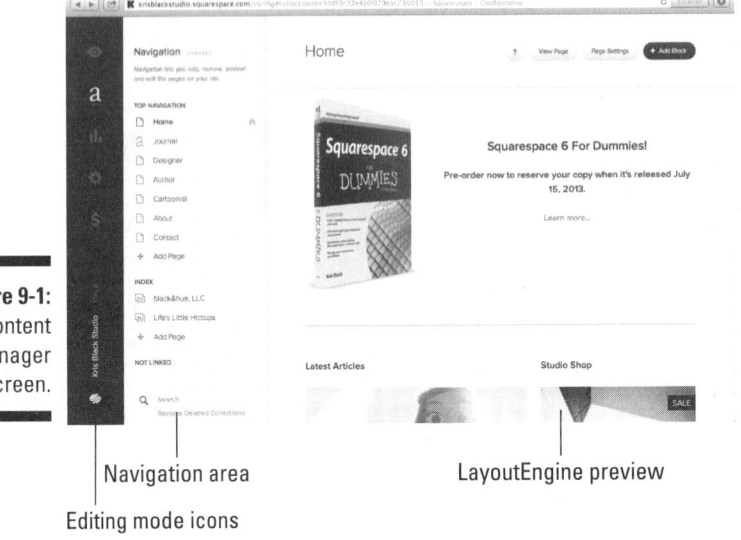

Figure 9-1:
Content
Manager
screen.

Navigation area

Editing mode icons

LayoutEngine preview

 Depending on the template you choose when you first created your Squarespace trial account, the pages and areas you see in the Navigation area can vary, as described in Chapter 4. All templates, however, utilize a main or top navigation containing the main pages of your site.

Determining Your Site's Navigation

The template you choose dictates the different navigation areas you have on your website. Your template may provide the following navigation areas in Content Manager:

- **Top/Main:** All templates have a top, or main, navigation.

- **Secondary:** Pages added to this navigation area are not the main focus of your site.

- **Footer:** Some templates have a footer navigation you can use for second-tier pages (those not as important as the pages in your main navigation).

- **Index:** Add any pages you want to display in an overview page, called an index page, on your site (see the preceding section). The index page pages are added in this navigational area to display the containing pages' content or page thumbnail to create image links.

- **Not Linked:** Add to this area pages that you don't want to appear in any navigation area.

All these areas are labeled in Figure 9-2.

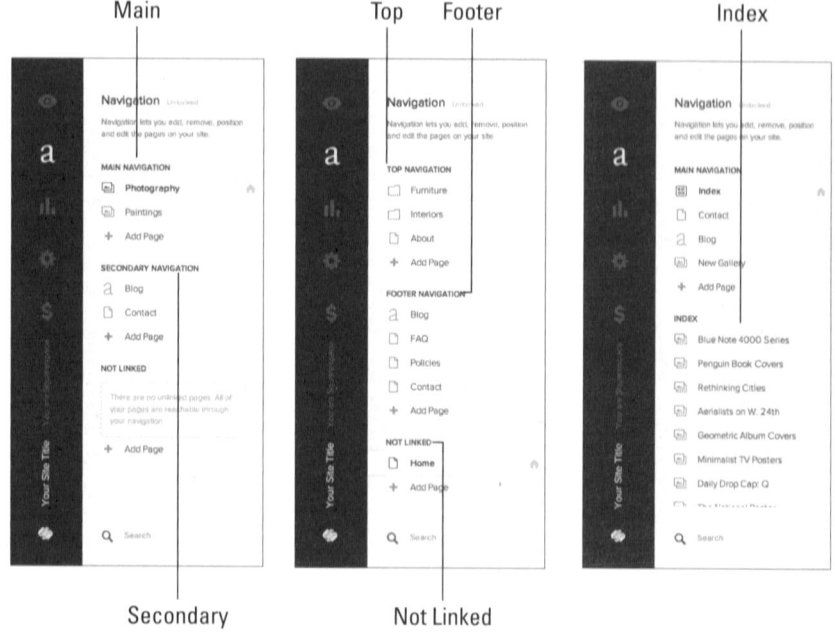

Figure 9-2:
Navigation
areas in the
Dovetail,
Wells, and
Qubert
templates.

If you are thinking about switching templates, your navigation areas may change, and you should be aware of a few issues. For example, remember the index page discussed in the preceding section? Well, an index page has an accompanying index navigation area. If you switch to a template that doesn't support the index page, the index navigation area won't be supported either and will be removed. Any pages in the index navigation area will be moved to the Not Linked navigation area.

Where do the pages go if you switch from a template with footer navigation to a template without footer navigation? If the template you're switching to has secondary navigation, the pages in the footer navigation will go there and vice versa. If the template has only a top or main navigation, the footer pages will be added to that navigation area.

You aren't limited in the number of pages you can add to your site or where you put them in your navigation. However, you'll want to limit the number of pages you place in your navigational areas based on how your site looks in preview mode. If you have too many pages, try the following:

✔ Add a folder to your navigation and move pages into that folder to create a pop-up menu in your navigation.

✔ Adjust the size of the navigation area, the font size, or the spacing between the navigation links.

✔ Consider moving pages to another navigation area if you have a secondary or footer navigation area.

✔ Hide pages in the Not Linked navigation area and link only to pages in text blocks.

The template you selected when you created your website added certain default pages in your navigation areas. You can add, modify, or remove these pages as needed, as you discover in this section.

Positioning pages in your navigation

You can move your pages to the different navigation areas just mentioned, or you can change the order in which the pages appear in a particular navigation area. The process is simple: Click and hold down on the page name you want to move, and then drag it to a new location in your navigation. As you drag, the pages you hover over split apart, opening up a space to drop your selected page, as shown in Figure 9-3.

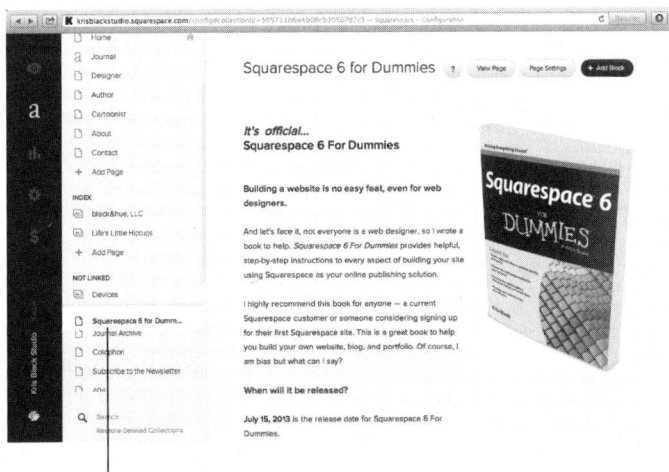

Figure 9-3:
Moving a page in your navigation.

I'm moving this page

Deleting pages from your navigation

If you decide you don't need a page and want to remove it from your site, follow these steps:

1. **Hover your mouse cursor over the page you want to remove.**

   A little x appears to the right of the page name in the navigation column.

2. **Click the x next to the page name.**

   A confirmation dialog box appears.

3. **Click the Delete button.**

   The page is removed from your site and from the navigation column in Content Manager.

You can delete a page from your site in another way:

1. **Open the Configure dialog box (see Figure 9-4) for the page you want to remove.**

   If you aren't already viewing the Configure dialog box, do the following: With the page you selected active in Content Manager, click the button at the top to open that page's settings. The button is labeled specifically for the type of page. For example, if you selected in a blog page, the button will be labeled Blog Settings.

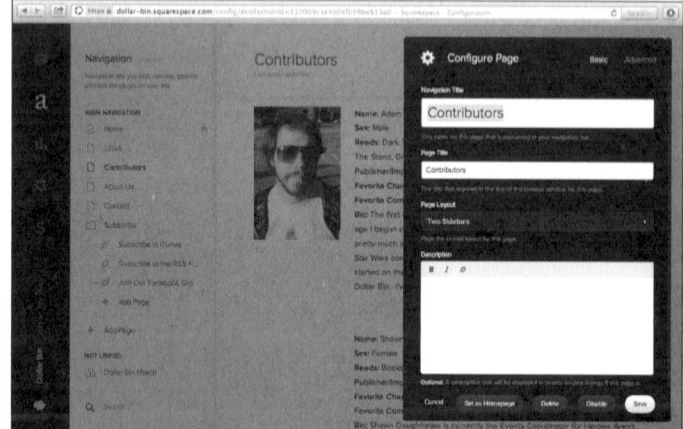

Figure 9-4: The Configure dialog box for a page.

2. **Click the Delete button, which is at the bottom of the Configure dialog box.**

   The Delete Page Confirmation dialog box appears.

3. **Confirm that you want to delete the page by clicking the Delete button.**

   Your page is deleted.

Deleting a page is not permanent. At the bottom of the navigation column in Content Manager, you'll find the Restore Deleted Collections link. Click this link to see a list of pages you've deleted. Click the Restore button next to the page you want to restore to your site's navigation.

If you're not certain that you want to delete a page, move it to the Not Linked navigation area. That way, the page won't be displayed in any of the navigation areas on your site.

Adding pages to your navigation

Adding pages to your site requires just a few clicks and a decision on where to place the page in your navigation. Here's how you add a new page:

1. **Click the Add Page link.**

   The Add Page link is at the bottom of the navigation area or at the bottom of a list of pages in a folder in your navigation area, as shown in Figure 9-5. The Create New Page dialog box appears.

Figure 9-5: Adding a new page to your navigation.

Add Page link

2. **Select the page type you want to add.**

   The types of pages (blog, events, folder, gallery, link, page, or products) are described in Chapter 8. After selecting a page, a configuration dialog box appears.

   If you're adding a page to a folder, you'll see all the page types except the folder option, because you can't add a folder within a folder in Squarespace.

3. **Name your page.**

4. **(Optional) Change the page's URL.**

   The page name is automatically applied to the page URL. You may want to change this to something else. If you don't know whether you want to change the page URL, don't worry — you can modify this later. (For details, see the "Changing the URL of the Page" section, later in the chapter.)

5. **(Optional) Set the new page as your home page by clicking the Set as Homepage button.**

   If you already have a home page, the new page replaces it.

6. **Save your new page.**

   After you save your page, you can begin adding content using blocks, as described in Chapter 10.

If you want to quickly edit an existing page's settings in the configuration dialog box, as described in the preceding steps, right-click the page name in the navigation column.

Configuring Pages with Basic Settings

For all page types, you use the Configure dialog box to configure the same core settings. Blog, events, and index pages provide a few additional settings in the Basic Settings area of the dialog box.

In this section, you explore what these settings do, but first you need to know how to open the Configure dialog box for any page on your site.

1. **In the navigation column, select the page you want to edit.**

2. **Open the Configure dialog box (refer to Figure 9-4).**

   With the page you selected active in Content Manager, click the button at the top right to open that page's settings. The button is labeled according to the page you're viewing, such as Gallery Settings for a gallery page.

In this section, you go through and modify the configuration settings for the page.

Choosing your navigation and page titles

When you add a new page to your site, you can give the page a unique name. That name will be used in two basic settings for the page:

✔ **Navigational Title:** The name that appears in your site's navigation

✔ **Page Title:** The name that appears at the top of the page's content area or is referenced from other features of the Squarespace system to create your site

By default, the navigation and page titles will be the same, but they can be different if you want. For example, let's say you wanted to use several structure blocks (see Chapter 13) to create a page that displays an archive of your blog with different options for site visitors to locate past blog posts. You may want *Search the Archive* for the page title but *Blog Archive* for the navigational title to conserve space in the navigation area.

Including a description of the page

The page description block is where you can write a brief description describing the page. This description serves two purposes in your site:

✔ **On-site display:** Some templates display page descriptions in the site. For example, in the Dovetail template, shown in Figure 9-6, the page description is displayed below the page title.

✔ **Search Engines:** A page description may be used and displayed in search results when search engines index your page.

If the page description will be used in the template of the site, you can take advantage of the limited text styling options available in Page Settings. Note the text styling options above the area where you type your description. You can make words bold or italic, or set a word or group of words to be a link to an external URL, a file on your site, or a specific page in your site. These text styling options are similar to how you edit text in a text block, as explained in Chapter 11.

Site title   Page title

Figure 9-6:
The Dovetail
template
uses the
page
description
on your site
pages.

Description

Changing the URL of the page

When you create a page, the page URL is a variation of the page title, modified to fit in the structure of how URLs can be written (see the upcoming Warning icon). You can modify the page URL if you want to change it to something different. For example, if your page and navigational titles are *Search the Archive* and *Blog Archive,* respectively, you may want to modify the page URL to simply *archive*. Then your page's URL would be displayed as follows in your browser: `http://www.`*yourdomain*`.com/archive`.

The page URL cannot contain spaces or special characters such as a question mark or exclamation point. Use only letters and numbers, and substitute spaces with dashes.

Search engines treat dashes as spaces when reading your URL, which helps with search engine optimization (SEO). What's SEO? Check out the end of Chapter 20.

Setting a password for the page

You may want to limit access to a page on your site. You can do this by giving the page a password. Then only someone who knows the password can view the page, as shown in Figure 9-7.

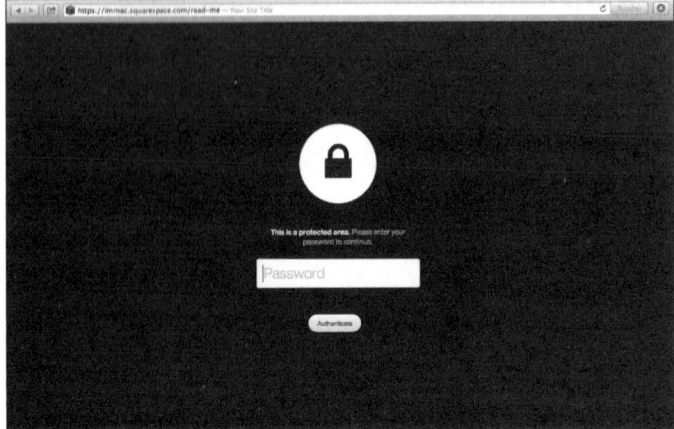

Figure 9-7:
A password-
protected
page.

Adding a password for your page

To password-protect a page on your site, type the password in the Password field. Make note of the password you type.

Do not use the same password as the one you use to log in as the site owner. Moreover, choose a password that you don't use for anything else online. Password security is important, and you want to make sure you don't jeopardize yourself by using a password you use for access to important online accounts.

Setting a password for a page is not an extremely secure way to password-protect pages on your site. When someone enters the correct password to view the page, their browser will continue to allow them to view the page even if you change the password. If they close their browser, their session ends and they must reenter the password the next time they visit the page.

To remove or change the password, you simply modify the Password field:

- ✔ **Change the password:** Select the password dots in the Password field and type in a new password.

- ✔ **Remove the password:** Select the password dots in the Password field and press the Delete key.

As mentioned, password-protecting individual pages is insecure. If you need to guarantee that someone can't see a particular page, you will need to do one of the following:

- ✔ Remove the page from your site.

- ✔ Disable the page so that it's no longer an active page on your site. (See the "Disabling a page" section, later in the chapter.)

- ✔ Password-protect your entire site (see Chapter 15).

Uploading a thumbnail for the page

Page thumbnails are used for certain features in your site. For example, some templates use them as

- The index view for pages added in the index navigational area
- A different website background image on individual pages (Peak template)
- A different header background image (Five template)

Also, the Collection Link structure block (see Chapter 13) uses the Page Thumbnail image to display an image link to the page. You can add an image as your page's thumbnail in three ways:

- **Drag an image from your computer.** If you have an image on your computer, drag and drop it over the thumbnail image area to instantly upload it to your site.
- **Click the large plus sign.** Click the plus sign in the thumbnail image area to open a system dialog box that enables you to select an image on your computer.
- **Click the Download icon in the lower-right corner of the thumbnail image area.** This action opens a dialog box where you can add a page URL to a location on the web with an image you want to use.

To add an image from a URL, do the following:

1. **Type the URL of the page with an image you want to use.**

   Make sure that you have authorization to use the page.

2. **Click the Find Images button.**

   A screen appears displaying all the images used on the page you added in Step 1.

3. **Hover your cursor over the image you want to use from the grid of images.**

   As you hover your mouse cursor over an image, horizontal and vertical rulers appear in the upper-left corner of the browser. These rulers show you the size of the image, which can help you determine whether an image is the right size for its intended use.

4. **Click the image to select it.**

   The image is pulled from the URL you referenced in Step 1 and added to the page thumbnail.

After you have an image uploaded to the Thumbnail Image setting, you can modify the image in Avery Image Editor, and you can change the focal point of the image.

Setting a page as your home page

You can set any page in your site as the home page, the page that first loads when someone goes to your Squarespace account URL (http://*your account*.squarespace.com) or to a custom domain (http://www.*your domain*.com) if you mapped your own domain (as explained in Chapter 15).

Setting your home page is as easy as clicking a button:

1. **Click the Set as Homepage button, at the bottom of the Configure dialog box.**

   If the page you selected is already the home page, you will not see the Set as Homepage button.

Yup, it's that easy.

You can also set a page as the home page when you create the page. See the previous section, "Adding pages to your navigation."

When you set a page as the home page, the page that was the homepage remains on your site. If you want to delete the old home page, see the "Deleting pages from your navigation" section, earlier in this chapter. What's that? You might want to disable the old home page or another page on your site? Glad you asked.

Disabling a page

If you want to disable a page on your site, you can do so in the Configure dialog box for the page. For example, if you are updating the content of a page, you may want to disable the page so that a site visitor doesn't stumble on the page mid-update. Or you might want to add, remove, or rearrange the page's blocks using the LayoutEngine (see Chapter 10).

Whatever your reason, follow these steps to disable your page:

1. **Open the Configure dialog box.**

2. **Click the Disable button, which appears at the bottom of the dialog box.**

   The Disable Page Confirmation dialog box appears.

3. **Click the Confirm button to disable the page.**

   Your page is disabled.

A disabled page remains in its location in your navigation, but the page link appears dimmed in Content Manager. In Preview Editor, the page will be hidden from your site's navigation, and your site visitors will not be able to see it. To navigate to the page when you are logged in (as the site owner), select the page in the navigation column and then click the View Page button at the top of Content Manager.

Oh, no! What if you want to enable the page you just disabled?

Enabling a page

Enabling a page is the same process as disabling a page. Your reasons for enabling a page are simple — you want people to be able to see it when they visit your site. If your page is disabled, it's probably because you disabled it. So you may be able to guess how you enable the page, but just in case you forgot, here's how.

1. **Open the Configure dialog box.**

2. **Click the Enable button, which is at the bottom of the Page Settings dialog box.**

   The page is enabled and the Configure dialog box closes, making the page available for your site visitors to see.

   Enabling a page is one step shorter than disabling a page because no confirmation window appears. Just make sure you are 100 percent sure you want to enable the page.

Configuring the Basic Settings for a Blog Page

If you're modifying a blog page, you have three additional settings to configure:

✔ **Posts per page:** Control the number of blog posts that appear on each page of your blog.

✔ **Post by email address:** Send blog posts to your site by e-mail.

✔ **Quickpost bookmarklet:** Instantly post to your blog from anywhere on the web, even if you're not logged into your website.

These settings are simple and easy to set up, as you see in this section.

Choosing the number of posts per page

You can think of a blog page, which is a collection page type, as a container that holds all the blog posts you add to the page. You can control the number of blog posts that appear per page. I realize this might be confusing, so let's look at how a blog page works.

A powerful feature of a blog page is its capability to filter and display blog posts in various configurations. Your blog can display posts in two types of views:

✓ **Filtered page view:** This view adapts to show only blog posts that are within a particular configuration or are organized by a specific category or tag.

✓ **Blog post page view:** Blog posts can be viewed at their own, unique URL. The unique URL is the page where people can comment about the blog post. See Chapter 16 about blog commenting on your site.

The difference between these two views is that the filtered page view is dynamic and adapts to show the number of posts you configured using the Posts per Page setting in the Configure dialog box. You can choose to display from 1 to 20 posts per page.

To adjust the number of posts per page, do the following:

1. **Open the Configure dialog box for your blog.**

2. **In the Posts per Page option, move the slider to adjust the number.**

   The Posts per Page option is just below the Page Title option. Click and drag the dot in the slider control to adjust the number of posts to display per page.

The type of content you put in your blog should determine the number of posts you display per filtered page view. Also consider how you want people to experience your content.

Following are some considerations when determining how many posts to display per filtered view:

✓ **Image-heavy posts:** If you add several photos or very large photos in your blog posts, consider limiting the number of posts that are displayed in the filtered view. Although Squarespace serves your website from a super-fast data center, consider those site visitors who may be accessing your site from a mobile device over a cellular Internet connection. Lots of images or large images can slow down their experience with your website.

✔ **Excerpts to preview your posts:** Consider using excerpts to show a preview of a blog post in a filtered view in which multiple blog posts are displayed on a page of your site. To view the entire blog post, a visitor would need to click the blog post title or a Read More link. Consider using the excerpt option of a blog post to generate more page views by your site visitors. (See the next section for details on blog post excerpts.) By using excerpts, you can display more blog posts per filtered view in a shorter page length.

✔ **Serialized content:** If you write, draw, or create serialized content, you may want to limit how many posts are displayed per page to better control the experience of your creation. For example, if you create sequential art (such as comic books, comic strips, or children's books) online for people to enjoy, limiting their exposure to one post at a time can help control the suspense of your stories.

✔ **High frequency of posting:** If you're a power blogger, you may find yourself publishing blog posts frequently. If this is the case, displaying more posts per page will make it easier to see more of your content on one filtered view. You may even want to consider using the excerpt feature.

Whatever your reason, controlling the number of filtered views can allow you to better control how the content on your site is consumed by your site visitors.

Establishing an e-mail address for posting

A neat Squarespace feature that I think many people overlook is that you can publish blog posts by e-mailing them to your blog page. This feature might seem odd because why not just log into your website and publish the post? Well, the following factors might be keeping you from publishing that way:

✔ **You're offline.** You don't have Internet access, but you want to go ahead and create a blog post while you're thinking of it. If your e-mail application allows you to create e-mails when you're offline, clicking the e-mail's send button should send the e-mail the next time you have Internet access automatically.

✔ **You don't have enough time.** You don't have enough time to publish the post through your website or from the Squarespace mobile app for Android or iOS devices (see Chapter 18). Sending an e-mail requires less involvement because you have to write only a subject and message in your e-mail app.

✔ **You want to let someone else post to your blog.** You can share your blog's secret e-mail address with people you trust but don't want to grant contributor access (see Chapter 15) so that they can send blog posts from their e-mail.

Publishing blog posts to your site by e-mail is easy. First, you must create your blog's e-mail address in the Configure dialog box.

1. **Open the Configure dialog box for your blog.**

2. **Click the Post by Email Address refresh icon (circular arrow) to generate your blog's e-mail address.**

   Clicking the refresh icon, on the far right of the Post by Email Address field, generates a random e-mail address in that field. This is the e-mail address you can use to send your blog posts.

3. **(Optional) Click the refresh icon again to change the e-mail address.**

   The old address is removed and a new e-mail address is generated.

4. **Save your page settings.**

   Click the Save button at the bottom of the blog settings configuration window.

Oh, did I mention you could e-mail photos to your blog? If you e-mail a single photo, it is displayed using the image block. Multiple photos are displayed in a single gallery block. For more on how Squarespace uses blocks to display images in your site, see Chapter 12.

If you want to post a picture to your site but don't have a lot of time, most smartphones (and some not-so-smart phones) enable you to e-mail photos on your device with a button click. Add your blog's e-mail address to your phone's address book to make the process even faster. Plus, the e-mail addresses Squarespace generates are not easy to remember.

If you don't want to allow blog posts to be posted by e-mail, you can disable the Post by Email Address feature. Click the X icon on the far right of the e-mail address to remove the current e-mail address. To enable the feature again, click the refresh icon to generate another e-mail address.

When posting by e-mail, remember the following:

- ✔ **Use the To field**. The e-mail address for the blog must be added to the To field of your e-mail message. You can't use the CC or BCC field.

- ✔ **Write in plain text.** Don't use font styling features (such as different font sizes, bold, or italic) in your e-mail message or HTML formatted e-mails. (Squarespace strips out your code.)

- ✔ **Posting can take a while.** You may have to wait from one to ten minutes for your e-mail to post to your site.

Installing the Quickpost bookmarklet

Are you a frequent blogger or someone who doesn't like to interrupt your web surfing by logging into your site? If you install the Quickpost bookmarklet, you can instantly publish to your blog from anywhere on the web.

To install the Quickpost bookmarklet in your web browser, do the following:

1. **Open the Configure dialog box for your blog.**

   Scroll to the bottom and locate the Quickpost bookmarklet setting.

2. **Drag the Post to Squarespace bookmarklet to your browser's bookmark bar.**

   After you install the bookmarklet, you can modify its name in your bookmark's settings. (In some browsers, you right-click the bookmark to rename it.) If you manage more than one Squarespace site, you may want to give each bookmarklet a unique name so you know which is which.

Using the bookmarklet is easy. When you want to post without having to load your site in your browser, do the following:

1. **Click the bookmarklet in your bookmarks bar or menu.**

   A new Edit Post pop-up window appears.

2. **If necessary, log into your site.**

   If you're not already logged in to your site from an older session, the login screen appears in the pop-up window.

3. **Start configuring your blog post.**

   You have access to all Edit Post features for composing your entry.

4. **When you're finished, save the post as a draft or publish it to your site.**

Utilizing Unlinked Pages to Add Hidden Content

As mentioned, not all templates provide the same navigation areas, but all templates do provide the Not Linked navigation area, where you can hide pages in your site.

You might want to have a hidden page to

- ✔ Document the creation process of a work shown in your portfolio

- ✔ Create a gallery page to show clients photos from an event they hired you to photograph

- ✔ Enable a colleague to critique a new page of your site without logging in to see it

- ✔ Develop a series of landing pages that are accessible only by links shared in different marketing campaigns

- ✔ Set up a portfolio for an interview that only your prospective employer can view — and that your current employer won't stumble upon

- ✔ Share free downloads with people who join your mailing list (through MailChimp integration using the form block, as detailed in Chapter 11)

Whatever your reason, the capability to hide pages is a useful feature. To let people find a hidden page, you can

- ✔ **Link to the hidden page in your content.** See Chapter 4 for steps on creating a link in a text block.

- ✔ **Share the URL by e-mail or social media.** To get the URL of the hidden page, click the View Page button at the top of the page when you are viewing it in Content Manager. Your hidden page will be loaded on your site, as a site visitor would see it, and you can then copy the URL from the URL field at the top of the browser.

Set your home page as a hidden page to save space in your navigation. Your site title, or your site logo, acts as a link to your home page.

Modifying Settings for Folders and Link Page Types

The folder and link page types are not pages on your site, but they help you structure a more robust navigation. Folders are useful for organizing pages within your navigation. Links can help you direct people to specific areas of your site or to other places on the web.

So what exactly can you do with these features? Let's find out.

Modifying folders

The folder is probably the simplest of any Squarespace item in Content Manager. You add a folder the same way you add any page to your Squarespace site: by clicking the Add Page link in Content Manager, as described earlier in this chapter. When you add a folder, you choose a folder name and a URL name.

If you want to modify the folder's settings, do the following:

1. **Hover your mouse cursor over the folder's name in the Navigation column, and then click the gear icon that appears.**

   The gear icon appears next to the x on the far right, as shown in Figure 9-8.

Figure 9-8: Hover your cursor over a folder (or any page, for that matter) to reveal the gear icon.

Gear icon

2. **If you want to rename the folder, type a new name in the white text field.**

3. **If you want to rename the folder URL, type a new name in the gray text field below the folder name.**

   Changing the folder URL will change the link to any page in the folder.

You can delete a folder in two ways:

✔ Hover your cursor over the folder name in the Navigation column, and then click the x that appears.

✔ Hover your cursor over the folder's name in the Navigation column, click the gear icon that appears, and then click the Delete button.

When you perform either of the deletion methods, you must confirm the deletion in the Delete Folder dialog box.

Deleting a folder will delete the pages in the folder. So make sure you either want to delete the pages in the folder or have moved the pages to another location in your navigation. See the "Positioning pages in your navigation" section, earlier in this chapter, on how to move pages.

Disabling a folder is just as easy as deleting it:

1. **Hover your cursor over the folder's name in the Navigation column, and click the gear icon that appears.**

2. **Click the Disable button.**

3. **In the dialog box that appears, confirm disabling of the folder.**

Disabling a folder only prevents the folder from appearing in your navigation. Any pages in the folder are not disabled and can still be accessed by a direct link.

Modifying link item settings

Adding links to your navigation can be a useful way to help direct people to specific web pages, whether or not the pages are on your site. Link pages do not have a page of their own; they simply allow you to link somewhere else.

You add a link item as you would a page:

1. **Hover your cursor over a link item in the Navigation column, and click the gear icon that appears.**

2. **Name the link.**

   This is the name that will appear in your navigation.

3. **Add the URL by selecting Click to Add URL (below the link name) and choosing one of the following:**

   • **External:** Type the URL for a web page that you want to link. Make sure you use the entire URL, including http://. To visit the URL you've typed, click the diagonal arrow to the far right of the URL field. If you want the link to open in a new window when someone clicks it, select the New Window option.

   • **Files:** Upload a new file to your site or select a file you've uploaded previously on another page of your site.

   • **Content:** Select a page to link to on your site.

If a link already appears in the link URL field, you can delete it by clicking the trash can icon on the far right of the field.

4. Click the Save button to save your link.

If you need to delete or remove a link you've created, do one of the following:

 ✔ **Hover your cursor over the link in the Navigation column, and then
    click the x that appears.**

 ✔ **Hover your cursor over the link in the Navigation column, click the
    gear icon that appears, and then click the Remove Link button.**

Both removal methods require that you confirm the deletion in the Delete
Link dialog box. Removing a link will delete the link from your navigation.

Well, there you have it. You've found out how to create and manage the
pages on your site. But how do you add content such as images, video, and
text to your pages? How do you publish content from your social profiles
such as Twitter and Facebook? Wouldn't it be great if these tasks were as
easy as building a tower with toy blocks, without it toppling over on you?
Actually, it is. Turn the page to find out.

Chapter 10

Building Your Pages with Items and Blocks

. . . .

In This Chapter

▶ Understanding pages, items, and blocks

▶ Adding and removing page items

▶ Reviewing Edit settings for posts, gallery images, and gallery videos

▶ Adding and removing blocks

▶ Rearranging blocks

. . . .

*A*dding content to your site is the most important part of creating a website. Without content, your website doesn't have a purpose. When you create a trial account on Squarespace, your site has placeholder content based on the template you chose. Now it's time to add your own content.

Certain page types in Squarespace allow you to organize your content into page items to create a blog, a gallery, or a store. You add and position content within pages by using blocks. In this chapter, you discover the different types of blocks you can use, and then add, remove, and configure them. Then you find out how to use LayoutEngine to rearrange blocks within your pages and page items.

Exploring How Pages, Items, and Blocks Work Together

We all know that a website is made up of individual web pages, much like a book is made up of individual pages. Squarespace has different types of pages you can add to your site. The simple page, called *page,* is a stand-alone page you add to your site. In other page types — the blog, events, gallery, and product pages — you can add special pages called *page items.*

Page items enable you to organize content by tagging and categorizing the content into related groups. On blog pages, page items are called blog posts. On events pages, page items are called events. On gallery pages, page items can contain either an image or a video, called media. In products pages, they are called products.

You use Squarespace blocks to add and organize the content on your pages for easy editing and rearranging. You add blocks directly to pages or, for blog, events, gallery, and products pages, directly within items.

All this adding and organizing of blocks takes place in Content Manager. You organize pages in the Content Manager's navigation lists (see Chapter 9). You organize blocks within the individual pages and items using LayoutEngine in Content Manager (as described later in the chapter).

Working with Page Items

On blog, events, gallery, and products pages, you can create five types of page items to categorize your content into related groupings:

- ✔ Blog posts
- ✔ Event listings
- ✔ Gallery images
- ✔ Gallery videos
- ✔ Products

First, you find out how to add an item to blog, events, and gallery pages. Then you look at the different settings for these items. (To find out how to add products to a products page and manage your store, see Chapter 17.)

Adding an item

To add an item to your blog, events, or gallery page, simply follow these steps:

1. **Select your blog, events, or gallery page in Content Manager.**

2. **Click the button to add an item.**

   On blog pages, the button is Add Post. On events pages, the button is Add Event. On gallery pages, click the Add Images or Videos button or the Add Media button.

If you have added a new page and are adding your first item, you can also click the large plus sign for blog and events pages in the middle of the item listing area.

Clicking the dotted-outlined box in the middle of the item listing area on new gallery pages will allow you to add only photos to the gallery page. If you need to add videos, be sure to click the Add Images or Videos button.

3. **If you're adding an image or a video to a gallery page, click the appropriate icon.**

4. **Add your content.**

   A blog post has a text block (see Chapter 11) added automatically in the content area so you can begin typing your content. If you want to add another type of block, see the "Adding a block to your page" section, later in the chapter.

   You can set your site to always use a Markdown block as the default block that appears in new page items instead of a text block. Change this in Site Manager➪Settings➪General as described in Chapter 15.

   If you're adding an image to your gallery page, see Chapter 4 for details. To add a video to your site, you will need to know the URL to the video hosted on the other website (such as YouTube or Vimeo).

5. **(Optional) Add a title.**

   I encourage you to add a title to blog posts and events. If you don't, Squarespace will generate a random, hard-to-remember sequence of letters and numbers for the page URL of the blog post or event.

   When you add a video's URL, as you do in Step 4, Squarespace will pull the video's title into the title for your video item. Make sure this title is what you want because the title will be used in the URL for the video page URL on your site.

   When you add an image to a gallery page, Squarespace automatically generates a random sequence of letters and numbers for the image's page URL. The URL will not match the title you give the image. This may not be an issue, depending on how your galleries are displayed in the template you are using.

   If you want to customize the page URL for any item, see the "Running Through the Edit Settings" section, later in the chapter.

6. **Save your item.**

   If you want to finalize the item later, click the Save button to save it as a work-in-progress item, called a draft. To instantly publish the item on your site, for site visitors to see, click the Save & Publish button. See the next section for more information about setting a page item's status manually.

Removing an item

To remove a blog post, an event, a gallery image, or a gallery video, simply do the following:

1. **Open the page item.**

   To open an item, double-click it.

2. **Click the Remove button.**

Setting the status of your page item

Maybe you prefer to write several blog posts and then locate images for them. You might have only the dates for events and need to come back and add the locations later. Or perhaps you want to add a few videos to your gallery and then have an assistant add descriptions later.

By setting the item's status, you can work on the item in stages. The following four status settings are available:

- ✔ **Published:** Sets your page item to be viewed by your site visitors.
- ✔ **Scheduled:** Publishes your page item on the date and time you choose.
- ✔ **Needs Review:** Indicates that the page item is ready for review, if you have contributors who have permission to edit page items.
- ✔ **Draft:** Sets the page item as unpublished, so you can edit it later.

For new page items, click the Draft status setting at the bottom of the Edit dialog box to change the status of your page item.

Running Through the Edit Settings

Blog, event, and gallery items have an assortment of settings and configurations to help you create the perfect content for your site. You may be asking yourself, "Where are all these settings?"

Although the settings for a blog post, an event, and a gallery item may differ, all the settings are contained in four navigational tabs at the top of the item's dialog box:

- ✔ **Item:** Add the content for the type of item you're adding to the page, such as a title, tags, categories, a description, and the main content.
- ✔ **Options:** Settings specific to the blog posts, events, and gallery images and videos.

✔ **Location:** This is an optional setting for blog posts and gallery items, but you can add the name of the location as the title along with an address, city, state, and zip code about the item you're posting.

✔ **Social:** Enable notifying your social profile accounts of new items on your site. The social accounts that appear here are configured in Site Manager⏴Settings⏴Connected Accounts (see Chapter 15).

The lists that follow describe the features offered in blog, events, and gallery page items.

Item section

The Edit dialog box contains the main configurations and settings for a particular item. This dialog box is also where you go to add content, tags, categories, a title, and more.

To open the Edit dialog box for a particular item — a blog post, an event, a gallery image, or a gallery video — first go to Content Manager and select the page that contains the item. Click a blog post or event, or double-click a gallery item to open the item.

Note the following settings for a blog post Edit dialog box, as shown in Figure 10-1:

✔ **Title:** The post title is used as a text link in other parts of your site, as the page title for the item's page, and to create the unique blog post URL to the item's page.

✔ **Content area:** You add your blog post content in blocks. See the "Adding a block to your page" section, later in the chapter, for information on adding blocks. See Part III for detailed information about each block type you can add.

✔ **Tags:** Use tags to highlight key topics or subjects in your blog post content.

✔ **Categories:** Use categories to organize blog posts into related groupings.

✔ **Comments:** Allow site visitors to add messages in an organized conversation on the same page as your blog post. Optionally, turn commenting on or off for individual blog posts.

✔ **Status:** Set the page item to be published or saved as a work-in-progress. See the previous section, "Setting the status of your page item."

Title   Content area

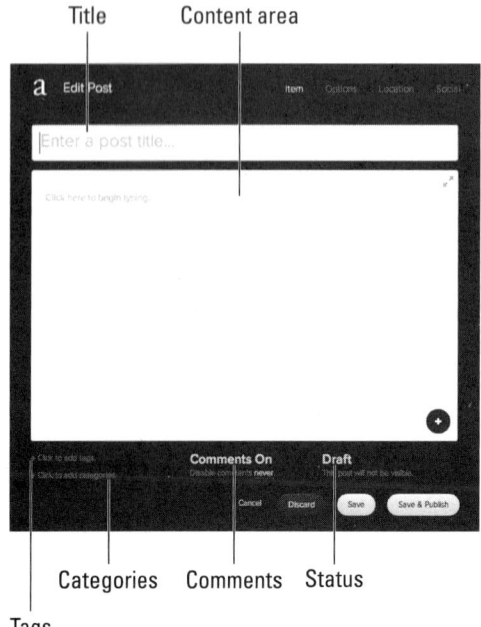

Figure 10-1:
A blog's
Edit Post
dialog box.

Categories   Comments   Status

Tags

The following options are available in the Edit Event dialog box, shown in Figure 10-2:

- ✔ **Title:** The event title is used as a text link in other parts of your site, as the page title for the item's unique page, and as the direct URL to the item's unique page.

- ✔ **Start Date:** Add the start date and time for the event.

- ✔ **End Date:** Add the end date and time for the event.

- ✔ **Content area:** You add your event content in blocks. See the "Adding a block to your page" section, later in the chapter, for information on adding blocks. See Part III for detailed information about each block type you can add.

- ✔ **Tags:** Use tags to highlight key topics or subjects for your event.

- ✔ **Categories:** Use categories to organize events into related groupings.

Title   Start date   End date

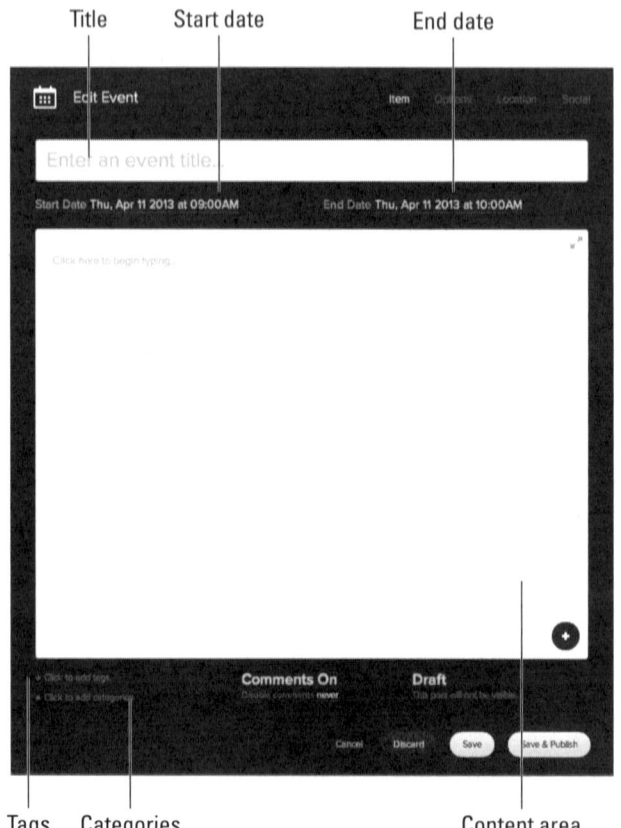

Figure 10-2:
An event's
Edit Event
dialog box.

Tags   Categories   Content area

The following options are available in the Edit Image dialog box, shown in Figure 10-3:

- ✔ **Title:** The image title is used as a text link in other parts of your site, as the page title for the item's unique page, and as the direct URL to the item's unique page.

- ✔ **Upload image area:** In the block to the left, upload the image you want to display.

- ✔ **Description:** In the block to the right, add a description about the image you uploaded.

- ✔ **Tags:** Use tags to highlight key topics or subjects in your image.

- ✔ **Categories:** Use categories to organize gallery media into related groupings.

Upload image area   Title   Description

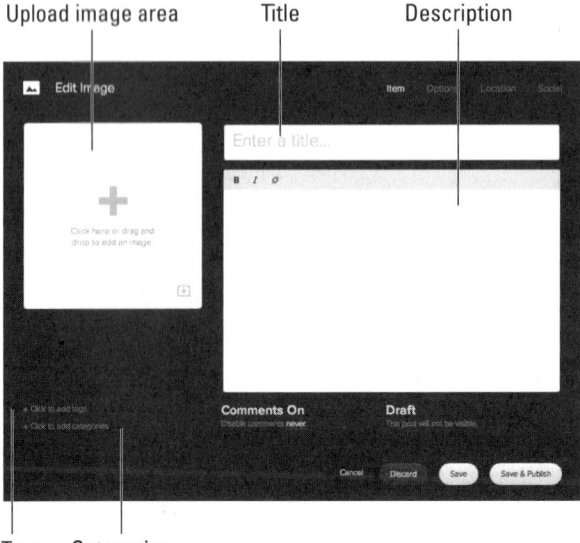

Figure 10-3:
A gallery's
Edit Image
dialog box.

Tags Categories

The Edit Video dialog box, shown in Figure 10-4, has the following settings:

- ✓ **Title:** Item titles are used as a text link on other parts of your site, as the page title for the item's unique page, and as the direct URL to the item's unique page.

- ✓ **Video URL or embed code:** Add the direct URL for the video (hosted on YouTube, Vimeo, or Wistia). Or add embed code from the video service hosting the video by clicking the gear icon to the right of the URL field to open a pop-up dialog box where you can paste your embed code. Chapter 12 offers more insight, which can be applied here, into using embed code when you are using the Embed block.

- ✓ **Content area:** A text block is already added in the content area, so you can begin typing. If you want to add more content with other blocks, see the later section, "Adding a block to your page." Also review Part IV for detailed information about each block type you can add.

- ✓ **Custom thumbnail:** You can include an image to represent the video.

- ✓ **Image overlay:** Select this option if you want to display the custom thumbnail in place of the video to speed up the loading of your page in a browser. When the visitor clicks the thumbnail, the video will begin playing.

- ✓ **Tags:** Use tags to highlight key topics or subjects in your video.

- ✓ **Categories:** Use categories to organize gallery media into related groupings.

Content area

Video URL or embed code

Title

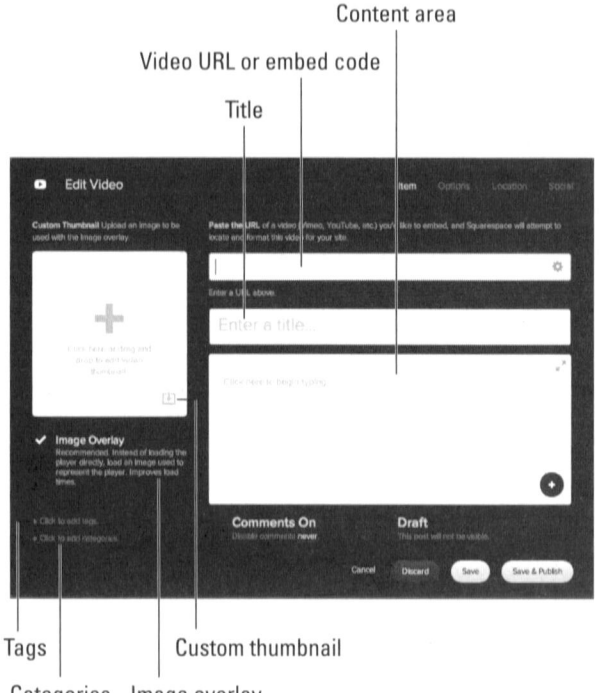

Figure 10-4:
A gallery's
Edit Video
dialog box.

Tags

Categories   Image overlay

Custom thumbnail

Not all templates support the display of gallery item features such as titles and descriptions. In addition, no templates allow comments on gallery, events, or products pages, even though the setting is available in the Edit dialog boxes.

Even though the commenting settings are present in the Edit dialog boxes for events and galleries, the commenting feature will not be available for your site visitors to comment on event and gallery pages.

Options section

The Options settings for an item can consist of a thumbnail image, the item's unique URL, the author of the item, and a clickthrough URL. To view the Options settings for the item you're adding, click the Options tab in the upper-right corner of the Edit dialog box. Figure 10-5 shows the Options settings for a blog post.

Thumbnail image   Post/image URL   Author   Source URL

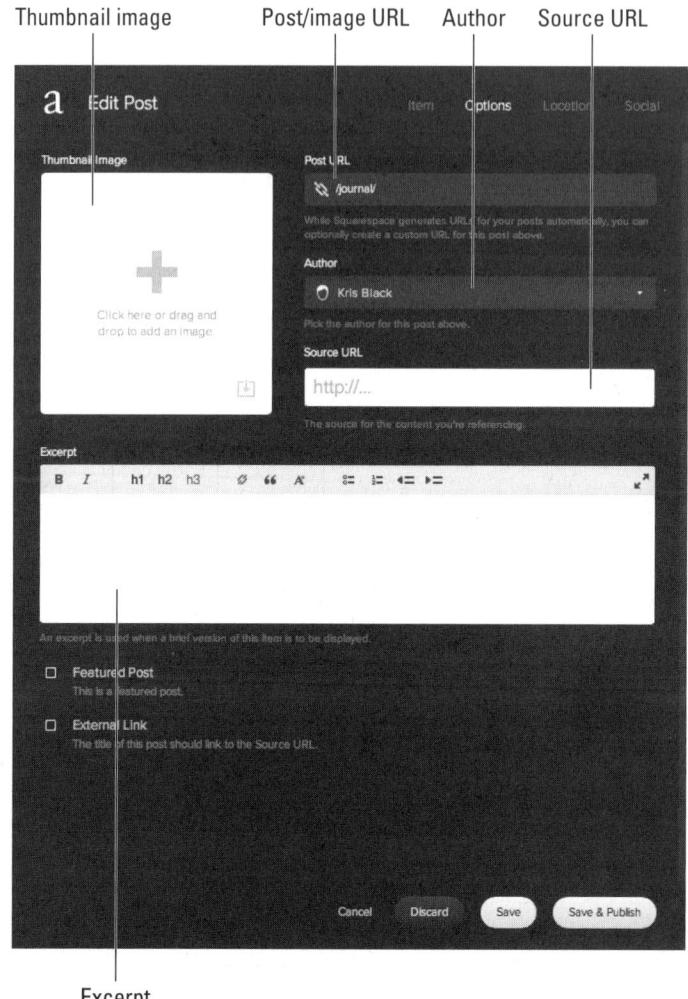

Figure 10-5:
The Options
screen for a
blog post.

Excerpt

The options for a blog post, a gallery image, or a gallery video follow:

✔ **Thumbnail image:** Blog post only. Add a thumbnail that represents your blog post. Some templates display the thumbnail in the blog post excerpt (see the "Excerpt" entry in this list) and in a summary block (see Chapter 13).

✔ **Post/event/image URL:** Squarespace automatically generates a unique URL for the item (blog post, event listing, gallery image, or gallery video). You can modify this cryptic string of numbers and letters to something that's easier to read.

✔ **Author:** The person who wrote the blog post, posted the event, or uploaded the gallery image or video. If you have multiple contributors on your site (see Chapter 15), you can set the author to a contributor.

✔ **Source URL:** If you are referencing someone else's material, add the URL to that source material here.

✔ **Clickthrough URL:** Gallery image only. Add a URL if you want to display a link to another site or a page or file within your site.

✔ **Excerpt:** Blog post, events, and gallery video only. Add a brief description about your blog post, event, or gallery video. You can copy and paste text from the main content area on the Item screen (refer to Figures 10-1 and 10-4) or add original content. Some templates display the excerpt on the main blog and event page view and in the summary block (see Chapter 13).

✔ **Featured post:** Blog post only. Select this option if you want to mark a post as a featured post. Some templates display featured posts differently than other blog posts.

✔ **External link:** Blog post only. Set the blog post title to link to the external website URL added to the Source URL setting (mentioned earlier in this list.)

Location section

If your blog post, event, or gallery image or video relates to a location, you can add the name, address, city, state, zip code, and country of the location. You can add the location of the item by clicking the Location tab at the top of the page item you are editing.

For event items, the location is used to provide a link to Google Maps for site visitors to get location information and driving directions to the event's venue. It's currently unclear whether this feature is being used in blog posts or gallery items because no templates take advantage of adding a location to blog post or gallery item pages. This may be a feature that will be offered in the future. If you think this would be a great feature to include for blog posts and gallery items, let Squarespace know by submitting a feature request to their support team (see Chapter 15 on how to submit a support ticket).

Social section

When you want to promote your blog or gallery item in your social accounts, select the last option, Social, in the upper-right corner of the Edit dialog box.

When you do, the social accounts you added in Site Settings (see Chapter 15) are displayed. Use the toggle buttons to determine which social accounts should receive a status update.

You can customize the message for each social account. Hover your mouse cursor over the question mark on the far right of the message field to display the pop-up window shown in Figure 10-6.

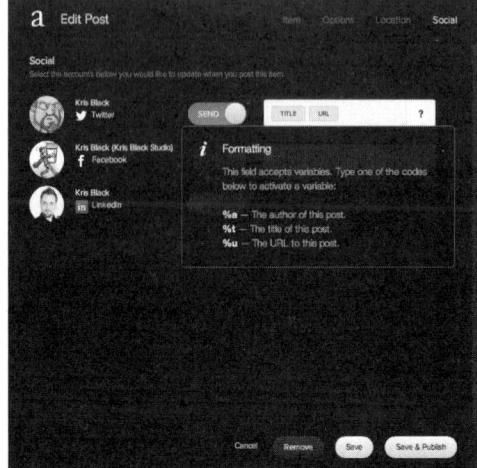

Figure 10-6:
Adding a social account to a blog post.

You use variables to include the following information in your status update:

- **Author:** The author you set in the Options settings for the item (see the preceding section)
- **Title:** The title of the item from the Item setting
- **URL:** The link back to your site for followers, friends, and connections on your social profiles

Adding content to a page item

When you add a gallery image to a gallery page, you can include a simple image description with basic text styling options (bold, italics, and creating a text link). When you add a blog post or a gallery video, however, you can also add blocks to the content area of the Edit dialog box. The next section briefly explains the types of blocks you can add to your site.

Working with Blocks

Blocks are containers for your content that enable you to easily separate different types of content.

You can add to your site three categories of blocks:

- ✔ **Content:** Add your own content. Generally, you use content blocks to add text, images, in-page galleries, videos, audio, custom code, forms, maps, links, and products. Chapter 11 outlines the different types of content text blocks, and Chapter 12 outlines the different types of media content blocks.

- ✔ **Structure:** Display content and features related to blog pages, such as category lists, summary excerpts, and a search feature. For more information on structure blocks, see Chapter 13.

- ✔ **Social:** Pull content and updates from social media profiles (such as Twitter, Instagram, and Foursquare) to display on your site. See Chapter 14 for details on social blocks.

You explore the individual types of blocks in Part IV.

Adding a block to your page

To add a block in a page, blog post, or gallery video, follow these steps:

1. **Select a page in Content Manager.**

   See Chapter 9 for details on accessing Content Manager and adding pages to your site.

2. **Click the Add Block button.**

   On pages, the Add Block button is in the upper right of Content Manager. In page items — blog posts and gallery videos — the Add Block button is in the lower right of the content area as a dark circle with a plus sign.

   The Add a Block selection window appears in the center of your browser, as shown in Figure 10-7.

   If you decide that you don't want to add a block, click anywhere outside the block selection window to close it.

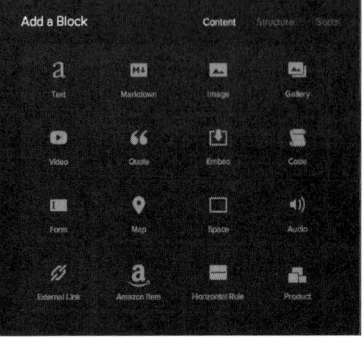

3. **(Optional) Switch to another block category (content, structure, or social).**

   The default set of blocks in the Add a Block window are the content blocks. If you want to add a structure block (see Chapter 13) or social block (see Chapter 14), you must click the respective tabs at the top of the Add a Block window to switch to that category. See the preceding section for information about the different block categories.

4. **Add the block to the page in one of the following ways:**

   • **Click the block you want to add.**

   Clicking the block places it at the bottom of your page.

   • **Drag the block to as needed.**

   You can place the block anywhere on the page. Click and hold down on the block, and then drag it away from the Add a Block dialog box. As you drag the block around, the Add a Block dialog box disappears and the edges of other blocks become highlighted in blue. Read the "Rearranging Blocks Using LayoutEngine" section, later in the chapter, to find out how to arrange your blocks.

   The configuration settings window for the block (if available) appears so you can configure the block.

The chapters in Part IV explore the different blocks and their configuration settings.

Removing a block

To remove a block, follow these steps:

1. **Double-click the block to open the block's configuration window.**

2. **Click the Remove button at the bottom of the configuration settings window.**

   A confirmation window appears.

3. **Click the Confirm button to finalize the removal of the block.**

When you remove a block, you can't get it back. The removal is permanent.

You can add blocks only to pages or within a blog post or a gallery video. You can't add blocks to gallery images.

The Text and Markdown content blocks do not have a configuration settings window. Instead, a formatting strip appears above the blocks to allow you to style text. On the far right of this strip, click the trash can icon to remove the block.

Rearranging Blocks Using LayoutEngine

LayoutEngine enables you to position blocks in several ways. The process is almost magical.

The root of LayoutEngine's magic is a column grid that governs how blocks are positioned on the page. You use the grid to perfectly align blocks to create neatly organized pages that are visually pleasing to the eye. Whoa! Is it really magic? I'll let you decide as I lift the curtain to reveal the wizardry of how LayoutEngine works.

To move and rearrange blocks on a page, do the following:

1. **Hover your mouse cursor over a block until the cursor changes to a multidirectional arrow, as shown in Figure 10-8.**

2. **Click and hold down your mouse button on the block you want to move.**

   All the blocks on your page become outlined in a faint, bluish glow so that you can see their edges and precisely position the block you are moving.

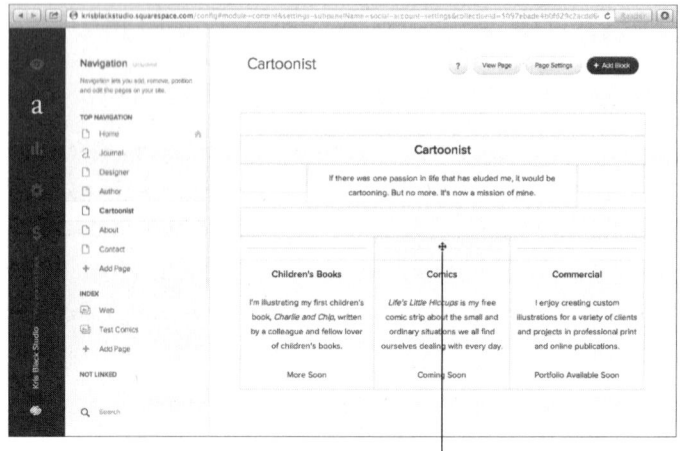

Figure 10-8:
Selecting a
block.

Multidirectional arrow

A multidirectional arrow icon appears in the upper-right corner of certain blocks when you hover your mouse cursor over them. If you see this icon, you must click it to drag that block.

3. Drag the block to another location on the page.

As you drag the block closer to the edge of another block, the edge is highlighted with a blue line, and one of four anchor options appears. You can control which option appears by the position of your cursor near the edge:

- **Row:** Adds the block to a new row. Position your cursor closer to the bottom or top edge of another block.

- **Insert:** Attaches the block to the top or bottom of another block. Position your cursor farther inward from the top or bottom edge of the block to which you want to attach the block you're moving.

- **Column:** Adds the block next to another block or set of blocks. Position your cursor close to the left or right edge of another block.

- **Float:** Allows you to place an image block or a map block within a text block so that the words wrap around the sides of the floating block. Position your cursor to the left or right of the paragraph that you want the image or map to float beside.

The following sections describe these options in detail.

4. Drop the block in place by releasing the mouse button.

Separating blocks into rows

When you add a block to a page, the block is added to a new row and spans from the far left to the far right of the page. The block's height is fluid, expanding to contain the content you add to it. You can rearrange blocks up and down the page.

If you're adding a block to a page that already contains blocks, the new block will be added below the existing ones.

When you create a new page or a new blog post, a text block is added automatically.

Creating columns of blocks

When you rearrange blocks, you can place them to the left or right of each other, creating columns within a row. (See the next section, "Inserting blocks," for information on adding a block above another block.) These columns affect only the row containing the blocks. For example, you might arrange three blocks on one row but five blocks on another row.

LayoutEngine uses a 12-column grid structure. If you're arranging blocks in a row and want them to be the same width, you must use 1, 2, 3, 4, or 6 blocks. (These numbers are evenly divisible into 12.)

To adjust the width of two adjacent blocks, position your cursor between the two blocks. A thin, vertical line appears and the cursor changes to a resize cursor. Click and drag to adjust the width of the blocks. Resizing one block affects the size of the adjacent block.

Inserting blocks

When you insert a block above or below another block, you connect those blocks within the same column. The blocks will be displayed together, which can be helpful when you create intricate page layouts.

In addition, when your site resizes to fit the width of a mobile device, the blocks will reflow to stack on top of each other. For example, the author page on my site features this book and a new blog, Squareverse. I set up this page so that the headers "A Book" and "A Blog" are positioned next to each other on the same row within their own columns. Then I inserted image blocks below the headers and text blocks below the image blocks. The columns will keep the inserted blocks together when the site resizes to fit on a smartphone.

I created a second page using the same content, but I didn't insert blocks above or below each other. Instead, I positioned the headers, the image blocks, and the descriptions next to each other on three separate rows. Both pages appear on my computer as shown in Figure 10-9. However, when you visit the two pages on a smartphone, the differences are readily apparent, as shown in Figure 10-10.

Typically, you insert blocks above or below another block. However, you can also divide text blocks with another block by inserting a block between paragraphs in the text block.

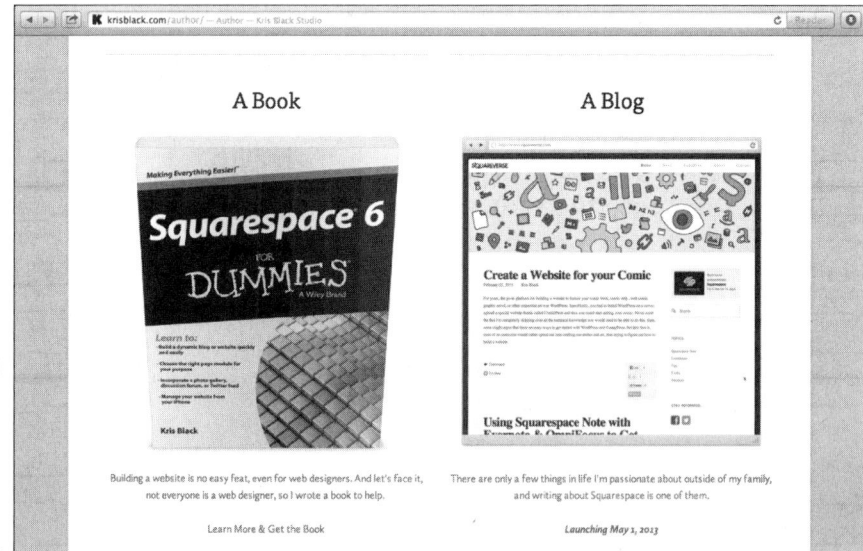

Figure 10-9: Pages with blocks displayed on a computer.

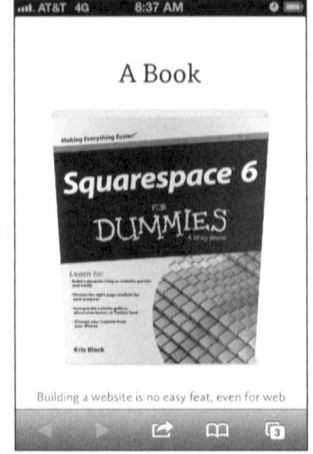 

Figure 10-10:
The same pages with blocks displayed on a smartphone.

Floating blocks within content

When you have a *floating* block, the text on the page wraps around the sides of the block. The only blocks that can float in a text block are image blocks (see Chapter 12) and map blocks (see Chapter 11).

You can float a block next to any paragraph of text in the text block. To position your block, you use the icons that appear at the top of the image or map block. Your floating options are

- ✔ **Left:** Floats the block to the left of the text.
- ✔ **No wrap:** Floats the block within the text but does not display text on the left or right side of the block. The map block will stretch to fill the full width of the text block. The image block will do the same unless the image is not large enough, in which case the image will be displayed at its largest size, centered in the full width of the text block.
- ✔ **Right:** Floats the block to the right of the text.

Now that you've looked at how to add, remove, and rearrange blocks within your pages, it's time to move on to Part IV, where you look at all the different types of blocks you can add to your site.

Part IV
Personalizing Your Website

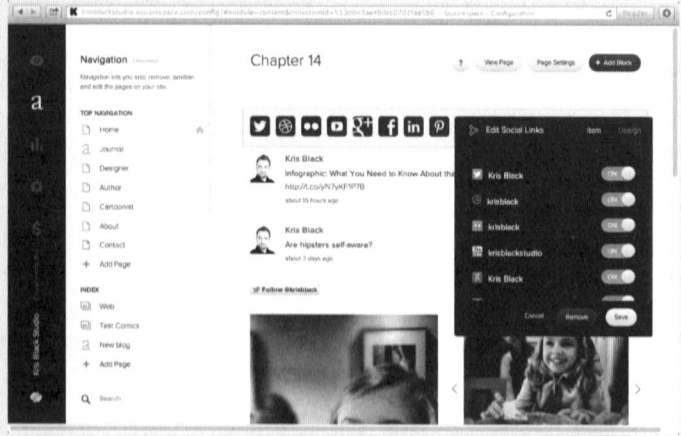

Discover the benefits of writing content for your site with a simple plain-text writing format called Markdown at www.dummies.com/extras/squarespace6.

In this part . . .

- ✔ Discover the different blocks you can use to add content to your site
- ✔ Create slideshows to display multiple images in one area of the page
- ✔ Spice up pages with YouTube videos
- ✔ Help readers discover more content with structure blocks
- ✔ Promote your site by sharing on your social media accounts
- ✔ Display all your social media activity with social blocks

Chapter 11

Creating Content with Content Blocks

In This Chapter

▶ Finding out about content blocks

▶ Creating advanced forms

▶ Spacing apart and dividing content

*C*ontent blocks are individual containers you use to add content on your pages. The three categories of blocks are content, structure, and social — as explored in Chapter 10. This chapter focuses on a group of content blocks that you use to add non-multimedia content, specifically text, code, forms, links, and products.

Some of these blocks are simple and straightforward. You'll easily understand what you can use them for and how they work. Other blocks are more robust, with customizable settings, and may require a little more effort to understand.

With the exception of form and product blocks, all blocks in this and the following three chapters are available with all pricing plans. If you need to review how to add, remove, and rearrange blocks on your pages, see Chapter 10.

Understanding Content Blocks

You use content blocks to add your own content to site pages, forming the style and personality of your site. Content blocks come in a variety of options from plain text blocks to robust galleries of images.

Following is a quick list of the types of content blocks:

- **Text:** Add text-based content with simple text styling that you apply by selecting text and clicking a style button.
- **Markdown:** Add content in a plain text format that will automatically be converted to the proper HTML for publishing on your site.
- **Quote:** Add a quote that is automatically styled and formatted for your site.
- **Code:** Add custom code to your pages or display example code for your readers with this free-form code editor.
- **Form:** Create a form to collect information from site visitors.
- **External link:** Add a single text link with a title to your page.
- **Amazon item:** Display on your site a product from Amazon.com with a buy button.
- **Products:** Display a product from your Squarespace site (Business plan only; see Chapter 17).
- **Space:** Add space between blocks on your pages.
- **Horizontal rule:** Display a single divider line between blocks.

You can't add content to the space and horizontal rule blocks. Instead, you use them to organize the layout of blocks on the page.

You add blocks to your pages in Content Manager (see Chapter 4) by clicking the Add Block button in the upper-right corner of the screen. If you're creating a blog post, you add blocks by clicking the plus icon in the lower-right corner of the Edit Post dialog box. See Chapter 10 for details about adding blocks.

Now let's look at each block in detail.

Text Block

The text block allows you to add your own text-based content in a WYSIWYG (What You See Is What You Get) format. The process is similar to how you write and style content in Microsoft Word or Apple Pages documents. A formatting bar appears above the text block when you are writing, as shown in Figure 11-1.

Bold
Italic
Link
Alignment
Headings
Quote

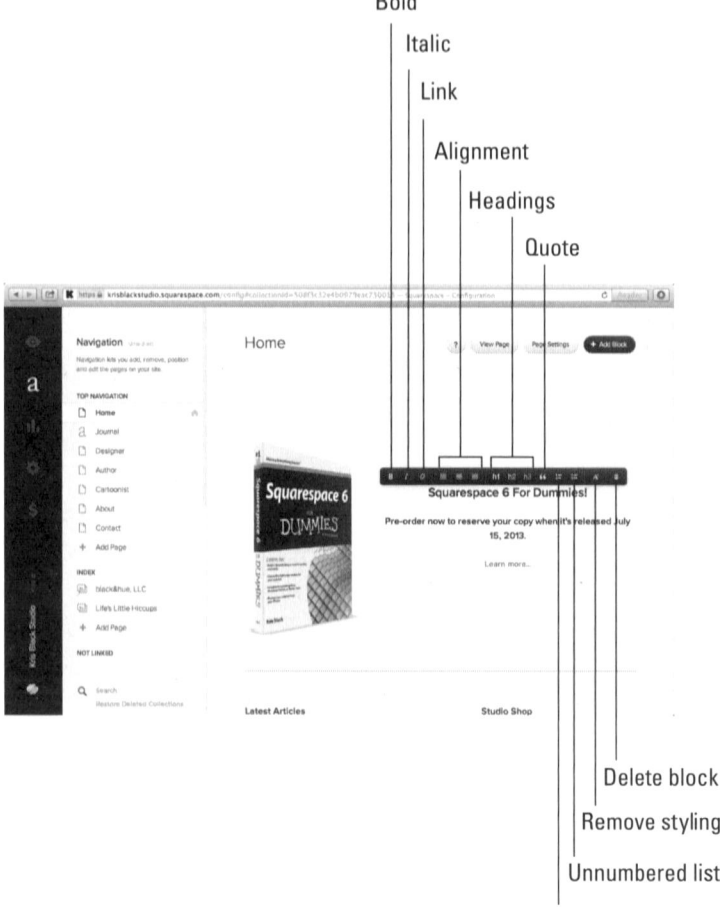

Delete block
Remove styling
Unnumbered list
Numbered list

Figure 11-1:
Text block
styling
options.

You can stylize your text with the following controls:

- ✔ **Bold and italic:** Emphasize the selected text.
- ✔ **Link:** Make text a link to another page or file on your site or to an external webpage.
- ✔ **Alignment:** Align paragraphs to the left, right, or centered.
- ✔ **Headings:** Set your text in one of three heading styles: h1, h2, and h3.
- ✔ **Quote:** Convert text to be displayed using the default quote styling applied by your template.
- ✔ **Numbered list:** Display numbered list items.
- ✔ **Unordered list:** Display a list of items that do not need to be in any specific order.

Would you like to start over with styling the text? Or want to remove a style from text in the text block? Simply select the text and click the capital A icon.

If you need to delete the text block, click the trash can icon on the far right of the style bar.

Markdown Block

Markdown is a plain text writing format developed by John Gruber of Daring Fireball (`http://daringfireball.net`). Markdown may appear a little weird, but I can tell you that it's a fun and easy writing format to grasp. You may prefer being able to see how your text will be formatted, like you can in the text block, but that's precisely the reason why the Markdown block is useful.

By removing the styling from your text while you type, you can focus on your thoughts and getting your content onto your site. You do have to get used to using the Markdown block, but once you do I'm betting you won't go back to using the text block.

Figure 11-2 shows a sample Markdown block used to create the content of a page in Content Manager (see Chapter 4 about the different editing modes in Squarespace, including Content Manager). Figure 11-3 shows the rendered text on your webpage.

Formatting text in Markdown is simple. Table 11-1 compares the basic text formatting available in a Markdown block to the formatting options available in the text block.

Figure 11-2:
The
Markdown
block as
content is
being typed
in it.

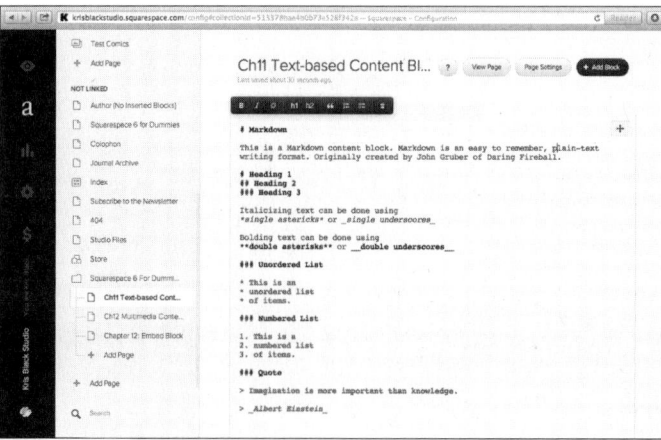

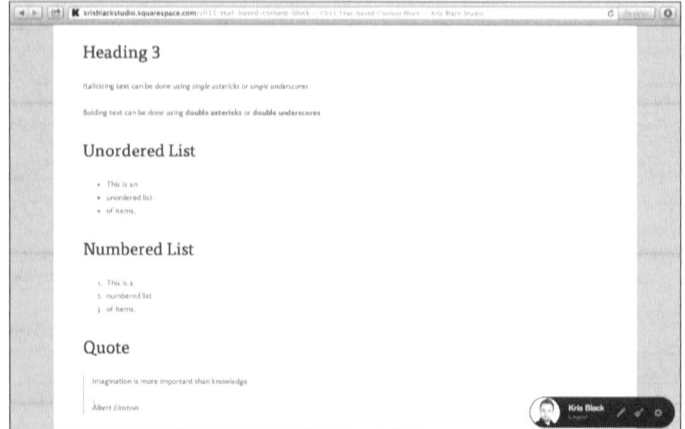

Figure 11-3:
The page
shown in
Figure 11-2
rendered on
your site.

Table 11-1		Text Styling in a Markdown Block	
Styling	**Syntax**	**Description**	**Example**
Bold	** or __	Wrap your text with two asterisks or two underscores	**bold** __bold__
Italics	* or _	Wrap your text with one asterisk or one underscore	*italic* _italic_
Link	[text](URL)	Link text inside square brackets followed by the URL inside parentheses	[Apple](http://apple.com)
Heading 1	#[space]	One pound character followed by a space	# Heading 1
Heading 2	##[space]	Two pound characters followed by a space	## Heading 2
Heading 3	###[space]	Three pound characters followed by a space	### Heading 3
Quote	>[space]	A greater than character followed by a space at the beginning of the line of text	> One more thing. > > Steve Jobs
Numbered list	Number. [space]	Number followed by a bullet and a space	1. This would be a 2. numbered list 3. of items
Unordered list	*[space]	Asterisk followed by a space	* This would be an * unordered list * of items

The table is just a small sampling of how you can style text in a Markdown block. For a complete list of options, visit John Gruber's Daring Fireball site at http://daringfireball.net/projects/markdown/syntax.

 As you format your text in Markdown on Squarespace, the Markdown block applies hinted styling, as shown in Figure 11-2, to indicate that the formatting is working. For example, when you create an unordered or ordered list (see Table 11-1), the list item text will turn blue. In addition, an abbreviated formatting bar appears as you type your text in a Markdown block.

Quote Block

The quote block enables you to add a quote on your page that uses the quote styling options of the template you have applied to your site. You add a quote in the Edit Quote dialog box, as shown in Figure 11-4.

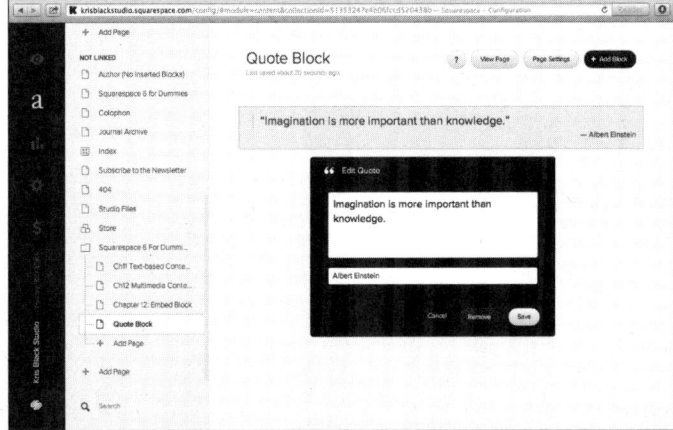

Figure 11-4: The Edit Quote text and the resulting quote block.

Type or paste the quote in the top, larger text area, and include the source of the quote in the bottom text area.

Not all templates offer settings in Style Editor to adjust block quotes. If you want to modify how the quote block appears on your site, switch to Style Edit mode (see Chapter 7) and see whether you have settings in Style Editor for block quotes.

Code Block

The code block allows you to add custom code to your pages. If you're a web developer or web designer with code experience, you can use the code block to retain complete control over the presentation of your content. The code block accepts the following types of code:

- ✔ CSS
- ✔ HTML
- ✔ JavaScript
- ✔ Markdown
- ✔ Plain text

The code block also enables you to display code on your site. For example, suppose you are writing a tutorial about designing websites and want to include example code in a blog post to demonstrate how to accomplish a particular effect with code. To do this with the code block, click the Display Source check box in the upper-left corner of the Edit Code dialog box shown in Figure 11-5. The code will be syntax highlighted — that is, Squarespace automatically colors certain elements of the code to make it easier to read.

Figure 11-5: The Edit Code dialog box.

Use of the code block is generally for advanced users of Squarespace. If you have code you need to embed on your site to display multimedia or other content from another website, check out the embed and video blocks in Chapter 12.

Form Block

The form block can be used to create a simple contact form or a robust form to collect specific information submitted by site visitors. The latter use is available only to Unlimited and Business plan customers. (You can find out more about Squarespace pricing plans in Chapter 3.)

When you first add a form block, the default form elements are those for a simple contact form:

- ✔ **Name:** Fields for the first and last names of the form submitter.

- ✔ **Email address:** A field for the e-mail address of the form submitter.

- ✔ **Message:** A multiple-line text field so that the form submitter can type a message.

If you have the Unlimited or Business plan, you can add any of the following form elements to the form block:

- ✔ **Text:** A single text field

- ✔ **Text Area:** A multiline text box

- ✔ **Select:** A drop-down menu list of options

- ✔ **Checkbox:** A list of options with check boxes to allow the selection of multiple options

- ✔ **Radio:** A list of options with radio buttons to allow the selection of only one option

- ✔ **Likert:** A survey-style list of questions with the following answer choices: Strongly Agree; Agree; Neutral; Disagree; Strongly Disagree

- ✔ **Name:** Two connected fields for someone to add a first and last name

- ✔ **Password:** Automatic display of security dots

- ✔ **Address:** Multiple connected fields for collecting addresses with the following fields: Address 1; Address 2; City; State/province; Zip/postal code; Country

- ✔ **Twitter:** An entry field preformatted with a Twitter @ symbol

- ✔ **Email:** A field that ensures that the e-mail address is formatted correctly

- ✔ **Website:** A field preformatted with *http://* for generating proper URLs in submissions

- ✔ **Date:** Three connected fields for collecting the month, day, and year

✔ **Time:** Four connected fields for collecting the hour, minutes, seconds, and *a.m.* or *p.m.*

✔ **Phone:** A field for collecting phone numbers with area codes and an optional country code field

✔ **Number:** A field that limits character entry to numbers only

✔ **Currency:** A field to which you can add your currency symbol in the field's configuration settings to indicate the currency that should be entered

✔ **Section Break:** A form element to divide your form into groups of fields

Customizing form elements

With the exception of the section break form element, all form elements offer the following optional configuration settings:

✔ **Title:** Your own name for each field.

✔ **Description:** A brief description about the type of information someone can submit for a particular field.

✔ **Required:** A check box to make the field required; the form can't be submitted if a required field is not filled in.

Some form elements allow you to add placeholder text. You might use this feature to display helpful information or an example of what should be entered in the field.

Moving form elements

Form elements stack one on top of the other. You can move the elements to rearrange them in an order that suits your needs. Follow these steps:

1. **Double-click a form block to open its Edit Form dialog box.**

2. **To move the form element, click and drag it.**

   Drag the element up and down the list of form elements in the Edit Form dialog box.

3. **Release the form element.**

   As you move a form element, the other elements will split apart. Drop the form element in an empty space.

Storing your form submissions

When you create a form, you can select one of the following three options for storing submissions from the form:

- ✔ **Google Docs:** Store all submissions in a Google Doc spreadsheet in your Google account.

- ✔ **MailChimp:** Capture e-mail addresses in your MailChimp account for use in an e-mail campaign. To can find out how to get a MailChimp account, visit www.mailchimp.com.

- ✔ **Email:** Send submissions to the e-mail address of the account owner of the website. (This is the e-mail address you used when you signed up for your Squarespace site.) This option is the default.

Switching storage options

To switch to another storage option, click the plug icon to the right of the option you want to use. Google Docs and MailChimp options require you to authenticate to connect to your account with their service.

After you're connected, the following options are available:

- ✔ **Google Docs:** The name of your form block is used for the name of the spreadsheet that will automatically be created in your Google Docs account to collect submissions. You can modify the name of the spreadsheet.

- ✔ **MailChimp:** Click Select List to show a drop-down menu of all subscriber lists in your MailChimp account. Choose the list you want the form information to be sent to when someone fills out your form.

If you just need to change the e-mail address of the Email option, click the x to the right of the current e-mail address. Then type the new e-mail address in the Email Address field, and click the plug icon to the right to apply the change.

Customizing the advanced settings of a form

You can modify two settings in the Advanced settings area of a form block:

- ✔ **Submit button title:** Change the default submit button title from *submit* to something more appropriate for your form.

- ✔ **Submission message:** Customize the text that will be displayed when someone fills out and submits your form. You can style your submission message with bold and italic, and you can add a link to a page or file in your site or to an external website.

External Link Block

The external link block is a simple block that you use to create a single text link. The settings for this block are

- ✔ **Link title:** The text that will be displayed on your page
- ✔ **URL:** The link to another website
- ✔ **Open in a new window:** Select if you want the link to open in a new window

If you want to display a list of links, consider using the text or Markdown block instead.

Amazon Item Block

Amazon.com sells just about anything imaginable. If you would like to display on your site an item that Amazon sells, use the Amazon item block.

You can display any of the following details about an item sold on Amazon in an Amazon item block:

- ✔ Title
- ✔ Thumbnail
- ✔ Author
- ✔ Price
- ✔ Buy button

You also have the option to set the alignment of the title, author, price, and buy button by using the Edit Amazon Item dialog box, as shown in Figure 11-6. You can also set the alignment of the block in the page layout by using the icons displayed at the top of the thumbnail in LayoutEngine. The process is the same as the one for aligning the image block (see Chapter 12).

If you have an Amazon Affiliate account, you can add your affiliate code in Site Settings (see Chapter 15). Then Squarespace will automatically add your affiliate code to any Amazon item you place on your site using the Amazon item block.

When you add an Amazon item block to your page, you need to search for the item that you want to display in the block. Type the name of the product in the Find a Product field. If more than one product is displayed, click to select the product you want.

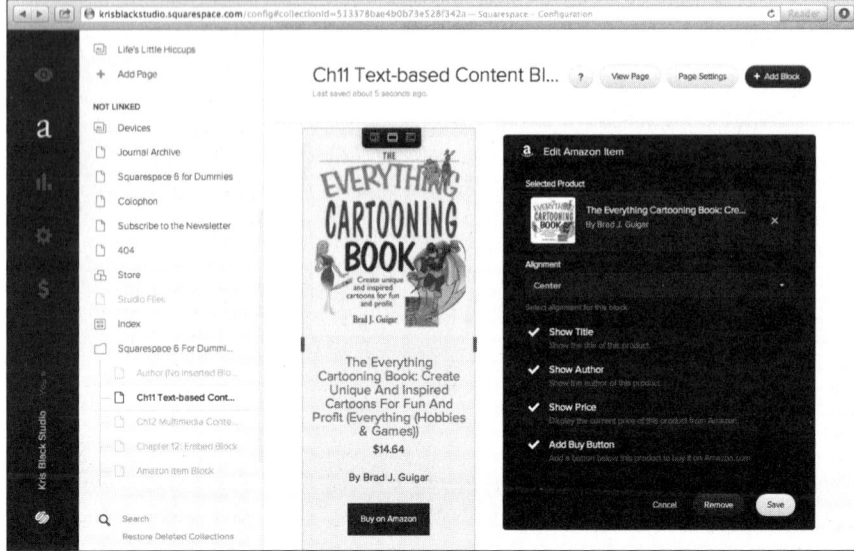

Figure 11-6:
Amazon
item block
configura-
tion settings.

If you want to display a different product in the Amazon item block, click the x to the right of the product title in the Edit Amazon Item dialog box. The product will be removed, and you can search for another product to display.

Product Block

If you have the Business plan for your Squarespace site (see Chapter 3), you can use the product block to display a product from the Inventory settings of Commerce in Site Manager. The product block will display a single item along with any of the following:

✔ Title

✔ Thumbnail

✔ Price

✔ Description

✔ Add to cart button

You don't configure or modify products with the product block. You merely display a product from your inventory. If you need to modify an aspect of the product you are displaying in the product block, do so in the Inventory settings of Commerce (see Chapter 17). To display additional products, add a product block for each.

If you want to display all your products, use a products page (not a product block). A products page displays all the products in your inventory as you add and remove them. For details on products pages, see Chapter 17.

When you add a product block to your page, you'll need to select the product to display in the block. Type the name of the product in the Find a Product field, as shown in Figure 11-7. If more than one product matches the search terms, click the product you want to display.

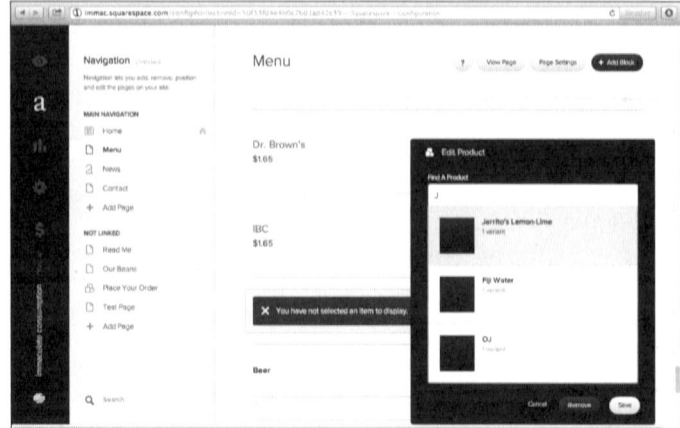

Figure 11-7: Finding a product to display in the product block.

Do you want to display a different product in the product block? Simply click the x to the right of the product title in the Edit Product dialog box to remove the current product and then search for another product to display.

Space Block

Space blocks are invisible and don't display any content. You can place space blocks beside, above, or below other blocks to separate them.

You can adjust the width and height of a space block. Hover your cursor over the space block until you see a handle on the bottom border, as shown in Figure 11-8. Drag that handle to adjust the height of the space block, pushing any blocks below it farther down the page. To adjust the width of a space block, see the section in Chapter 10 on adjusting column widths.

When your site is viewed on a small screen (like the one on a smartphone), space blocks disappear because Squarespace templates are designed to reflow blocks so that they are stacked. Disappearing space blocks usually don't disrupt the visual appeal of your site. However, if you don't like the effect consider using a horizontal rule block instead (see the next section).

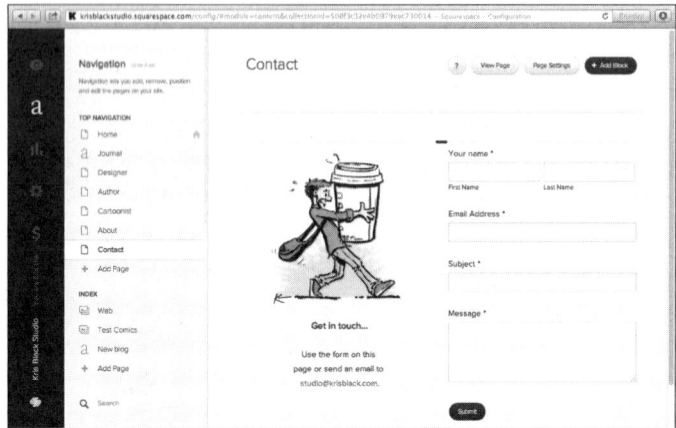

Figure 11-8:
Using a han-
dle to resize
a space
block.

If you have a non-space block on a row by itself and would like to keep the block from stretching the full width of the page, place a space block on either side of the block. With the non-space block in the middle of the two space blocks, adjust the space blocks' widths to make the center block narrower.

Horizontal Rule Block

You use the horizontal rule block to divide content on the page with a single horizontal line. The horizontal rule block doesn't offer customization options in the Edit Horizontal Rule dialog box. However, some templates enable you to modify the line in Style Editor. See Chapter 7 for information on styling your site with Style Editor.

The horizontal rule block is a handy little design element that separates content in a visually appealing way. You can rearrange horizontal rule blocks in LayoutEngine (see Chapter 10) just like any other block.

One useful arrangement is to insert horizontal rule blocks at the bottom of each column in a row. When your site resizes to fit in the screen of a mobile phone, the rules help separate the columns as they reflow to stack one on top of the other. Without the horizontal rules, the columns might appear to run together.

Chapter 12

Adding Multimedia with Content Blocks

- -

In This Chapter

▶ Using multimedia content blocks

▶ Uploading images

▶ Showcasing video

▶ Adding content from another site

▶ Adding an audio file

▶ Providing a map

- -

*C*ombine powerful imagery, videos, and other media to create a website with a distinctive look and a powerful message. In Chapter 11, you work with text-based content in content blocks. In this chapter, you look at content blocks that enable you to add multimedia content such as images, videos, embedded content from other sites, and audio players.

If you need a refresher course on adding blocks to your site, review Chapter 10.

Understanding Multimedia Content Blocks

Multimedia is more important than ever when attempting to engage site visitors. To that end, Squarespace provides the following multimedia-based blocks:

✓ **Image:** Add an image to your page or blog.

✓ **Gallery:** Create galleries anywhere on your site in a variety of presentation styles.

✓ **Video:** Add a video from video services such as YouTube, Vimeo, and Wistia.

↳ **Embed:** Add embed code from third-party services to display their media.

↳ **Audio:** Add an audio player to your page to play a podcast, a song you recorded, and more.

↳ **Map:** Enter an address to display its location on an interactive map.

Now let's look at each of these blocks in detail to see what they can do.

Image Block

Images you add to your site should be relevant to your content and can greatly spice up the experience visitors have on your site.

The image block displays a single image on your page. You add the image to the image upload box in the Edit Image dialog box, as shown in Figure 12-1. See Chapter 4 for details on adding an image using the image upload box.

Caption display

Description

Upload image area

Filename

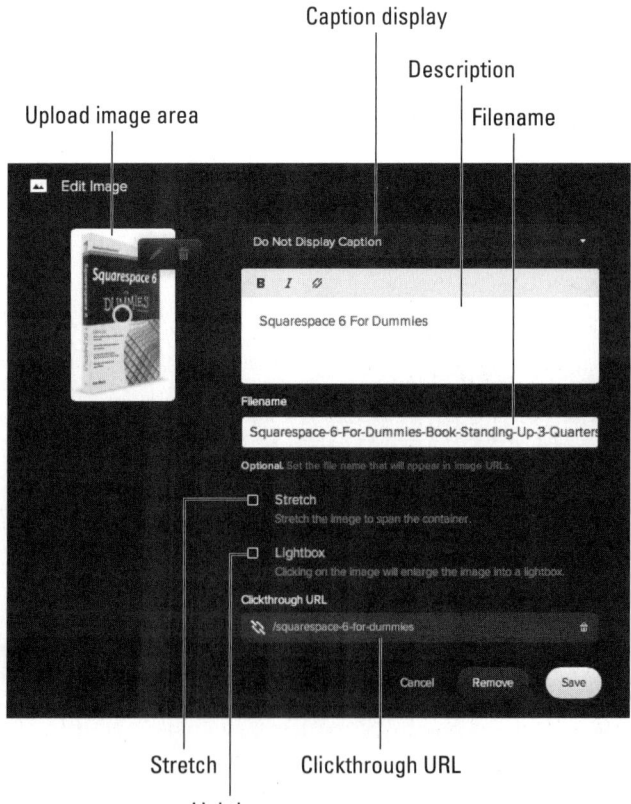

Figure 12-1:
The Edit
Image
dialog box
for an image
block.

Stretch

Clickthrough URL

Lightbox

The following options are available:

- ✔ **Upload image area:** Upload the image you want to display.

- ✔ **Caption display:** Select a display position for the image's caption. Your choices are Caption Below (the default); Do Not Display Caption; Caption Overlay; and Caption Overlay on Hover.

- ✔ **Description:** Add a description about the image. The caption will be used as part of the HTML alt tag, which search engines use to help identify the image.

- ✔ **Filename:** By default, the filename will match the filename of the image you uploaded. You can rename it, which will also rename the image URL.

- ✔ **Stretch:** Force a small image to stretch and fill the full width of the block in your layout. With this option deselected, the image will be displayed no larger than its actual size.

  Smaller images that are stretched to fill the full width of the block may look blurry and blotchy on your site.

- ✔ **Lightbox:** Allow the image to be clicked to display it full size in presentation mode, in which the website darkens and the image appears on top of the website.

- ✔ **Clickthrough URL:** Make the image a link to a page on your site, a file on your site, or an external website.

When you upload an image to the image block, you can edit the image directly in your Squarespace site using Aviary. See Chapter 4 for details on using the Aviary Photo Editor.

Gallery Block

When you add a gallery block (see Chapter 10 for details on adding blocks to your site), you can quickly add multiple images at once and adjust the gallery's design to create enjoyable and simple galleries for your site visitors.

The Edit Gallery dialog box has two tabs in the upper-right corner for setting up the gallery block:

- ✔ **Design:** Choose from four display options: Slideshow, Slider, Grid, and Stacked. Each offers different choices for displaying gallery images.

- ✔ **Content:** Add images to the gallery block by uploading images from your computer or by pulling images from a gallery page.

Before we look at the different display options in more detail, let's add images to the gallery block.

Uploading images to the gallery block

As in other image uploading areas of your Squarespace site, you can upload images to the gallery block in two ways. Click the plus sign to open a system dialog box to locate the images on your computer, or drag and drop images to the image upload area of the gallery block.

After you upload your images, double-click an image or click the gear icon that appears when you hover your cursor over the thumbnail of the image. The following settings appear, as shown in Figure 12-2:

- ✔ **Title:** Give the image a title.

- ✔ **Description:** Add a short description about the image.

- ✔ **Clickthrough URL:** Add a link to your image to allow someone to click the image to open a page or a file on your site or go to another website.

Figure 12-2: Uploading images to a gallery block.

Squarespace uses the image title to add alternative text for the image. Search engines use this text to get descriptive information about the image, increasing your search engine optimization.

Pulling images from a Gallery page

An alternative method of getting images in your gallery block is to pull them from a gallery page on your site. When you display images from a gallery page (as shown in Figure 12-3), you can't modify or configure the images from within the gallery block. Instead, you must make your changes on the gallery page.

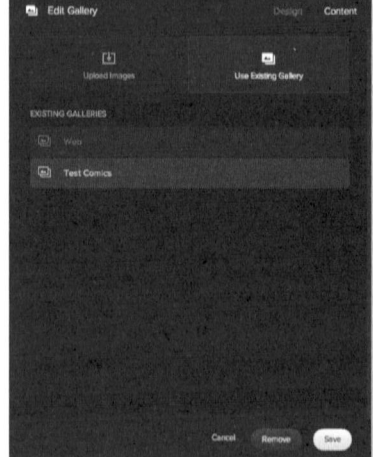

Figure 12-3:
Selecting a gallery page to display images in a gallery block.

Choosing a display option

Now that you have images in the gallery block, you need to configure the gallery block to display the images. Four display choices are available:

- ✔ Slideshow
- ✔ Slider
- ✔ Grid
- ✔ Stacked

Let's look at each one of these in more detail.

Slideshow

The Slideshow display option offers the most configuration settings. In a slideshow, one image is displayed at a time, and navigation controls appear so that visitors can advance through the images.

You can modify the following settings for the Slideshow display option:

- **Autoplay:** Automatically begin transitioning between images when the page loads. Use the slider control to set the delay between image transitions from 1 to 10 seconds.

- **Controls:** Display arrows on either side of the current image (except the first and last image) to allow someone to manually change images.

- **Auto Crop:** Automatically scale and crop the images so that they are the same size.

- **Thumbnails:** Display all the images in the gallery block in a row of thumbnails below the slideshow. Use the slider controls to set the height of the thumbnails and the distance of the thumbnail row from the slideshow.

- **Show Title and Description:** Display the title and description of each image.

- **Title and Description Position:** Reposition the title and description in one of several locations.

- **Show on Hover:** Display the title and description only when someone hovers the cursor over an image in the slideshow.

Slider

The Slider display option, like Slideshow, displays the images in a slideshow format. However, the Slider option also displays faded portions of the previous and next image on either side of the current image.

- **Autoplay:** Automatically begin transitioning between images when the page loads. Use the slider control to set the delay between image transitions from 1 to 10 seconds.

- **Controls:** Display arrows on either side of the slider to allow someone to manually change images.

- **Active Alignment:** Position the full image to the left, right, or center of the gallery block.

Grid

The Grid display option shows all your images as thumbnails aligned in a grid. This feature is useful when you want to display all your images at once and let the visitors decide which one they want to view larger. The following options are available:

- **Square Thumbnails:** Display your images as square thumbnails, creating a grid of images that are all the same size.

- **Thumbnails per Row:** Use the slider to adjust how many thumbnails are displayed on each row.

✔ **Padding around the Thumbnails:** Add more space around your thumb-nail images. Note that doing this will decrease the size of the thumbnail.

✔ **Lightbox:** Allow thumbnails to be clicked to display larger versions of the images in a presentation-style format. The website darkens and images are displayed in the center of the window.

Stacked

Stacked is the simplest display option, presenting the images one after the other down the page. It has no settings to configure.

If you don't have any blocks arranged to the left or right of the gallery block and you choose Stacked, the images will be sized to the full width of the page.

Video Block

Watching videos online has become a normal activity for many of us. Whether you want to share your own videos or the latest Grumpy Cat video, using the video block makes it easy to add video to your site.

You can use the video block to add video from many popular video services, including the following:

✔ YouTube: www.youtube.com

✔ Vimeo: www.vimeo.com

✔ Wistia: www.wistia.com

When you add a video block, the Edit Video dialog box appears, as shown in Figure 12-4. This dialog box is similar to the Edit Video dialog box for a gal-lery page (see Chapter 10).

The following settings are available:

✔ **Video URL or Embed Code:** Add the direct URL to the page containing the video. Alternatively, add the embed code from the service hosting the video. (Click the gear icon on the far right of the URL field to open a pop-up dialog box for pasting the embed code.)

✔ **Title:** Squarespace adds the title automatically if it can pull the video from the URL you pasted in the Video URL field.

✔ **Description:** Add descriptive content to display along with the video.

✔ **Custom Thumbnail:** Use custom thumbnails to display a specific image you want to use to represent the video.

✔ **Image Overlay:** Display the custom thumbnail in place of the video to speed up the loading of your page in a browser. To begin playing the video, the site visitor clicks the thumbnail image.

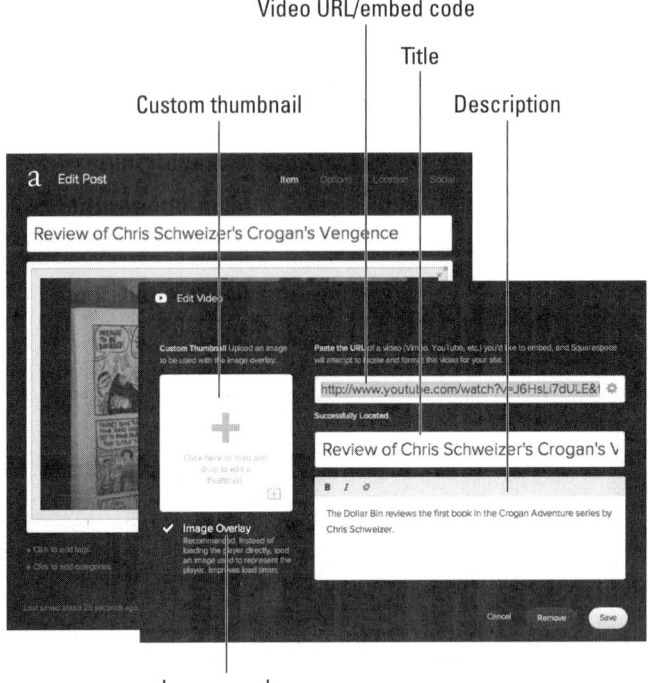

Figure 12-4:
The Edit
Video dialog
box for a
video block.

Embed Block

To add content to your site from another site, use the embed block. Squarespace has made this process as easy as providing the direct link to the content you want to add.

For example, if you want to embed a Tweet from Twitter on your site, simply paste the direct URL to the Tweet in the Edit Embed dialog box, as shown in Figure 12-5.

To find the direct URL of a Tweet, click the Tweet's date when viewing someone's Twitter profile on the Twitter website.

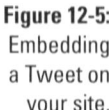

Figure 12-5:
Embedding
a Tweet on
your site.

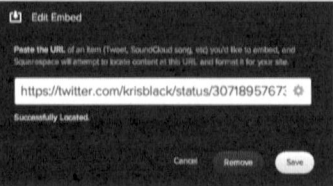

If the content you want to embed doesn't have a direct URL, click the gear icon on the far right of the URL field in the Edit Embed dialog box. Another dialog box appears so that you can paste embed code from a third-party service.

Many third parties provide embed code so that you can display their content on your site. For example, the following services allow you to put digital files such as presentations, academic papers, and even catalogs online:

✔ **Issuu** (www.issuu.com): Publish your own digital magazine, newspaper, or catalog.

✔ **Scribd** (www.scribd.com): Read, share, and publish documents and written works.

✔ **Slideshare** (www.slideshare.com): Share your presentations with the largest online community for this service.

Advanced form-building services may be useful if you find yourself needing more form features than those offered by the form block (see Chapter 11). Consider the following three options:

✔ **Formstack** (www.formstack.com): Integrate this robust form-building service with other business apps you may use.

✔ **JotForm** (www.jotform.com): Take advantage of the tons of features in this easy-to-use form builder.

✔ **Wufoo** (www.wufoo.com): Check out the robust set of design customization features that web designers will find useful.

If you use one of the following e-mail newsletter services to manage subscribers and send e-mail newsletters, you can use the embed block to display their sign-up forms on your site:

✔ **Campaign Monitor** (www.campaignmonitor.com): Manage client campaigns.

✔ **Constant Contact** (www.constantcontact.com): Manage e-mail, event, and social marketing with this leading small-business solution.

✔ **MailChimp** (www.mailchimp.com): Use their sign-up form code if you need to add a customized form to your site. MailChimp is already integrated with the form block (see Chapter 11).

Audio Block

Adding audio to your Squarespace site used to be a huge pain in the you-know-what. Now, however, the audio block makes the process just about as easy as adding any other media to your site.

Enhance your website by adding podcasts, songs, lectures, and more. When you add an audio block to your site, you'll need to complete the following settings:

- ✔ **Track Title:** A name describing the audio
- ✔ **Track Author:** The person or group who created the audio

Then you embed your .mp3, .m4a, or .ogg audio file in one of two ways:

- ✔ Upload the file
- ✔ Link to a file hosted on another site

To embed an audio file by uploading, drag the file over the upload area of the Edit Audio dialog box, or click the plus sign to open a file select window to locate a file on your computer to select and upload. For this method, audio files must be smaller than 120MB. If the file is larger, you must embed your audio file by using the second option, which is shown in Figure 12-6.

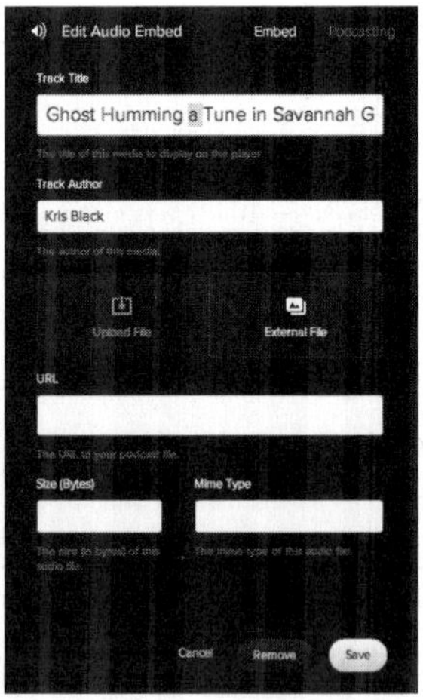

Figure 12-6:
Link an external audio file to the audio block.

To link to a file hosted on another site, you provide the following:

✓ The URL to the file hosted on the other service

✓ The size of the file in bytes

✓ The file's mime type if you're going to be podcasting with iTunes

To find the size of your audio file in bytes, ask Google. Seriously, go to www.google.com and type

> convert ##MB to bytes

substituting ## with the size of your audio file. Google will display the answer on the search results page, as shown in Figure 12-7.

Figure 12-7: Using Google to find the size of a file in bytes.

Providing the mime type of a file will help Squarespace know how to handle the file. You can add the following file types to an audio block:

✓ **mp3:** audio/mpeg

✓ **m4a:** audio/mp4a-latm

✓ **ogg:** audio/ogg

The second screen of options in the Edit Audio dialog box, shown in Figure 12-8, contains the podcast settings.

Figure 12-8:
Podcast settings for the audio block.

Fill in the following settings:

- ✔ **iTunes Subtitle:** A brief description about the audio file.
- ✔ **iTunes Summary:** A longer description about the audio file.
- ✔ **iTunes Search Keywords:** Any important words that describe the audio file that someone may search for in iTunes. Separate the search words with commas.
- ✔ **iTunes Episode Duration:** The duration of the audio file in the following format: hh:mm:ss.
- ✔ **Explicit content:** Display a message if your show has foul language or content not suitable for young listeners.

Podcasting with the audio block will work only when you add the audio block to a blog post. See Chapter 10 for details on creating blog posts.

Map Block

The map block is useful for many reasons, such as providing a map to a business or a location you are promoting. To add a map to your site, you simply add a location name and the address of the location in the Edit Map dialog box, as shown in Figure 12-9.

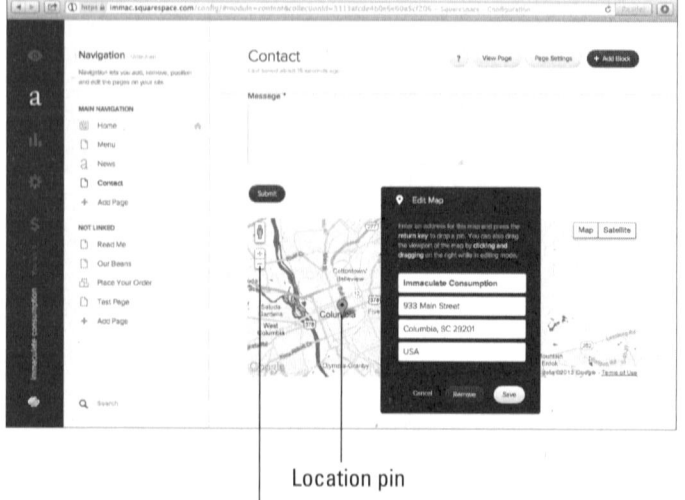

Figure 12-9:
Adding a
map with
the map
block.

Location pin

Zoom in and out

As the site owner, you can adjust the following aspects of the map when
you're configuring the map with its Edit Map dialog box open:

- **Reposition the location pin:** If you want to move the location pin in
  the map, you can drag it to a new location on the map. Doing this will
  update the address fields in the Edit Map dialog box.

- **Zoom:** Use the controls in the upper left of the map to zoom in and out
  on map.

- **View:** Click anywhere on the map (other than the location pin) and drag
  the map to adjust view.

The Map and Satellite buttons (in the upper-right corner) switch to a color
map view and a satellite view, respectively. Although you can click the buttons to see the map change, neither setting is permanent. The map reverts to
a black-and-white view when you refresh the page or view the page on your
site.

Just like the image block, you can also resize the map using handles on the
left, right, and bottom edges while hovering your mouse cursor over the map
block in LayoutEngine in Content Manager. You can also use the left, right,
and centered alignment icons at the top of the map to position it accordingly
within your page.

Chapter 13

Navigating with Structure Blocks

In This Chapter

▶ Understanding structure blocks

▶ Helping people search for your content

▶ Showing a summary listing of your latest blog or gallery posts

▶ Publicizing how often you post new content in a month

▶ Displaying an index of your tags and categories

*I*n Chapters 11 and 12, you looked at content blocks, which you use to add text and multimedia-based content to your site. In this chapter, I introduce structure blocks, which you use to pull and display specific information from pages within your site. Ultimately, these blocks will be updated automatically, displaying new content you create on another page.

Using some of these structure blocks, such as the summary block, you can create features on your home page that promote updates on pages deeper in your site. In this way, you help move site visitors throughout your site as well as keep them coming back for more. Remember, though, that you also need to have a plan for updating your content. For more on this topic, see Chapter 2.

Understanding How Structure Blocks Work

You can pull information using structure blocks only from pages that let you add items:

✔ Blog pages

✔ Events pages

✔ Gallery pages

✔ Products pages

These types of pages allow you to organize items such as blog posts, gallery images, and products into similar groupings by using tags and categories. Page items contain settings that determine when they are published to your site and who's credited with creating them (called authors). The content stored on these pages is searchable and can be used in other areas.

Chapter 10 explains how to add blog, events, and gallery items to these types of pages. See Chapter 17 for details on adding products to a products page.

You use structure blocks to pull content stored in blog posts, events, gallery images, gallery videos, and products pages to display elsewhere on your site. Some blocks display previews of content with links to view the rest of the content on another page. Other blocks display a list of information.

You can add the following types of structure blocks to your site:

- **Search:** A search box
- **Collection link:** The page thumbnail and page description of any page in your site
- **Calendar:** A calendar that indicates which days of the month a particular page's items have been published
- **Summary:** Page item updates
- **Tag cloud:** Tags applied to page items in different display styles
- **Author index:** Authors who have published items on a page
- **Tag index:** The tags used across all items on a page
- **Category index:** The categories used to group similar items
- **Month index:** The months when page items were published

All structure blocks, except the search block, pull information from a single page of your site. The steps are the same for any structure block:

1. **Add a structure block to a page.**

   See Chapter 10 for details on adding a block to a page of your site.

2. **Select the page from which the structure block will pull information.**

   In the block's configuration dialog box, select a page from the list. Figure 13-1 is an example of a list of pages in a structure block. The pages are listed and organized by page type:

   - Blog
   - Gallery

- Events
- Products
- Pages

In the rest of the chapter, you explore each of these blocks in detail.

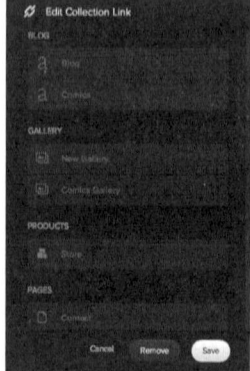

Figure 13-1:
An example
of a list of
pages in a
structure
block.

Search Block

The search block enables you to add a search box to your site. Search boxes are useful when your site has a lot of pages with information that could be too difficult to find by going through the site page by page.

You don't configure any settings when you add a search block to your site because the search box searches your entire site.

If your site is made up of only a handful of pages, you probably won't need to use the search block. Instead, make sure that the content of your site is organized in such a way that finding information is intuitive.

The remaining blocks that I describe in this chapter can pull information only from pages that allow you to add page items (blog posts, gallery images and videos, and products).

Collection Link Block

The collection link block can connect to any page in your site, including the non-item page type, and display the page thumbnail and page description of the selected page. The collection link block doesn't discriminate because all pages of your site allow you to add a page thumbnail and description, as explained in Chapter 9.

When you add a collection link block, you must choose the page you want the block to display on your page. When you select a page in the list in the Edit Collection Link dialog box, that page's thumbnail and description are displayed in LayoutEngine.

 If you don't see a page thumbnail and description in LayoutEngine, check that page's Page Settings and make sure a thumbnail and description are included. (See Chapter 8 for information on adding pages to your site and configuring page settings.)

Calendar Block

The calendar block displays a small calendar, perfect for page sidebars or footers, which highlights the days in the month when page items for blog and gallery pages were published, or the days of an event from an event listing on an events page. When site visitors hover their mouse cursor over a day in the month, the title of the page item appears in a pop-up window, as shown in Figure 13-2.

Blog posts and gallery item titles in the pop-up window are organized by the time of day that they were published. Click a title to go view the item on its original page.

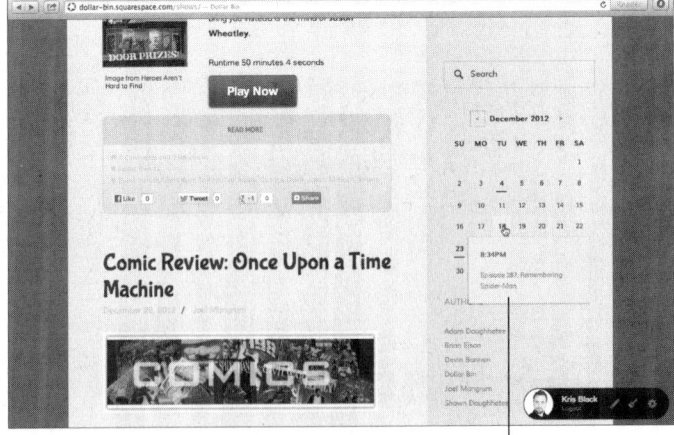

Figure 13-2:
A page item published on a particular day of the month.

Pop-up window

The only setting in the Edit Calendar dialog box is the page from which you want the calendar block to display information. If you want to display multiple pages, you must add a calendar block for each page.

The calendar block has a set minimum and maximum width. It will not stretch to fill the full width of a page, which is why it's a perfect block for a sidebar or footer.

Summary Block

The summary block displays a preview of 1 to 20 pages. You might want to use this block to show the latest published page items from a particular page on your site.

The display in a summary block depends on the page type you select in the Edit Summary dialog box. Generally, the block displays the following content:

- ✔ Title
- ✔ Published date
- ✔ Thumbnail for blog posts and events, or the main image for galleries and products
- ✔ Excerpt or description

If a page item doesn't have content for one of these features, the summary block will display the labeled field but it will be blank. It will still show the item but will display only what information it does find. Figure 13-3 shows a summary block on the left side of my home page that displays content from my blog.

Summary block

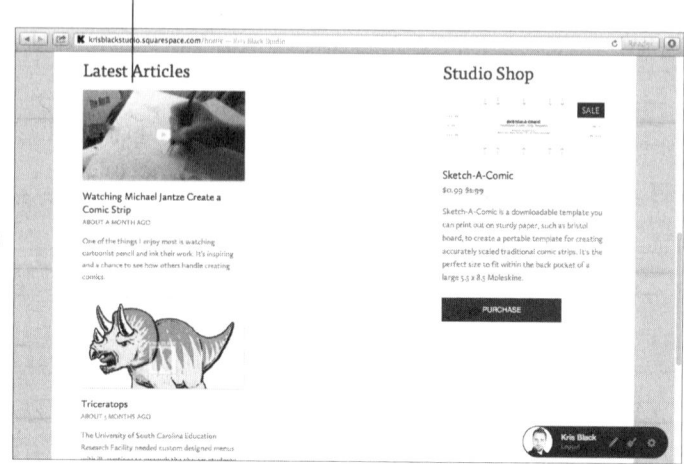

Figure 13-3: Summary block displaying content on my website.

As mentioned, you could adjust the number of items that the summary block will display. When you open the Edit Summary dialog box, the following two tabs are in the upper-right corner:

✔ **Content:** Choose the page you're targeting and adjust the number of items to display in the block. This is the default view.

✔ **Filters:** Reduce the items displayed in the block by adjusting the following settings:

- **Tag:** A tag you used on a published page item in the page you selected in the Content tab

- **Category:** A category you used on a published page item in the page you selected in the Content tab

- **Featured:** Display only page items designated as featured posts

You can enter both a tag and a category in the Filters settings. The summary block will filter out the page items that match both.

Tag Cloud Block

Despite the tag cloud block's name, this block displays tags or categories. The tags or categories are those you applied to page items on a page you selected in the Edit Tag Cloud dialog box. The tags or categories are displayed in a weighted style, in which the more frequently applied tags or categories are displayed in a larger typeface, as shown in Figure 13-4.

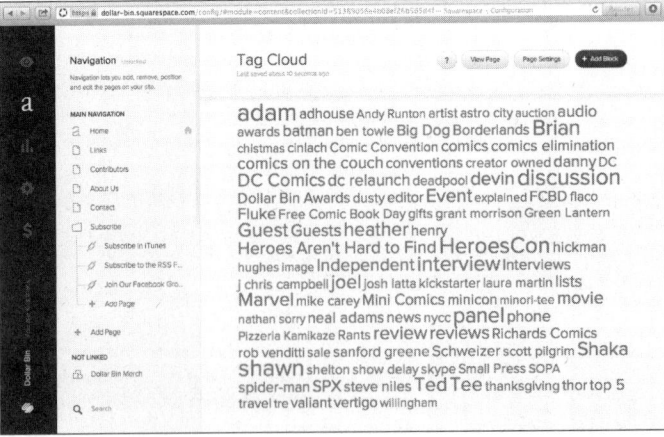

Figure 13-4:
A weighted tag cloud on the Dollar Bin Comics Podcast site.

You can make the following adjustments for the tag cloud block:

- ✔ **Display Type:** Display a page's tags or categories.
- ✔ **Sort By:** Sort the tags by choosing A–Z (alphabetically); Weight (most commonly used); or Activity (most recently used).
- ✔ **Tag Limit:** Using the slider, set the block to display from 5 to 100 tags or categories.

Author Index Block

The author index block displays a list of all the site contributors who have been assigned as authors of page items for the page from which the block is pulling information. (For more on contributors, see Chapter 15.)

Some templates will display a number in parentheses following the author name. This number represents how many page items the author has published. Clicking an author's name will load a filtered view that displays all the page items where the person is credited as the author.

The only configuration setting for the author index block is choosing the page from which this block will pull information. If you're the only author of content on your site, you will probably not find this block useful. But if you're part of a team of contributors who create content for a blog or gallery, the author index block enables you to easily display all contributors in a simple list.

Tag, Category, and Month Index Blocks

The index blocks display lists of tags, categories, or published date:

- ✔ **Tag:** Displays a list of tags applied to page items
- ✔ **Category:** Displays a list of categories applied to page items
- ✔ **Month:** Displays a list of months when page items were published

The only configuration setting for these blocks is selecting the page you want to target and connect with the blocks.

Unlike the tag cloud block, the index blocks don't apply a visual hierarchy to the words in the lists. Instead, the lists are presented in a simple list format. Depending on the template you're using, your lists might have bullets or another visual style applied to them.

In LayoutEngine (see Chapter 10), you may notice numbers in parentheses following the words in the lists created by the index blocks. These numbers represent the number of times the words were applied to the tag or category in all the page items of the page to which the tag or category index block is connected. For the month index block, the numbers reflect how many page items were published during the month. Depending on the template you're using, the index blocks may or may not display these numbers on your site for your site visitors.

Chapter 14

Automating Updates with Social Blocks

In This Chapter

▶ Sharing photos from photo-sharing sites

▶ Displaying your tweets on your site

▶ Creating links to your social accounts

*H*ere you are in the last chapter of Part IV. In the previous chapters in this part, you found out about the following types of blocks that you can add to personalize your site:

✔ Text-based content blocks (Chapter 11)

✔ Multimedia content blocks (Chapter 12)

✔ Structure blocks (Chapter 13)

In this chapter, you review social blocks, which are the blocks you use to pull in content you've added to your social accounts on sites such as Flickr, Instagram, and Twitter. With social blocks, you can effortlessly keep new content automatically flowing through to your site without actually having to update your website.

Furthermore, most of the social accounts these blocks connect to have apps you can install on a mobile device, such as an iPhone, Android phone, or iPad. This means that your site can be updated while you're away from your computer. Speaking of mobile apps, make sure to check out Chapter 18, which explores the mobile possibilities with the Squarespace apps. Now let's look at these social apps and what they can do.

Understanding How Social Blocks Work

When you have a social block on your site, you don't have to constantly update them with new content. Instead, the social blocks display content that you've added to your social accounts on the following websites:

- 500px (www.500px.com)
- Flickr (www.flickr.com)
- Foursquare (www.foursquare.com)
- Instagram (www.instagram.com)
- Twitter (www.twitter.com)

Each of these sites has its own social block in Squarespace. One more social block, social links, is unlike the other social blocks. This block doesn't pull information from any of your social accounts. Instead, it displays links to your social accounts so people can go directly to your account profiles on those sites.

You can also link to other popular social sites, including the following:

- Facebook
- Google+
- LinkedIn
- Pinterest

You look at the social blocks in more detail later in the chapter. First, you find out how to connect your social accounts to your blocks.

Connecting a Social Account to a Social Block

You can add all social accounts that are supported by Squarespace to the Connected Accounts area. Find details about how to add social accounts in

Chapter 15. To save you some page turning, here are the general steps to follow:

1. **Log in and go to the Connected Accounts area of Site Settings.**

   Choose Site Manager⟳Site Settings⟳Connected Accounts.

2. **Click the Add Account button in the top-right of the window and select a social account from the list that appears.**

3. **Repeat Step 2 to add additional accounts.**

All social blocks look to the Connected Accounts settings to see if you have an account already connected for the social block you are adding. You can add multiple accounts for the same social site. For example, if you have two Twitter accounts, you can add both to your site.

When you add a social block, you need to choose the social account from which it will pull content to display on your site. Here's how:

1. **Add a social block to a page.**

   When you add a social block to a page on your site, the block's configuration dialog box will open, as shown in Figure 14-1. See Chapter 10 for the steps for adding a block to a page of your site.

Figure 14-1:
A social block's configuration settings.

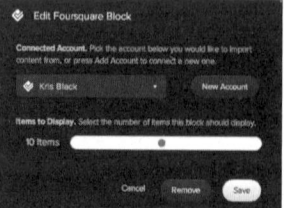

2. **Connect your social account.**

   • Social accounts that you've already added to your site are displayed in a menu to the left of the New Account button.

   • For a social account that hasn't been added to your site, click the New Account button (see Figure 14-2). Then log in to your social account and give Squarespace permission to pull information and updates from the account. The account will be automatically added to your Connected Accounts settings.

3. **Save the block.**

   Click the Save button to save your new block and add it to your page.

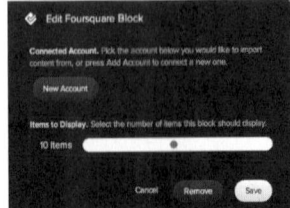

Figure 14-2:
Connecting
a new
account to a
social block.

When you add a new account to a social block, the new account will be added also to the Connect Accounts settings in Site Settings.

All social blocks except the social links block provide you with a way to import content to your website from your social accounts.

Now that you know how to connect a social account to a social block, let's look at the social blocks in more detail.

Creating Galleries from Photo-Sharing Sites

Three social blocks provide the same feature — they display a gallery of images pulled from a photo-sharing site. The three photo-sharing social blocks and the sites they pull photos from are

- ✓ **500px:** A community for discovering, sharing, buying, and selling photos by creative professionals
- ✓ **Flickr:** An online photo-management and photo-sharing site
- ✓ **Instagram:** A photo-sharing app used on mobile phones to share your life with your friends

When you add one of these blocks to your site and their configuration dialog box opens, you will see two tabs in the upper-right corner, as shown in Figure 14-3:

- ✓ **Account:** Set the social account from which you will pull images. Use the Items to Display slider to set the number of photos to display.
- ✓ **Design:** Set the gallery design to one of four display options: Slideshow, Slider, Grid, or Stacked. These are the same features found in the Gallery block, which is covered in Chapter 12.

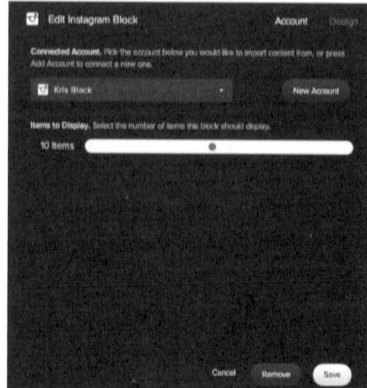

Figure 14-3:
The
Account
and Design
tabs in the
Instagram
block.

When you click an image displayed by one of these blocks, you will be taken to the original page that hosts the image in the social account from which it was imported. The only way to prevent this behavior is to use the Lightbox setting in the Grid display option. When the Lightbox setting is selected, thumbnails can be clicked to display larger versions of the images in a presentation-style format, in which the website darkens and the images are displayed in the center of the window.

Using photo-sharing social blocks is a great way to instantly update your site with the latest photos you share in your social accounts.

Streaming Your Latest Tweets

The Twitter block is a great way to share your latest Tweets. The Tweets are rendered directly in the page and integrate seamlessly with the rest of your website. This display method differs from third-party code and Twitter's own widget, which embed Tweets in a container that uses a scroll bar and a preset design that may or may not match your site.

The Twitter block uses the same slider control as the other social blocks to set the number of Tweets to display from 1 to 20. You can use three other settings to customize the Twitter block, as shown in Figure 14-4:

- ✔ **Show Avatar:** Show or hide your Twitter avatar.
- ✔ **Show Username:** Show or hide your user name in your Tweets.
- ✔ **Show Follow Button:** Show or hide the Twitter Follow button below all your Tweets.

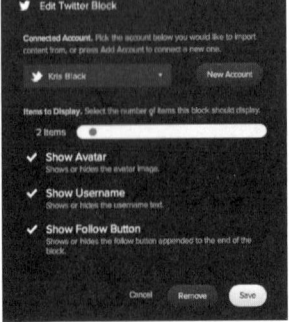

Figure 14-4:
The Twitter block con-figuration settings.

Clicking the avatar or user name will take you to the Twitter account on the Twitter website. If you click a Tweet's time stamp displayed on your site (which indicates when the Tweet was posted), you load that Tweet's page on Twitter in your browser window.

The Twitter block displays the latest tweets from your Twitterstream. If you are interested in placing a specific Tweet on your site, check out the embed block in Chapter 12.

Checking in with Foursquare

Foursquare is a mobile app you use to "check in" with locations when you visit them and then share those locations with your friends.

Foursquare will list from 1 to 20 of your latest check-ins. You set the number of check-ins by adjusting the Items to Display slider in the Edit Foursquare Block configuration dialog box.

The Foursquare block displays the following information, as shown in Figure 14-5:

- ✔ **Icons:** These icons represent the type of location you checked into.
- ✔ **Name and Location:** The name, city, and state of the place you checked into.
- ✔ **Date:** A relative time stamp of when you checked in.

The Foursquare block can do more than just display your check-ins. If you click any of the location updates, you will be taken to that check-in's page on Foursquare.

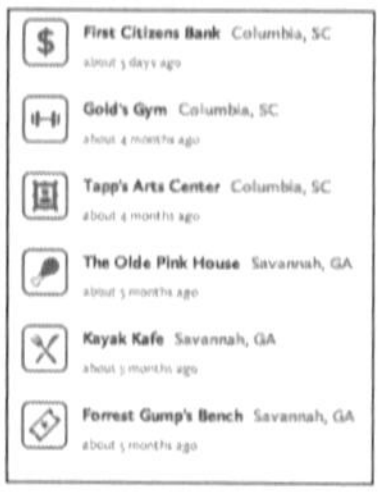

Figure 14-5:
The
Foursquare
block.

Listing Your Social Accounts

Now that we've covered pulling information from your social accounts in
blocks, let's look at the social links block, which displays a list of your social
accounts. You may want to list your social accounts on your site in one place
so people can see the different options they have for connecting with you.

When you add this type of block to your site and its configuration dialog box
opens, you'll see two tabs in the upper-right corner, as shown in Figure 14-6:

✔ **Item:** Set the social accounts you want to display on your site. The list of
social accounts you see is pulled from the Connected Accounts settings
in Site Settings of Site Manager. You can find out more about connected
accounts in Chapter 15.

✔ **Design:** Set how the social links will be styled and displayed on your
site. You can adjust the following settings:

• **Style:** Choose a Round, Square or Icon Only display option for the
icon.

• **Size:** Choose from small, medium, or large icons.

• **Alignment:** Align the icons to the left, right, or center of the block.

• **Color:** Choose from either black or white icons.

When you click one of the social icons, you will be taken to your profile on
that social site.

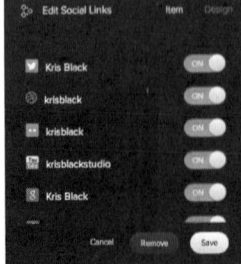

Figure 14-6:
Displaying
your social
accounts
with the
social links
block.

When you connect new social accounts in Site Settings➪Connect Accounts,
any social links blocks you have on your site will not automatically display the
icons for the newly added social accounts. Instead, you need to open a social
links block's configuration dialog box to turn on the new accounts so that they
are displayed on your site.

Part V
Extending Your Website

In this part . . .

- ✔ Configure your site settings and include billing information
- ✔ Add your own custom domains
- ✔ Monitor your site's activity
- ✔ Discover the Squarespace mobile apps: Note and Portfolio
- ✔ Sell stuff on your site with Commerce

Chapter 15

Configuring Site Settings

. . . .

In This Chapter

▶ Configuring basic and general settings

▶ Adding contributors to help manage your site

▶ Previewing and choosing a new template

▶ Getting your own custom domain

▶ Updating your billing information

. . . .

*T*here's more to building a website than just adding content and designing your site's template. You should also consider settings that affect your entire site, such as:

✔ Adding site titles and descriptions

✔ Connecting third-party services such as Google Analytics and Disqus

✔ Connecting social accounts such as Facebook and Twitter

✔ Inviting someone to be a contributor

✔ Adding a custom domain

✔ Applying code to all your site pages

In this chapter, you explore Settings (gear icon) in Site Manager. You find at least a brief explanation of each setting, with a few more robust settings described in more detail.

Getting to Know Your Site's Settings

Settings is divided into many different groups of settings. Although Settings may appear to contain a hodge-podge of features that don't go together, there is some logic to the different categories. Each setting has a specific purpose to help you configure your site the way you want.

To get to the Settings area in Squarespace, do the following:

1. **Log in to your site.**

   You are taken to Content Manager. If you were already logged in and in Preview mode, click the gear icon in the Preview Toolbar to go to Content Manager.

2. **Click Settings (the gear icon), which appears in the black bar to the left side of the screen.**

   When Settings loads in your browser, you see a sidebar directly to the right of the black bar.

The Settings navigation sidebar displays a list of all the different groups of configuration settings available:

- ✔ **Site:** Add a site title, description, and logo.

- ✔ **General:** Configure third-party integrations, commenting, posting to blogs, and page title formats.

- ✔ **Time/Geography:** Set date presentation across your site.

- ✔ **Connected Accounts:** Connect your site to your social accounts to push and pull data.

- ✔ **Facebook Page:** Publish a page on your site to your Facebook Page.

- ✔ **Share Buttons:** Allow visitors to share your site's content on a social network such as Facebook, Twitter, or Google+.

- ✔ **Contributors:** Invite people to help contribute to or maintain your site.

- ✔ **Domains:** Use your own custom domain instead of your squarespace.com domain.

- ✔ **Templates:** Switch between all the templates to change your site's design.

- ✔ **Import/Export:** Import your old site from various other web-publishing services such as WordPress, Shopify, or even your old Squarespace 5 account.

- ✔ **Code Injection:** Insert custom snippets of code into your site.

- ✔ **Advanced:** Create URL redirects (mappings) that help direct people to the correct content.

- ✔ **Developer:** Find useful data for developers who sign up to use the Squarespace developer platform.

- ✔ **Sessions:** See which of your computers are being used to log in to your site.

- ✔ **Mobile Apps:** Find out about mobile apps available from Squarespace.

✔ **Billing:** Upgrade your account and update your billing information.

✔ **Help & Support:** Contact Squarespace Customer Support.

When you go to any of these settings and update the information they contain, be sure to click the Save Settings button at the top right of the screen to save your changes.

Now let's look at each of these settings in more detail.

Configuring Basic Site Settings

At the top of navigation column in Settings is the Site option. Click it and the screen in Figure 15-1 appears.

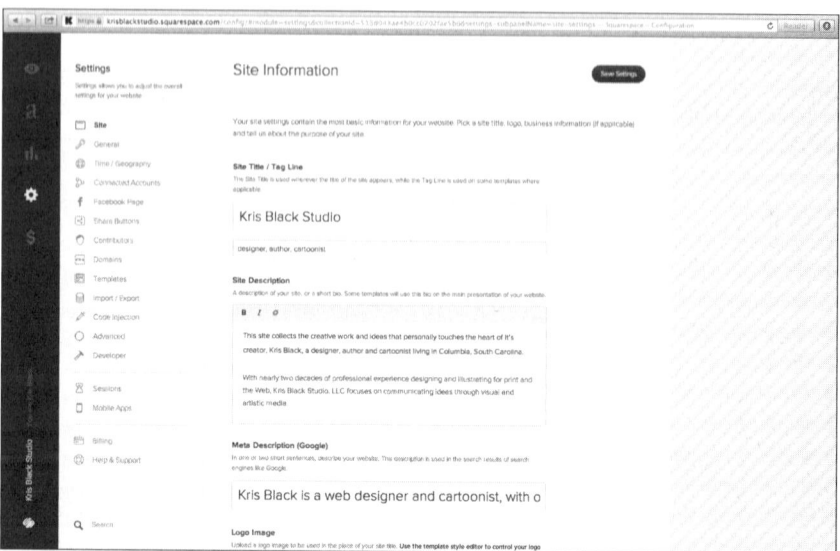

Figure 15-1:
The Site
settings
screen.

The Site option has the following basic settings for configuring your site:

✔ **Site Title:** Enter a title for your site. The site title will appear anywhere that the title needs to be displayed in your site, such as directly in your site pages, and in the name of page titles configured in General Settings (see the Homepage Title, Collection Title, and Item Title formats in the next section).

✔ **Tag Line:** Enter a tag line that describes your site. Some templates use the tag line in the site layout.

✔ **Site Description:** Add a description of your site. Some templates use the description in the site layout.

✔ **Meta Description:** Type a short description about your site. Google and other search engines display this information in their search results.

✔ **Logo:** Upload your logo to replace the site title in the layout of your site.

✔ **Browser Icon:** Customize the little image that appears in the URL bar or window tab of a browser.

✔ **Subject/Type:** Help Squarespace categorize your site for their records.

✔ **Contact Information:** Add contact information for you or your business, including an e-mail address, a phone number, and a mailing address. Some templates display this information in your site.

Make sure you fill in the site title and meta description. These important settings help search engines categorize and index your site for display in search results.

See Chapter 4 for directions on adding images to the Logo and Browser Icon settings. These settings utilize the Squarespace image uploader feature found in other areas of your Squarespace site.

Configuring General Settings

You'll find a variety of settings to configure in the General screen. This catch-all area collects some one-off settings as well as groups of settings that affect your entire site.

Third-party services

Squarespace understands that you may want to use third-party services to enhance or customize your site. These services typically provide the same code for any website owner to add to their site, with a unique identifier in the code for each website.

The first group of settings in the General screen enables you to add your unique identifier for the following third-party services:

✔ **Google Analytics** (www.google.com/analytics): Provides more robust website traffic and statistics information than what you have available in Activity (see Chapter 16).

✔ **Typekit Kit ID** (www.typekit.com): Fonts added in a kit in your Typekit account will be available to select in Style Editor.

✔ **Disqus Shortname** (www.disqus.com): Replace the Squarespace commenting system and add more features for commenting on your site.

✔ **Amazon Associate Tag** (affiliate-program.amazon.com): Earn money when someone buys a product on Amazon.com from a link on your site.

Although you don't need to use any of these third-party services, they can provide you with more options to analyze your site's activity (Google Analytics), customize your site's design (Typekit), engage more with site commenters (Disqus), and earn some sweet, sweet cash (Amazon Associates).

Overall site configurations

These next few settings are only similar in that they can have an effect on your entire site:

✔ **Site-Wide Password:** Temporarily block access to your entire site by requiring visitors to use a password to view your website.

✔ **Template Settings:** Adjust a couple of settings affecting your site's template:

- Disable promoted blocks used by some templates to give special treatment to the following blocks if they're placed first in a blog post: image, gallery, map, quote, and video.

- Disable mobile styles so your site looks the same on mobile devices as it does on computers.

✔ **404 Page:** If visitors come to your site and the page they link to is no longer available, they will get a missing page message error, known as a 404 page error. You can use the Squarespace default page for this, or you can choose a page you created in Content Manager by selecting it in the drop-down menu.

✔ **Homepage Title Format:** Configure how the site and page title appears in the browser when viewing your home page.

✔ **Collection Title Format:** Configure how the title of collection pages (blog, gallery, and products pages) appears in a browser.

See Chapters 9 and 10 for more detailed explanations about collection pages (blog, gallery, and products pages) and the items you add to them.

✔ **Item Title Format:** Configure how the title of your item pages (blog posts) appears in the browser on your home page.

- **Markdown Editing:** When a text block (pages and blog posts) appears by default, replace it with a markdown block (see Chapter 11).

- **Post URL Format:** Configure the format of the URL for a blog post.

- **Simple Liking:** Disable the Simple Liking feature on blog posts.

- **Comments:** Configure the comment settings. See the next section for details.

- **Promotion/Indexing:** Allow Squarespace to feature your site in promotional areas of their site, such as the Templates page.

- **Escape Key to Login:** Disable the use of the Esc key to display the login page for your site.

Comment settings

If you have a blog page on your site, you may have enabled commenting in your blog posts. As you discover in Chapter 10, you can allow or disallow commenting for each individual blog post in the Edit Post window. In the General screen, however, you can control many more aspects of commenting than just switching commenting on and off per post:

- **Enable Comments:** Turn commenting on or off for your entire site.

- **Comment Likes Allowed:** Allow commenters to like someone's comment.

- **Comment Flags Allowed:** Allow commenters to flag a comment, typically to indicate inappropriate conduct.

- **Approval required:** Require your approval before a comment is posted to your site (see Chapter 16).

- **Anonymous Comments Allowed:** Allow commenters to post without providing identifying information. If anonymous comments are not allowed, commenters will need to verify themselves with one of the four account types: Squarespace, Twitter, Facebook, or Google+.

- **Threaded:** Allow commenters to directly respond to a specific comment.

- **Avatars Visible:** Show a commenter's avatar next to his or her comment.

- **Enable Comments by Default when Posting:** Comments are allowed by default when creating a new blog post.

- **Auto-Disable Comments Default Value:** Disable comments after a set time period ranging from never to 90 days.

✓ **Default Comment Sort Order:** Sort comments in blog posts by newest first, oldest first, most liked, or least liked.

✓ **Auto-Moderation Flag Count Threshold:** Choose how many flags a comment can receive, ranging from off to 20 flags, before being set to Awaiting Moderation.

These comment settings will affect commenting across all blog pages you have added to your site.

Setting the Time and Geography

The Time/Geography settings enable you to customize how the date and time appear in certain pages of your site such as blog posts. You may customize the following settings:

✓ **Choose the Nearest City:** Click the map in the approximate location of where you live. Your time zone will be highlighted on the map, and the nearest largest city will be indicated by a dot.

✓ **Time and Date:** Below the map on the left you will see the time for your time zone and the current date.

✓ **Nearest City:** To the right of the time and date is the name of the nearest city indicated by the dot in the map. Click the city name to reveal a pop-up menu to select a city that may be closer to you.

Other features on this page are

✓ **Language:** Select the language you use to write the content of your site.

✓ **Geography:** Select your country and state in the drop-down menu.

Adding Connected Accounts

You can connect your social accounts to your Squarespace site in the Connected Accounts settings. When you do this you are able to

✓ Push updates from your site to your social accounts

✓ Pull updates from your social accounts to display on your site in social blocks (see Chapter 14)

To connect one of your social accounts in Connected Accounts, do the following:

1. **Click the Add Account button, which is at the top right.**

   A pop-up box appears with all the social accounts you can add to your site.

2. **Click the social account to which you want to connect.**

3. **If Squarespace will be pulling updates from the social account, you must add your account information, as shown in Figure 15-2.**

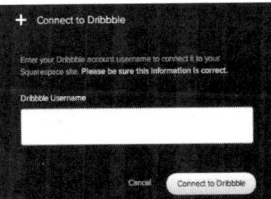

Figure 15-2:
Connecting to a social account.

4. **If Squarespace can push updates to your social account (such as Facebook and Twitter), you must give Squarespace permission to post updates on your behalf.**

   You will need to authorize Squarespace to connect to your social account by logging into your social account in a new window that opens, as shown in Figure 15-3.

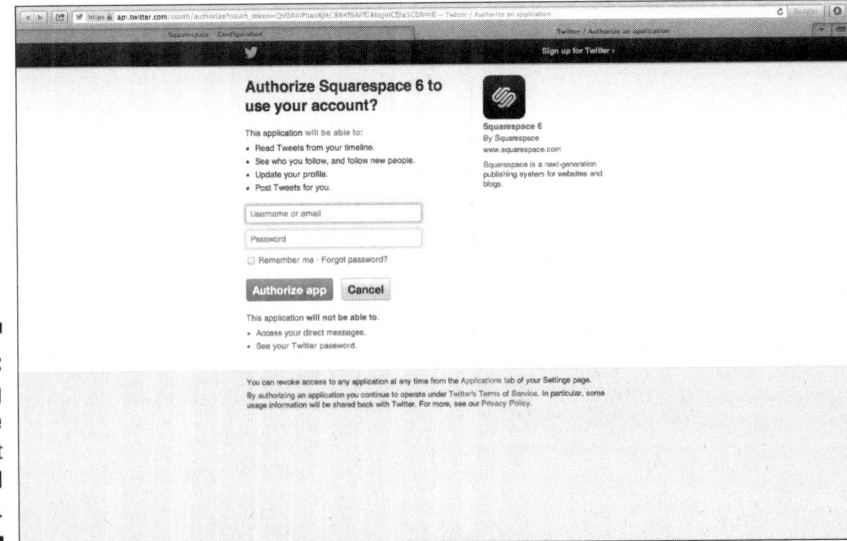

Figure 15-3:
Authorizing your site to connect to a social account.

The social accounts you can connect to your site vary, from the popular Facebook, Twitter, and Google+ to photo-sharing services such as Flickr to specialty websites such as Dribbble (yes, three *b*'s). Each social account you add has its own settings for adjusting how your site pushes and pulls content.

The two basic settings available for all social accounts are

- ✓ **Show social icon:** Choose to display the social account in any social links block added to your site. For more information, see the section on listing your social accounts in Chapter 14.

- ✓ **Profile URL:** The URL to your social account profile.

The following social sites use the previous two settings only to allow you to add them as links in a social links block. They don't provide any further features:

- ✓ **Dribbble:** www.dribbble.com

- ✓ **Google+:** www.plus.google.com

- ✓ **Pinterest:** www.pinterest.com

- ✓ **Vimeo:** www.vimeo.com

- ✓ **YouTube:** www.youtube.com

Three additional settings found in several of the social account configurations are

- ✓ **Show Push Option:** Allows you to set an option in collection page items (blog posts, gallery images, gallery videos, and products) to publish updates to your social sites. See Chapter 10 for details.

- ✓ **Download Data:** Squarespace will download data from your social account to store and be used for displaying on your site in blocks.

- ✓ **Default Posting Format:** Configure updates so that they are preformatted with the title, author, and URL of the post you are pushing to the social account.

The following social accounts include one or more of the preceding settings along with an explanation of any additional features they may offer:

- ✓ **500px** (www.500px.com): Sync your latest updates to a 500px block for display on your site.

- ✓ **Facebook** (www.facebook.com): Select to push preformatted updates to your Facebook profile or a Facebook page you manage.

- ✓ **Flickr** (www.flickr.com): Sync your latest updates to a Flickr block for display on your site.

✔ **Foursquare** (www.foursquare.com): Download your location data to the Foursquare block for display on your site.

✔ **GitHub** (www.github.com): Display a link to your account on GitHub.

✔ **Instagram** (www.instagram.com): Sync your latest updates to an Instagram block for display on your site.

✔ **LinkedIn** (www.linkedin.com): Push preformatted updates to your LinkedIn account.

✔ **SmugMug** (www.smugmug.com): Import albums from your SmugMug account for display on your site.

✔ **Tumblr** (www.tumblr.com): Cross-publish your Squarespace blog posts to a blog on your Tumblr account.

✔ **Twitter** (www.twitter.com): Add multiple Twitter accounts to your Connected Accounts, while choosing to push preformatted updates to each account. Also download data to display in the Twitter block.

The two most different social accounts that offer unique features are

✔ **Dropbox** (www.dropbox.com): Create new gallery pages or update current gallery pages with images you import from your Dropbox account.

✔ **Email:** Display a link with your e-mail address in the social links block.

To disconnect one of your social accounts from your site, do the following:

1. **Click your social account.**

   The configuration dialog box appears.

2. **Click the Disconnect Account button.**

   A confirmation window appears.

3. **Confirm the disconnection.**

   Click the Confirm button to disconnect your social account from your site.

Publishing Pages to Your Facebook Page

If you signed up for the Unlimited or Business plan (see Chapter 3), you can publish a gallery and page to your Facebook page. If you don't have a Facebook page, you can sign up for one at www.facebook.com/about/pages.

To be able to publish your pages to your Facebook page, you must first connect your Facebook account in Connected Accounts, as explained in the preceding section. Then you'll have the following options in the Facebook Page section of Settings, as shown in Figure 15-4:

✔ **Linked Facebook Page:** Select the Facebook page to which you want to publish your Squarespace gallery or page. When your gallery or page is published to your Facebook page, it will be added as a feature called a tab. Tabs appear below the cover photo of your Facebook page.

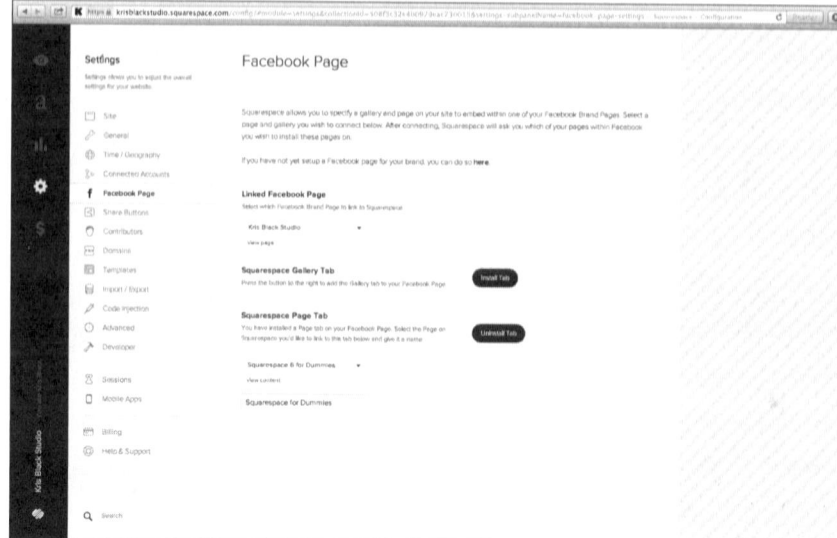

Figure 15-4: Square-space pages will appear as tabs on a Facebook page.

✔ **Squarespace Gallery Tab:** Click the Install Tab button to select the gallery page from your site in the drop-down menu to publish to your Facebook page. Add a gallery title to be displayed on the Facebook page.

✔ **Squarespace Page Tab:** Select the page from your site in the drop-down menu to publish it to your Facebook page. Add a page title to be displayed on the Facebook page.

Activating Share Buttons

Do you want to provide your visitors with the ability to share your blog posts on their social accounts? Simply activate the specific social accounts to allow the display of their share buttons on your blog posts on your site.

To activate a social account, click the social account's icon in the Share Buttons options screen. The following social accounts are currently supported:

- ✔ Facebook
- ✔ Google
- ✔ LinkedIn
- ✔ Pinterest
- ✔ Reddit
- ✔ StumbleUpon
- ✔ Tumblr
- ✔ Twitter

Pinterest sharing will work only for blog posts to which you've added a thumbnail image in the Options settings of the Edit Post window. See Chapter 10 for more information about adding a thumbnail image to a post.

These sharing buttons will be displayed at the end of your blog posts. To access a sharing button, you typically hover your cursor over the Share link to reveal a pop-up menu of share buttons, as shown in Figure 15-5.

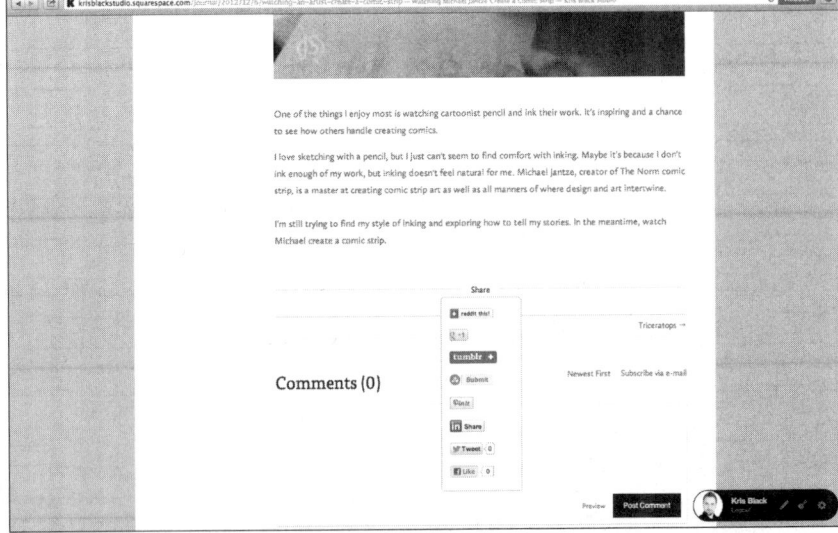

Figure 15-5: Share buttons allow visitors to help promote your posts.

Inviting Contributors to Your Site

You can add other people as contributors to your site to allow them access
with permission to do certain tasks. Squarespace allows you to grant the following different types of permissions to contributors for your site:

- ✔ **Administrator:** Full permission access, the same as the account owner
- ✔ **Billing:** Update credit card information
- ✔ **Comment Moderator:** Edit, approve, mark as spam, and help manage
  comments on your blog
- ✔ **Content Editor:** Edit content on your site.
- ✔ **Reporting:** View website statistics in Activity (see Chapter 16)
- ✔ **Store Manager:** Receive store notifications and manage orders
- ✔ **Trusted Commenter:** Bypass comment moderation

You can select multiple permissions for each contributor you add to your
site. For example, if you need someone to manage comments and have access
to update billing information, you would grant them Billing and Comment
Moderator permissions.

Adding a contributor

To add a contributor to your site, start from the Contributors screen in your
site's Settings area:

1. **Click the Add Contributor button.**

   The Invite Contributor dialog box appears, as shown in Figure 15-6.

2. **Provide the name and e-mail address.**

   Type the name and e-mail address of the person you are inviting in the
   provided fields at the top of the dialog box.

E-mail address of invite

Name of invite

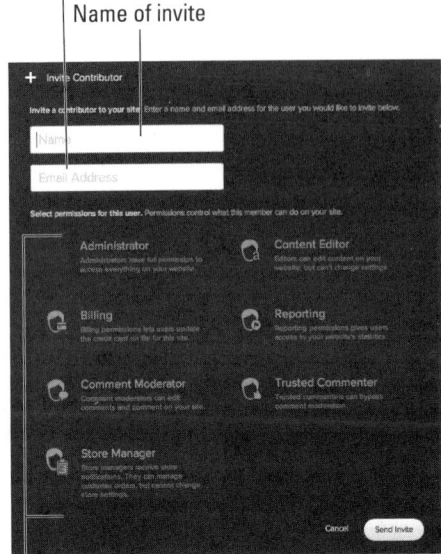

Figure 15-6:
Inviting
someone
to be a
contributor.

Permissions

3. **Select the permission(s) you want to assign to the contributor.**

Click each permission type you want to assign.

4. **Click the Send Invite button.**

An e-mail invitation is sent to the person using the e-mail address you entered in Step 2.

When the person you're inviting receives your invitation, he or she will need to click a link in the e-mail to accept your invite. A window will open in the person's browser and with one of two options:

✓ **Log in with an existing Squarespace account:** If the person already has a Squarespace account on another site, he or she can use that account's e-mail address and password to log in to your site.

✓ **Create a new Squarespace account:** The person will need to create a Squarespace account.

If the person you invited didn't receive or can't find the invitation, you can copy the Invitation Link at the top of the Modify Invitation dialog box (see the next section) and e-mail it to the person in an e-mail you send from your e-mail account.

Removing a contributor

To remove a contributor and revoke all permissions, do the following in the Contributors screen of your site's Settings area:

1. **In the Contributors area, click a contributor.**

   The Modify Permissions dialog box opens.

2. **Click the Remove Access button.**

   The person is removed from your site, and all permissions assigned to that person are revoked.

Modifying a contributor's invitation

If you need to update the invitation permissions sent to someone, you have the opportunity to do so before the person accepts the invitation. Here's how you modify the invitation:

1. **In the Contributors area, click a contributor.**

   The Modify Invitation dialog box appears.

2. **Click the permission types in the person's invitation to add or remove assigned permissions.**

   See the next section for steps on how to do this.

3. **Click the Save button.**

   Save your changes and close the window to return to the Contributor screen.

If you want to uninvite a person rather than change his or her permissions, click the Remove Invite button. The invitation link in the e-mail the person received will be disabled, and the person will not be able to create a contributor account on your site.

Modifying a contributor's permissions

If you want to add or revoke particular permissions for a contributor, do the following:

1. **In the Contributors area, click a contributor.**

   The Modify Permissions dialog box appears.

2. **Click a permission type to add or revoke it.**

   If the permission type is not assigned to the contributor, selecting it will highlight the permission and assign it. If the permission type was assigned, selecting it will remove the permission.

3. **Click the Save button.**

   Your changes are saved and you return to the Contributor screen.

If you modify a contributor such that he or she ends up with no permissions, you might as well remove the person as a contributor.

Adding contributors to your site is a great way to help pass the burden of managing multiple aspects of your site. If you're running a business, for example, you can assign specific permissions to key employees that match their job duties.

Using Your Own Domain

When you sign up for your Squarespace account, you are given a unique Squarespace URL that looks like this: `http://youraccountname.square-space.com`. If you want complete control over the branding of your site or simply want a unique URL, you can *map,* or point, a custom domain to your Squarespace account.

You have three options for setting up a custom domain for your site:

✔ Transfer a Squarespace-managed domain from your Squarespace 5 site.

✔ Register for a free domain from Squarespace.

✔ Link an existing domain you already own.

You begin the process of setting up a custom domain by clicking one of three buttons at the top of the Domains screen, as shown in Figure 15-7. You find the Domains screen in Site Manager⇨Settings⇨Domains.

You will not see the Register Free Domain button if you did not sign up for annual or biannual billing.

Let's look at each of these options in more detail.

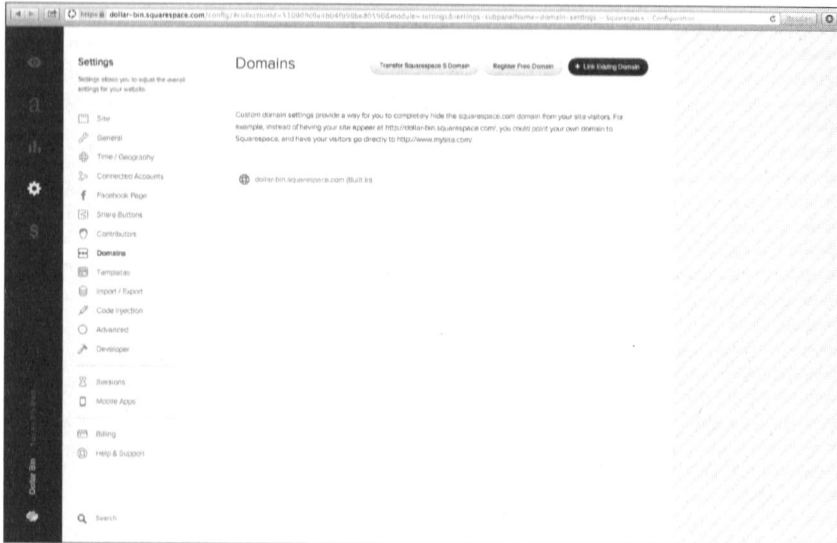

Figure 15-7:
Add your
custom
domain.

Transferring a Squarespace-managed domain

You can transfer a domain you registered through Squarespace, called a Squarespace-managed domain, from your Squarespace 5 website to your Squarespace 6 site. This works best when you're replacing your Squarespace 5 website with your new Squarespace 6 site because you won't need to use your domain with your old site on Squarespace 5.

To move your Squarespace-managed domain from your Squarespace 5 site to your Squarespace 6 site, do the following:

1. **Click the Transfer Squarespace 5 Domain button at the top of the Domains screen.**

   A transfer domain dialog box appears.

2. **Enter the Squarespace-managed domain you are transferring.**

3. **Enter the login and password information for your Squarespace 5 site.**

4. **Click the Transfer Domain button.**

   The domain is added to your list of domains as a domain managed by Squarespace.

With this option, you can transfer only domains registered through Squarespace from your Squarespace 5 website. If you need to transfer a domain you register with a domain provider, such as Godaddy.com, see the "Pointing an existing domain to Squarespace" section, later in this chapter.

Registering your free domain from Squarespace

If you sign up for annual or biannual billing (see Chapter 3), you can register for a free domain through Squarespace, called a Squarespace-managed domain. If you already registered a domain through Squarespace on your old Squarespace 5 site, see the preceding section.

To register for your free domain through Squarespace, do the following:

1. **Click the Register Free Domain button at the top of the Domains screen.**

   The Register Free Domain dialog box appears.

2. **Enter a domain you want to register.**

   Type the domain you want to register and choose the extension (.com, .org, .net, .biz, .info) in the drop-down menu in the domain field.

3. **If you see a notice telling you that the domain is not available, repeat Step 2 with another domain name**.

4. **Click the Add button.**

   A confirmation dialog box appears, indicating that the domain is available.

5. **Click the Register button.**

   The domain is registered and added to your list of domains.

It can take up to 72 hours for a newly registered domain to begin working. A blue clock icon appears next to the domain to indicate that it's not available to use yet. When the domain is available and working, the blue icon disappears.

With annual or biannual billing, you can register only one domain through Squarespace. Make sure you choose the domain you want. If you want to register another domain, you'll need to follow the steps in the next section.

Pointing an existing domain to Squarespace

To point an existing domain to Squarespace, you must first purchase a domain from a domain provider. Following are three top domain providers:

- ✔ Go Daddy: `www.godaddy.com`
- ✔ Nettica: `www.nettica.com`
- ✔ Network Solutions: `www.networksolutions.com`

Each of these domain registrars offers services in addition to registering your domain, such as getting your own e-mail address at your domain. See your domain provider for details after you've registered your domain.

To point your domain to Squarespace, you must modify your domain's DNS settings. Typically, you'll need to set the DNS CNAME to the following Squarespace URL:

```
www.squarespace6.com
```

and then set your domain's DNS A record to Squarespace's IP address:

```
65.39.205.57
```

Contact your domain provider for details on how to point your domain in its system. Squarespace provides some guidelines on pointing domains for the three providers just listed as well as a few other popular domain providers at `http://help.squarespace.com`.

After you've pointed your domain's DNS settings to Squarespace, you have essentially pointed the domain to Squarespace's front door. To finish the domain pointing, you need to claim your domain in your Squarespace account by adding your domain to the Domains setting:

1. **Click the Link Existing Domain button.**

   The Link Existing Domain dialog box appears.

2. **Type your domain.**

   You do not need to type the http:// part of the domain name.

3. **Click the Add button.**

   The domain is added to your list of domains.

Your domains will work with and without the www. prefix, so that your site can be found at http://www.*yourdomain*.com and http://*yourdomain*.com.

Your website automatically uses a custom domain as the default domain for your account. If you have more variations of your domain, you can point those to your Squarespace account and then choose which domain to use as your primary domain by clicking its Make Primary link, which you see when you hover your mouse cursor over the domain.

Your Squarespace URL is never removed from your account, and your site will still be accessible from your Squarespace URL. If you have external links pointing back to your site using your Squarespace URL, you may want to change these to use your custom domain.

If you create your own links to pages or resources on your site, use a site-relative URL instead of a full URL. A *site-relative URL* does not include the domain at the beginning of the URL. For example, the following is a full URL:

```
http://youraccount.squarespace.com/gallery/
```

If you point a custom domain and have a link to a page using the full URL, anyone clicking that link will be redirected to that page using your Squarespace URL and not your custom domain. Instead, create links to internal pages using the relative URL:

```
/gallery/
```

A web browser will know to go to the page under the domain being used to view the site.

Any Squarespace-generated links in your site create site-relative URLs, so switching full URLs to site-relative URLs will need to be addressed only if you manually create your own links within your content. Some common areas where people create their own links are in the content of pages, in the configuration settings of a Link page type, and in the content of Text blocks.

Switching Templates

In Chapter 7, you find out how to style your website using Style Editor. If you decide that the template you're using is not the best one for your site, you can switch to another template. Switching templates is easy, and you have access to all the templates Squarespace offers.

In Chapter 5, you determine your template needs while signing up for your Squarespace website. You might want to review that chapter first.

To choose a different template after you've created your site, simply

- ✔ Review the template thumbnails.
- ✔ Check out the template preview.
- ✔ Read the template preview's Read Me page for details about the template.

When you first go to the Templates area of Settings, your current template will be highlighted as such. The initial set of templates that are displayed will be from one of three categories:

- ✔ Blog
- ✔ Business
- ✔ Portfolio

The category that loads will depend on which template you're using, but you can switch categories by choosing another category in the Browse menu that appears at the upper right of the screen.

Just like when you were signing up for your site, don't be surprised if you notice a template appearing in different categories because some templates fall into more than one.

While you are previewing a template, you can switch to Style Editor (see Chapter 7) and experiment with customizing the template. Any changes you make in Style Editor will be applied only to the template you are previewing. If you cancel previewing the template, your site will revert to the template you are using.

After you preview the templates (see Chapter 5 for details) and find one you like, click the Enable Template button in the Previewing toolbar (see Figure 15-8) to apply the template to your site. Enabling the template will switch out the current template for the one you are previewing.

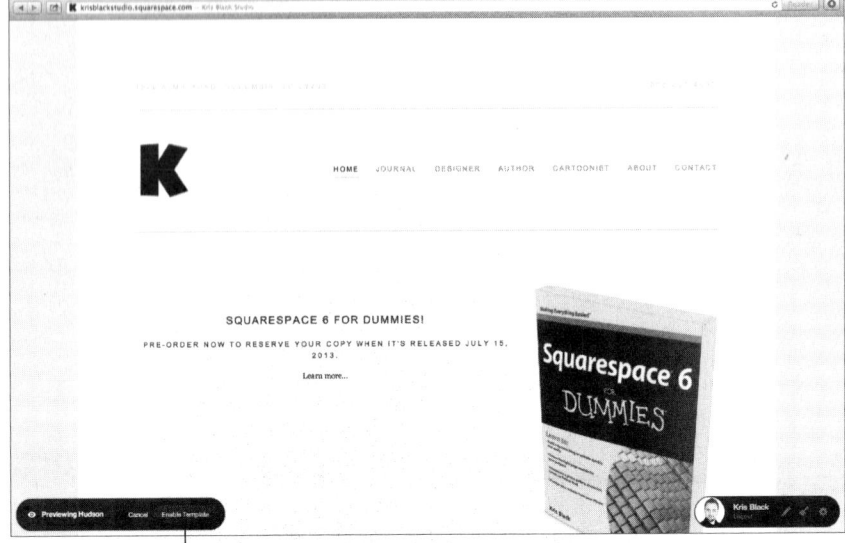

Figure 15-8:
Click the
Enable
Template
button to
set another
template
as your
new site
template.

Click here to apply the template

Importing and Exporting

If you're switching from another blogging or website builder, you may be able to import your site's content in the Import/Export screen, shown in Figure 15-9.

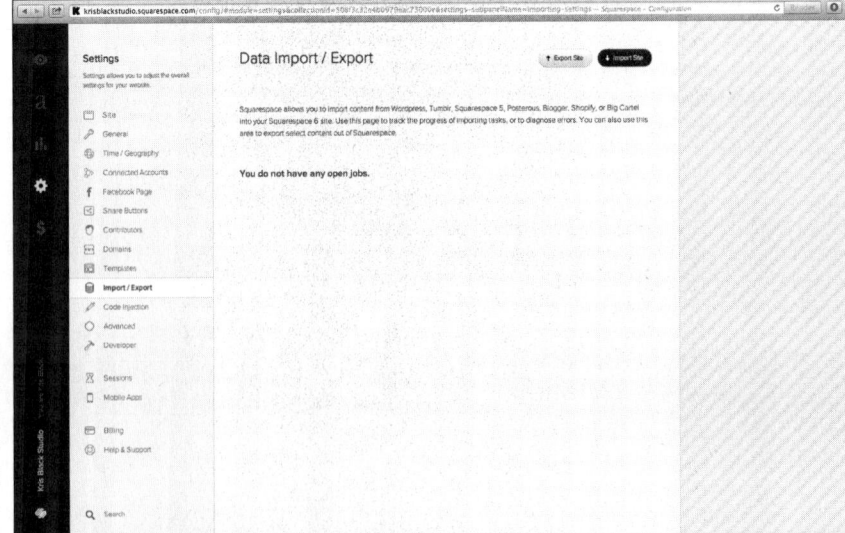

Figure 15-9:
Importing
and export-
ing content
to your site.

To get to the Import/Export screen, choose Site Manager⟳Settings⟳Import/Export. You can also export your Squarespace 6 website content from the Import/Export screen. Let's look at these options in more detail.

Importing content from another website

The website builders you can currently import from are

- ✔ **Big Cartel:** www.bigcartel.com
- ✔ **Blogger:** www.blogger.com
- ✔ **Shopify:** www.shopify.com
- ✔ **Squarespace 5:** Previous version of Squarespace.
- ✔ **Tumblr:** www.tumblr.com
- ✔ **WordPress:** www.wordpress.com or www.wordpress.org

With each service, the import process varies, but the general steps follow:

1. **Choose Site Manager⟳Settings⟳Import/Export.**

   The Import/Export screen appears (refer to Figure 15-9).

2. **Click the Import Site button.**

   The Import Site dialog box appears.

3. **Select the website builder from which you'll be importing content to your site.**

4. **Following the instructions from the website builder.**

   You'll be asked to enter login credentials, a URL, or import settings.

By importing your content, Squarespace can maintain old links and create redirects to your content's new location on your site.

Exporting your content from Squarespace

You can export your site's content for importing to another site. Currently, your site's blog content can be exported as-is for importing into a WordPress site either at www.wordpress.com or a self-hosted solution from www.wordpress.org.

To export your site's blogs and pages, do the following:

1. **Choose Site Manager➪Settings➪Import/Export.**

   The Import/Export screen appears (refer to Figure 15-9).

2. **Click the Export button at the top of the screen.**

   The Export Site dialog box appears.

3. **Click the WordPress logo.**

4. **If you have more than one blog page:**

   a. **Select the blog page on your site that you want to export.**

   The Select Primary Blog dialog box appears, as shown in Figure 15-10. *Note:* WordPress, unlike Squarespace, doesn't support multiple blogs.

   b. **Click the Export button.**

   The Select Primary Blog dialog box closes and the exporting process begins, preparing an export file for downloading.

5. **Click the Download button.**

   Your export file is downloaded and stored on your computer.

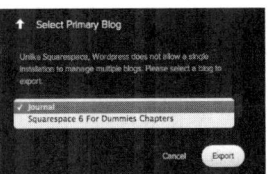

Figure 15-10:
Exporting
your blog.

See the following WordPress help sites for information about importing your Squarespace export file into WordPress:

✔ http://en.support.wordpress.com for Wordpress.com hosted sites

✔ http://codex.wordpress.org for WordPress.org hosted sites

Injecting Code into Your Site

You use the Code Injection area of Settings to add custom HTML and JavaScript to your site's layout, as shown in Figure 15-11.

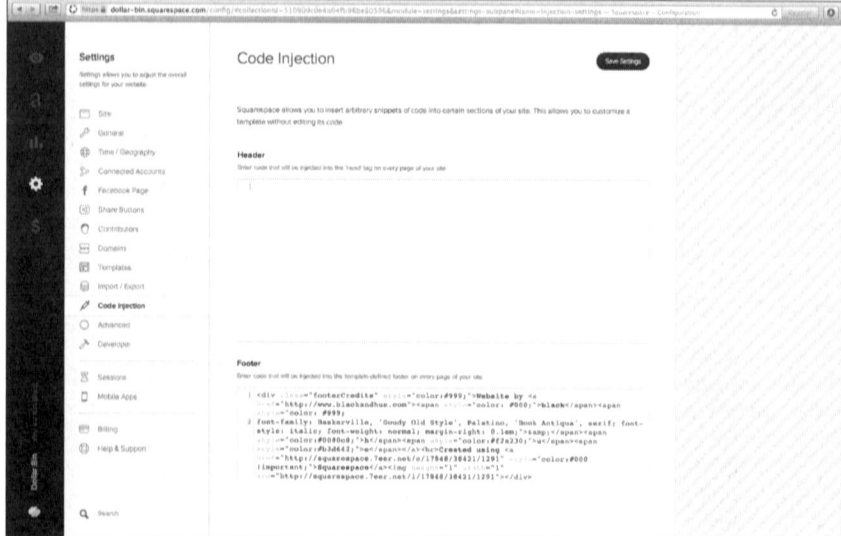

Figure 15-11:
Be careful
when enter-
ing code on
this screen.

You can insert code in three areas:

✓ **Header:** Code is added in the HTML <head> area, but the code doesn't appear on your site. Use this option for third-party code that requires you to place JavaScript in your site between the <head> and </head> tags in your site's HTML. Sometimes you need to add code in your site's <head> area to verify that you own the site.

✓ **Footer:** Code added here appears at the very bottom of your site.

Any code added to the Header and Footer will be applied to your entire site.

✓ **Lock Page:** Add your own message in properly formatted HTML to appear on the Lock page if you password-protect your entire site. See the "Configuring General Settings" section, earlier in this chapter, for details on password-protecting your entire site.

Following is a boilerplate of the HTML code you can use on your Lock page to add your message in a single paragraph:

```
<p>Add your message here. You can add multiple sentences
            separated by spaces.</p>
```

Redirecting a URL with Advanced Settings

If you want to create a URL that is easier to remember or to redirect people from outdated URLs to newer content on your site, choose Site Manager➪Settings➪Advanced. The Advanced screen appears, as shown in Figure 15-12.

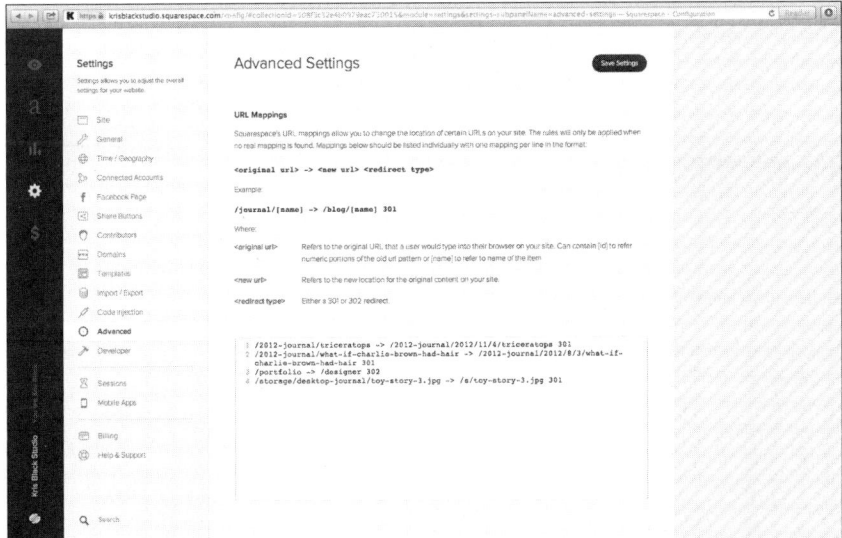

Figure 15-12: Creating a URL mapping.

To use the URL mapping feature, you will need to know the following:

- ✔ **Original URL:** The part of the URL after the domain (www.yourdomain. com) that someone types to be redirected to a page on your site
- ✔ **New URL:** The URL to which the shortcut will be redirected
- ✔ **Redirect Type:** Either a 301 or a 302 redirect

You can't redirect URL mappings to pages outside your website. The page to which you are redirecting must be hosted by Squarespace in your Squarespace website.

The URL mapping can be a new URL you made for creating an easier-to-remember URL or an old URL that used to be available on your site. Perhaps you're removing a page but want external links to that page to be redirected to another page with newer content; you can create a mapping that links

the old URL to the new page. For example, if you delete a page located at
`http://www.`_`yourdomain`_`.com/myoldpage/` and want to redirect external
links to your new page at `http://www.`_`yourdomain`_`.com/mynewpage/`,
you would add `/myoldpage/` to the Original URL field and `/mynewpage/` to
the New URL field.

When you create a URL mapping, you have two options to dictate the type of
redirect you are creating:

- **301 Redirect:** Indicates to search engines that the URL mapping to
  which you are redirecting is the new URL to be used for the content on
  that page. You would use this option to redirect from an outdated or a
  deleted URL to the active URL with current content.

- **302 Redirect:** Tells search engines that the content at the mapped URL
  is temporary. You can use this option to point the URL mapping to a
  page and then change it to point to another page later. Search engines
  will know to come back to the page to index the content again and on a
  routine basis.

To add mappings in the Advanced screen, you use a plain text format, with
one mapping per line:

```
/original-URL/ -> /new-URL/ redirect-type
```

Using our example, the following is what you would enter as the URL mapping in the text box in the Advanced screen if you wanted the redirect to be
permanent (301 Redirect):

```
/myoldpage/ -> /mynewpage/ 301
```

You can add as many URL mappings to your site as needed. Make sure any
mappings you create are site-relative URLs. For more information on site-
relative URLs, see the previous section, "Pointing an Existing Domain to
Squarespace."

Checking Out Developer Information

If you're an advanced web designer or developer, you may be interested in
building sites on Squarespace using the developer platform. This platform
gives you access to the underlying HTML, CSS, and JavaScript code so that
you can build custom templates.

The great thing about the developer platform is that you can still add content
to pages with blocks and customize your site configuration in Settings as you
normally would.

The Developer screen in Site Manager⇨Settings doesn't provide any features for you to adjust or configure. Instead, you see information about your Developer Platform account, as shown in Figure 15-13.

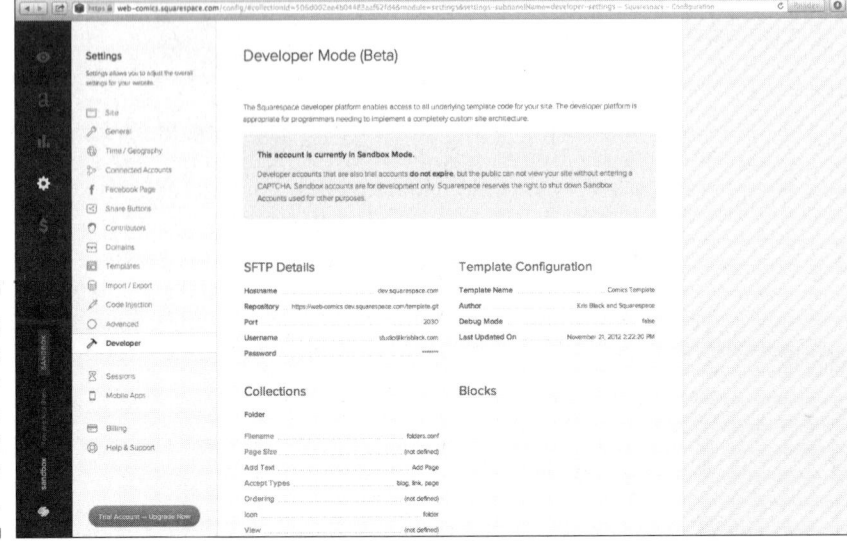

Figure 15-13:
The
Developer
screen in a
developer
platform
account.

The developer platform is beyond the scope of this book. However, you can visit the incredible Developer Center website at developers. squarespace.com and find loads of information and documentation to help you get started using the developer platform.

Reviewing Your Active Sessions

You can use the Remember Me option to log in to Squarespace without typing your password. This is a great way log in to your site quickly from your personal computer.

However, you might need to access your site from someone else's computer, such as at a friend's house or at your local library. If you forget to log out of your site, someone else could gain access to it. (Closing the browser window doesn't guarantee that your session on the site has ended.)

In Site Manager⇨Settings⇨Sessions, you can see all active login sessions currently in effect for your site. Your current session is marked as such, and any other sessions from previous logins may be in the list as well.

Each session tracks the following information:

- ✔ **Browser:** The web browser used to log in for that session
- ✔ **Operating system (OS):** The operating system used on the computer for that session
- ✔ **Date created:** The date the session began
- ✔ **Date expires:** The date the session will automatically be terminated by Squarespace
- ✔ **IP address:** The Internet location of the computer for that session

If you want to remove any of the sessions instantly, click Delete on the right side for the session row you want to terminate. Any user that tries to access your site from the computer at the IP address for that session (including you) will be asked to provide a user name and password to log in.

Upgrading Your Trial Account

If you're still on your trial account, you'll need to update to a paid plan if you want to keep the site you've built. Choose Site Manager➪Settings➪Billing to display the Billing screen, as shown in Figure 15-14.

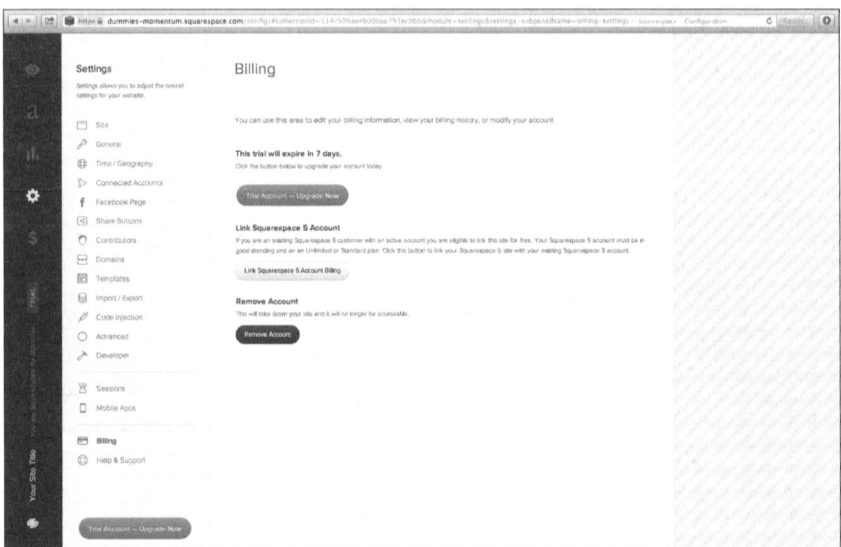

Figure 15-14:
Upgrade your trial and sign up for a paid plan.

Click the green Trial Account — Upgrade Now button. A screen appears so that you can select one of three pricing plans:

- Business
- Unlimited
- Standard

Review Chapter 3 for the details on these pricing plans, and select the plan that best fits your needs. A form appears for you to enter your credit card information.

Above the credit card form are three payment options:

- **Monthly:** Your credit card is charged every month.
- **Yearly:** Your credit card is charged once a year, and you get a 20 percent discount.
- **Two Year:** Your credit card is charged once every two years, and you get a 25 percent discount.

Click the payment option you want, enter your credit card information, and then click the Subscribe button.

Updating Your Billing Information

If you need to update your billing information, choose Site Manager⇨ Settings⇨Billing. A screen appears, with two tabs at the top: Payment Information and Invoices.

On the Payment Information screen, shown in Figure 15-15, you can

- Modify your credit card information
- Select a different pricing plan level
- Switch to a different billing period
- Change the billing contact person if you have a contributor with permissions set to Administrator or Billing
- Review when your next bill is due
- Cancel your account

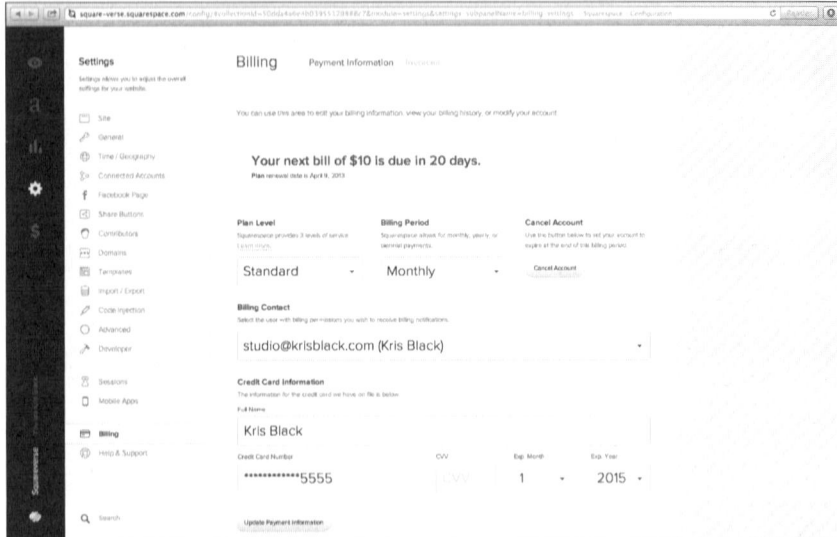

Figure 15-15:
Update your
billing
information.

The Invoices screen displays all the invoices for the charges your site has incurred since you signed up for the account. You can click an invoice to view the details.

When you update your billing information, your account will be charged (if you're upgrading) or refunded (if you're downgrading) a prorated amount based on when your account renews.

Getting Help from Support 24/7

In addition to the community forum (http://answers.squarespace.com) and the Help manual (http://help.squarespace.com), one of the best benefits of using Squarespace is the wonderful support staff. They are available to help 24 hours a day, seven days a week, all year round.

You have a couple of options for contacting them:

✔ **Contact form:** The form is located in the Help and Support screen, as shown in Figure 15-16.

✔ **E-mail:** Use your e-mail program to send a message to support@squarespace.com.

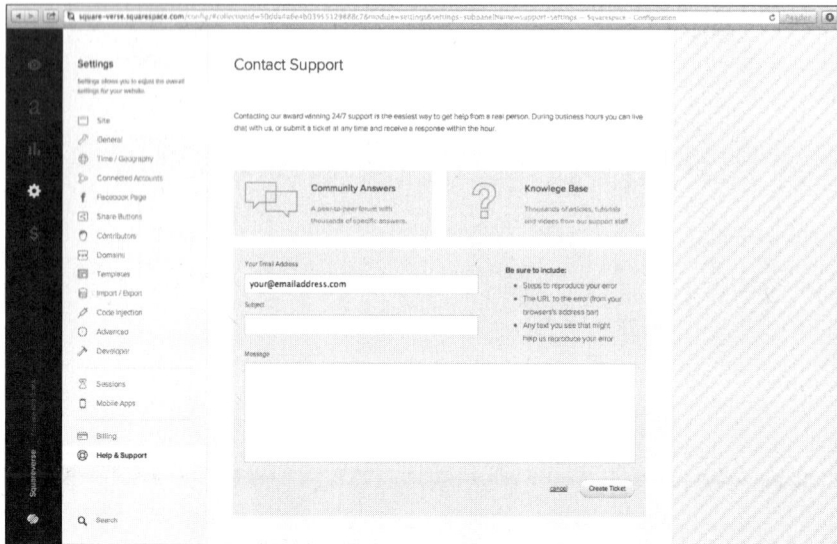

Figure 15-16:
Contacting
Square-
space
Support.

Be sure to provide Squarespace Support with detailed information about why you're contacting them. You may want to include a URL to the page on your site, the steps to reproduce a problem, and any other detailed information to help them understand the issue. Squarespace Support generally responds within a few minutes.

Chapter 16

Monitoring Site Activity

. . . .

In This Chapter

▶ Discovering who is visiting your site

▶ Seeing where visitors are coming from

▶ Hanging with the popular content

▶ Digging into detailed activity

▶ Taking action on comments

. . . .

Do you lay awake at night wondering how many people are visiting your site, how they are finding out about your site, and what they find to be the most important content on your site? Yeah, probably not, but I bet you have pondered these questions at some point.

Whether or not you worry about such things, wouldn't this information be nice to know? You're putting lots of effort into your site, and it sure would be nice to know if that effort is paying off.

In this chapter, you review all the site activity (statistics) that Squarespace collects for you to review and explore. This information is in the Activity area of Site Manager. In Activity, you can discover detailed information such as the following:

✔ The number of pages viewed on your site

✔ The number of visitors to those pages

✔ How many robots (search engines) are indexing your pages

✔ The websites that are referring visitors to your site

✔ Your most popular site pages

✔ The specific search queries used to find your site's content

Also in this chapter, you look at how you manage comments left by site visitors on your blog pages. Now let's get started finding out more about your site visitors.

Tracking Site Activity

When you look at your site's traffic, it's easy to assume that people's activities are being tracked and collected to generate your site's statistics. But that assumption isn't quite right. IP addresses, not the people themselves, are being tracked. For example, the IP address for the Starbucks Wi-Fi Internet access I'm using while typing this chapter is 64.134.182.104. All IP addresses are written this way, as four sets of numbers separated by periods.

Understanding IP addresses can help you understand more about your site's traffic. Although it would be easy to assume that an IP address is representative of a single person, that's not always the case. For example, suppose I were to visit your website right now. Your site would track me by the IP address here at Starbucks. If I then wanted to look at your site on my iPhone, my visit would be tracked as a different IP address, 166.205.49.163, because I would be using my cellular connection with AT&T. Therefore, your site would show me as two visitors accessing your site because it would track the two IP addresses.

Understanding how this works takes a little mystery out of the magic, but at the same time it means you shouldn't worry too much about the specific numbers in your site's activity. Instead, observe the trends in your site's traffic over a period time.

Now let's dive into the first area of activity, Traffic Overview.

Observing Your Traffic

One of the most important numbers in your site's activity is the number of visitors to your website. Then you want to know how many pages these visitors are viewing. Are Google, Bing, and Yahoo! finding your site?

To find the answers to these questions, begin by choosing Site Manager⇨Activity. The screen shown in Figure 16-1 appears. The first area in Activity, Traffic Overview, is selected by default.

At the top of Traffic Overview is a graph showing you an overview of the following in a given period of time:

✔ **Page views:** The number of pages viewed on your site

✔ **Unique visitors:** The number of individuals who come to your site

Above the graph are four options you can click to view the site traffic for a given period of time:

✔ **Hourly:** The last 24 hours of traffic

✔ **Daily:** The last 30 days of traffic

✔ **Weekly:** The last 13 weeks of traffic

✔ **Monthly:** The last 12 months of traffic

Selecting one of these time periods will change the graph at the top of the page in Traffic Overview to reflect that time period. Below the graph you'll see a detailed list comparing the number of page views to unique visitors as well as the number of robots (search engines) that came to your site. An example of weekly traffic on my site can be seen in Figure 16-2.

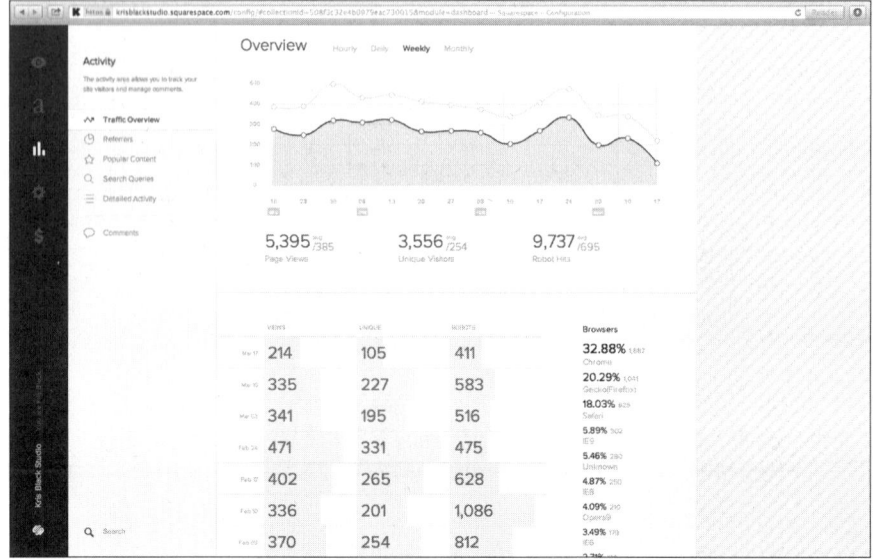

Figure 16-2:
Weekly traffic overview for www.krisblack.com.

On the right side of Traffic Overview, below the graph and to the left of the table, are three columns of detailed information about

- **Browsers:** The browsers visitors are using to visit your site

- **Operating Systems:** The operating systems visitors are using on their computers

- **Robot Hits:** Which search engines are coming to your site and the number of pages they're indexing

The entries are shown with the percentage of traffic each represents compared to the others in their lists.

Traffic Overview represents the traffic on your site, but what if you want to find out where the visitors came from before they got to your site? You need to find out who is referring visitors to your site.

Finding Where Visitors Come From

Who's linking to your site? Knowing where people are coming from to get to your site can help you learn a little bit more about your site visitors. And if you promote your site on other websites, you can see whether your efforts are paying off.

The Referrers area of Activity, shown in Figure 16-3, helps you find the top referring websites sending visitors to your pages. At the top of the page is a pie chart, with the total number of page views below the pie chart. Hover your cursor over the pie chart slices to highlight one of the top ten referrers in the list to the right of the pie chart.

Figure 16-3:
The refer-
rers to my
site over a
three-day
period.

The referrers display their percentage of page views by visitors they sent to your site in a given time period. Above the pie chart you can click one of five time period options: 1 Day, 2 Days, 3 Days, Week, and Month.

Below the pie chart and the top ten referrers is a detailed list of all the refer-rers in the selected time period. The first ten referrers will be the same as the referrers in the pie chart. Click one of the referrers in this list to reveal the URL of the web page that sent visitors to your site (as shown in Figure 16-3).

Discovering Your Popular Content

Wouldn't it be nice to know what content on your site is the most popular? That knowledge could help you make decisions about the type of content you put on your site. For example, if you found out that your most popular con-tent was about guinea pigs and not hamsters, you would know that writing more blog posts about guinea pigs might increase your traffic.

The Popular Content area of Activity is where you can discover your site's most popular content. At the top of the Popular Content page is a pie chart, with the total number of page views that the pie represents below the chart. As you hover your cursor over a slice in the pie, one of the top ten popular pages on your site will be highlighted to the right of the pie.

You can change the time period for the data represented by selecting one of five options at the top of the page: 1 Day, 2 Days, 3 Days, Week, and Month.

Below the pie chart and the top ten popular pages is a detailed list of all the popular pages and the number of visits those pages received on your site in the specified time period. The first ten pages will be the same as the pages in the pie chart and top ten list to the right of the pie chart.

Finding How Visitors Search for You

In the Traffic Overview area of Activity, you can find out which search engines, called robots, are coming to your site and indexing your pages. Search engines index your pages for use in answering search queries. Squarespace can share with you the search queries that people use to find your site.

In the Search Queries area of Activity, you can discover the most popular search terms that get visitors to your site. Just like the Referrers and Popular Content areas of Activity, the Search Queries area has a pie chart divided into slices. Hover your cursor over a slice to highlight one of the top ten search terms used to find your site in a search engine. The total number of page views that the pie represents is below the pie chart.

You can change the time period for the data represented by selecting one of five options at the top of the page. Below the pie chart is a detailed list of all the search terms and the number of page views those search queries sent to your site in the time period you set. To the right of a search term in the list is the referring search engine.

Getting the Details of Site Visitors

The Detailed Activity area of Activity displays a list of all the activity on your site. This information can be helpful to determine when pages were accessed. The following information is collected:

- **Date and time:** The date and time of the activity
- **Visitor:** The IP address where the visitor is located

✔ **Page title:** The page on your site where the activity took place

✔ **Country:** The originating country where the IP address is tracked to

✔ **Referrer:** The web page that referred the visitor to your site

✔ **Browser and operating system:** Detailed browser and operating system information

Initially, all you see is the date and time, the visitor's IP address, and the page they were visiting. To see additional information, click one of the visits in the list. If you want to see even more activity, click the Load More button at the bottom of the page.

You can also search for specific activity on your site. At the top right of the Detailed Activity area, click the magnifying glass icon to open a search dialog box. You can filter the search results with the following criteria:

✔ **Visitor:** The IP address of the visitor you are searching

✔ **Activity:** The page title visited on your site

✔ **Referrer:** The web page that sent a visitor to your site

✔ **Date:** Adjust the before and after dates to specific time frames

You don't have to be specific with the terms you use to search your detailed activity. For example, if you want to see all activity referred by a specific website, just enter the site's domain name. For example, Figure 16-4 shows my site's activity filtering the referrer to only webcomics.com.

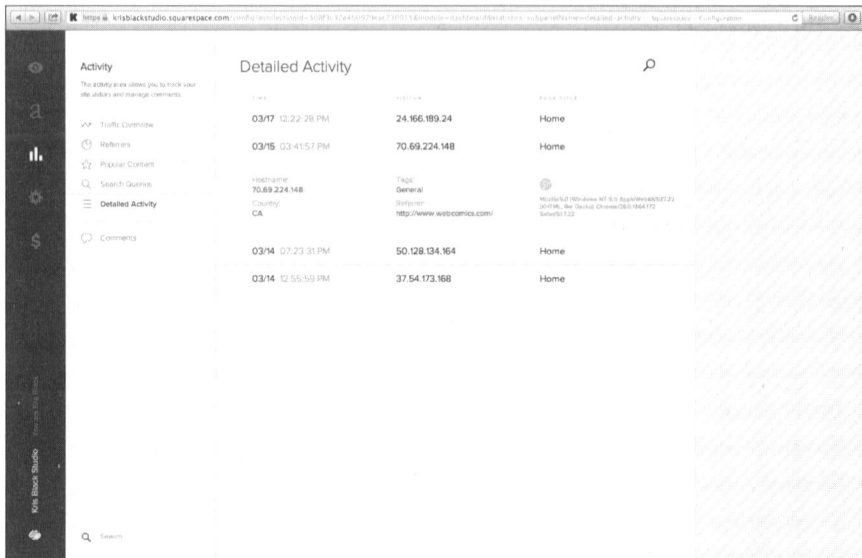

Figure 16-4:
Filtering
detailed
activity.

Managing Comments on Your Site

If you have a blog on your site, you can allow site visitors to comment on your blog posts. Allowing people to comment on your site is a great way to connect with others. It also allows them to share their ideas and thoughts with you.

You manage comments by choosing Site Manager⇨Activity⇨Comments or by using the Squarespace mobile app (see Chapter 18).

The Comments screen in Activity, shown in Figure 16-5, has three management areas:

- ✔ **Unmoderated:** Comments needing approval to be shown on your site
- ✔ **Approved:** Comments that are displayed on your site
- ✔ **Flagged:** Comments flagged for inappropriateness by other commenters

Commenting is enabled by default. If you want to disable it sitewide, go to Site Manager⇨Settings⇨General. See Chapter 15 for details. You can also disable commenting on a per-post basis, as described in Chapter 10.

In this section, you look at the actions you can take on your comments.

Replying to comments

You can reply directly to individual comments in any of the areas on the Comments screen:

1. **Hover your mouse cursor over the comment to which you want to reply. When the left-pointing arrow appears, click it.**

   The comment expands to reveal a comment box.

2. **In the comment box, type your reply.**

   If you change your mind about commenting after clicking the icon, click the icon again to close the comment box.

3. **Click the Post Reply button.**

   A Post Comment dialog box appears, asking you to confirm your decision.

4. **Click the Post Comment button to save your reply.**

   Your reply appears below the original comment.

Deleting comments

You can delete comments from your site in two ways. You can delete individual comments one by one, or you can select multiple comments and delete them all at once. You can also delete comments and report them as spam to Squarespace to help block these types of comments in the future.

To remove a single comment from your site:

1. **Hover your mouse cursor over the comment you want to delete. When the x icon appears, click it.**

   A Delete Comment dialog box appears.

2. **Click the Delete button or the Delete & Report Spam button.**

   The comment is removed from your site. If you clicked Delete & Report Spam, the comment is also reported as spam to Squarespace.

To remove multiple comments from your site at once:

1. **Select the comments you want to delete.**

   Select multiple comments by simply clicking each one. (You don't need to hold down any special keys.) You can select any number of comments, whether they are adjacent or not.

   The comments become highlighted and a toolbar appears at the bottom of the screen with three buttons:

   - **Select All:** Selects all comments on the screen.
   - **Deselect:** Deselects all comments you selected, hiding the toolbar in the process.
   - **Delete:** Removes the comments from your site.

2. **Click the Delete button in the toolbar.**

   A Delete Comment dialog box appears.

3. **Click the Delete button or the Delete & Report Spam button.**

   The comments are removed from your site. If you clicked Delete & Report Spam, the comments are also reported as spam to Squarespace.

Approving comments

Comments needing your approval before they are posted to your site are added to the Unmoderated area. Comments are displayed in this area because you selected the Approval Required setting in the General area of Settings.

To approve a single comment, hover your mouse cursor over the comment and click the check mark icon that appears. The comment is instantly approved and posted to your site.

To approve multiple comments from your site at once, do the following:

1. **Select the comments.**

   The comments become highlighted and a toolbar appears at the bottom of the screen with three buttons:

   - **Select All:** Selects all comments on the screen.
   - **Deselect:** Deselects all comments you selected, hiding the toolbar in the process.
   - **Delete:** Removes comments from your site.
   - **Approve:** Approves comments and displays them on your site.

2. **Click the Approve button in the toolbar.**

   The selected comments are instantly approved, moved to the Approved area, and posted to your site.

The number of comments that need moderating is displayed next to the following in Site Manager as shown in Figure 16-5:

✔ Activity icon

✔ Comments setting link

✔ Unmoderated area link

Although flagged comments are indicated with a number next to the Flagged link (refer to Figure 16-5), that number is not indicated in the number next to the Comments link in the Activity navigation column or the Activity icon.

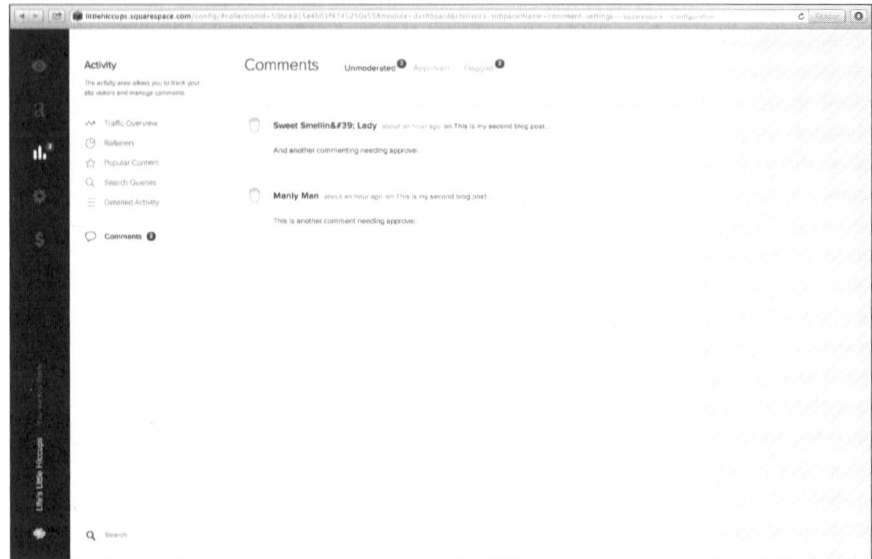

Figure 16-5:
Unmoder-
ated
comments
needing
approval.

Handling flagged comments

Site visitors can flag comments that they find offensive or inappropriate. It's your decision as the site owner to decide whether the comment should be removed from the site.

If you don't approve of a comment someone flags, you can

- ✔ **Delete the comment:** Follow the steps in the previous "Deleting comments" section to remove a flagged comment.

- ✔ **Reply to the comment:** Follow the steps in the previous "Replying to comments" section to post a reply, letting the commenter know that the comment was flagged as offensive or inappropriate.

- ✔ **Clear comments:** Click the Clear Flags button at the top of the Flagged comments screen to remove flags from all comments on the screen.

You may want to provide commenting guidelines that explain what is and is not allowed on your site and the consequences of breaking these guidelines.

Chapter 17

Setting Up Shop with Commerce

. . . .

In This Chapter

▶ Configuring store settings

▶ Managing orders received from customers

▶ Stocking your inventory

▶ Creating shipping options

▶ Creating coupons to offer discounts

▶ Determining taxes to apply to orders

▶ Modifying e-mail notifications

. . . .

*W*ho doesn't want to make a little bit of money with their website? What if you could easily create an online store where you could sell your artwork, crafts, or digital products? Wouldn't that be awesome? And what if you could do all this on your Squarespace website? In fact, you can do this thanks to Commerce, Squarespace's simple online store solution.

You no longer have to set up a shop with another service such as Big Cartel, Shopify, or eBay. Sell your stuff directly on your site with a shopping cart or with express checkout. Accept credit cards, track inventory, manage shipping, generate coupon codes, and even customize e-mail notifications sent from your store. Find out how in this chapter.

Preparing to Set Up Shop

Before you begin creating your site's store, I want to share a few tips that will help you be better prepared to set up shop:

✔ **Pricing plan:** Commerce is available only with the Business pricing plan. You can read more about the pricing plans in Chapter 3. If you need to upgrade, see the section in Chapter 15 about upgrading your site in the Billing area of Site Manager➪Settings.

✔ **Photos:** Go ahead and have some product images available to upload. Although you don't need to have photos to sell items on your site, it makes your store and items look much more appealing.

✔ **Shipping Prices:** To use the shipping settings, you need to know your shipping costs. Squarespace doesn't automatically calculate shipping for different carriers based on weight and package size, but instead allows you to determine your own shipping and handling formulas.

My suggestion is to research the different shipping options with the major carriers, including the following:

- **United States Postal Service (USPS):** www.usps.com

- **UPS:** www.ups.com

- **FedEx:** www.fedex.com

The USPS has a flat rate for each sized Priority Mail box and envelope. You can find out more at http://postcalc.usps.com.

Adding Products to Your Site

The first step when creating a shop on your site is to add your products to a products page. If your site doesn't have a products page, review the process of adding this page in Chapter 9. Following is an abbreviated refresher of the steps involved:

1. **Log in to your site.**

2. **Go to Site Manager➪Content Manager.**

3. **Click the Add Page button.**

   Add your page in the navigation area of your site if you want the store link displayed in your site's navigation. If you want to keep your store hidden for now, add the page to the Not Linked navigation area.

You can add more than one products page. For example, you might want a separate products page for each category of product you sell.

After you have a products page on your site, you can begin adding your items.

Adding an item to a products page

The process of adding a product is similar to adding a blog post or a gallery item, as described in Chapter 10. You can add products to two locations in your site:

- ✔ **Products page:** Add products directly to the products page from Site Manager⟳Content Manager.

- ✔ **Inventory area:** Add products to any products page in your site from Site Manager⟳Commerce.

The Inventory area is just one settings area in Commerce. We'll go through all the areas in Commerce later in this chapter. For now, let's look at the two types of products you can add to your store:

- ✔ **Digital:** Digital products are files you upload to your site for downloading after they have been purchased. When a customer purchases a digital product on your site, Squarespace will send the customer a link to download the file. The download link works for only 24 hours after the purchase is processed. Digital products can be any type of file you have on your computer, such as music, videos, photos, design templates, or model schematics. Just make sure you are the copyright owner of what you are selling. You don't want anyone taking legal action against you.

- ✔ **Physical:** Physical products must be shipped by a carrier for your customer to receive them. Some examples of physical products you can sell are t-shirts, crafts, artwork, prints, antiques, and collectibles.

To add a product to a products page, follow these steps:

1. **Click the Add Product button.**

   A small dialog box appears with icons and a brief explanation of the two types of products you can sell.

2. **Choose whether you are adding a physical product or a digital download.**

   The Edit Product dialog box appears, as shown in Figure 17-1.

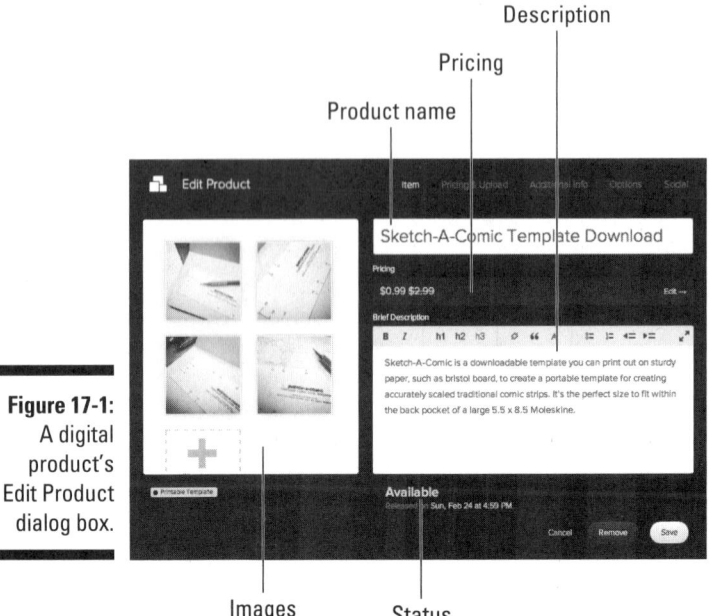

Description

Pricing

Product name

Figure 17-1:
A digital
product's
Edit Product
dialog box.

Images   Status

3. **Add your product content:**

   • **Product name:** Product names are used as text links on other parts of your site, the page title for the product's unique page, and the direct URL to the item's unique page.

   • **Pricing and variants (physical products only):** Displays the price of your physical product and the number of variants of the product. Clicking this will take you to the Pricing and Variants configuration screen, described later in the chapter.

   • **Pricing and Upload (digital products only):** Displays the price of your digital product. Clicking this will take you to the Pricing and Upload configuration screen, described later in the chapter.

   • **Description:** Add a description about the product you're selling.

   • **Images:** Upload multiple images of your product. See Chapter 4 for details on uploading images to your site.

   • **Categories:** Use categories to organize products into related groupings. Then you can target specific groups of products when you display them in a content block, such as a summary block. You can also apply coupon codes to a particular group of products, as described later in this chapter in the "Coupons" section.

   • **Status:** Set the product as Available or Not Listed. Details follow.

4. **Save your product.**

   If you want to finalize your product later, click the Save button to save it as a Not Listed item. To instantly publish the product on your site to sell, click the Save & Publish button. See the next section for more information about setting a product's status.

When you're working with products, you can set the status to one of two options:

- ✔ **Available:** Sets your product as available for purchase on your site.

- ✔ **Not Listed:** Saves the product in your inventory but does not list the product for sale on your site. This status is similar to the Draft status for blog posts (see Chapter 10).

The ability to set the status of a product to Not Listed can be helpful. For example, you might want to add all the title and descriptions of your products one day, photograph the products another day, and upload the photos all at once on yet another day.

Configuring a product item

In addition to the Item screen, the Edit Product dialog box offers four additional screens of configuration settings.

- ✔ **Pricing and Variants:** Physical products only. Set the price and create variants of your product.

- ✔ **Pricing and Upload:** Digital products only. Set the price for your product and upload the digital file that is being sold.

- ✔ **Additional Info:** Use blocks to add more customized content about your product. The chapters in Part IV describe the different blocks you can use to customize content on your site.

- ✔ **Options:** Add a thumbnail image and create a custom URL.

- ✔ **Social:** Enable notifying your social profile accounts of new items on your site. The social accounts that appear here are configured in Site Settings (see Chapter 15).

Pricing and Variants screen for physical products

Physical products have attributes that you assign for selling on your site. Basic attributes include the price of the product and whether it is in stock.

Following is a list of the default attributes provided when you create a physical product:

- ✔ **SKU:** An abbreviation for *stock-keeping unit*. This unique identifier is used to refer to an item being sold. Squarespace will automatically assign a SKU (for example, SQ1234567), or you can customize the SKU with your own identifier.

- ✔ **Price:** Enter the price a customer will pay for the product.

- ✔ **On Sale:** Select this attribute if the item is on sale.

- ✔ **Sale Price:** If you marked your item as on sale, enter the sale price.

- ✔ **In Stock:** Enter the total number of units you have to sell for the product.

- ✔ **Unlimited:** Select this if you have an unlimited supply of your product.

- ✔ **Weight:** Enter the weight of the unit being sold.

Physical products can come in multiple variations, called *variants,* depending on what you are selling. For instance, if you're selling a t-shirt design, you may want to offer the shirt in different sizes (small, medium, large, and extra large).

To differentiate one variant from another, you generally add an attribute of the product called an *option.* You can add custom options to your products such as color or size.

To add an option, follow these steps after opening the Edit Product dialog window:

1. **Go to the Pricing and Variants settings.**

2. **Click the plus sign at the end of the attribute header row, as shown in Figure 17-2.**

   The Edit Option dialog box appears.

3. **Type the name of the option.**

4. **Click Save**

   Your option is added in a new column to your list of variants.

To add a new variant, click the plus sign at the bottom-left of the variant rows (labeled in Figure 17-2). The new variant will be a duplicate of the previous variant. You can change the attributes as needed.

Click here to add a variant   Click here to add an option

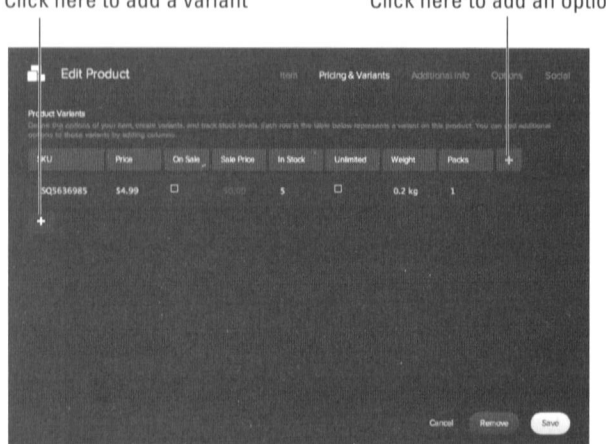

Figure 17-2:
Adding a
variant and
a custom
option.

Pricing and Upload screen for digital products

Digital products are relatively simple and require only a few attributes, as
shown in Figure 17-3:

- ✔ **Price:** Enter the price a customer will pay for the product.

- ✔ **On Sale:** Select this attribute if the item is on sale.

- ✔ **Sale Price:** If you've marked your item as on sale, provide the sale price.

- ✔ **Digital File:** Upload the digital file that is being sold for this product.

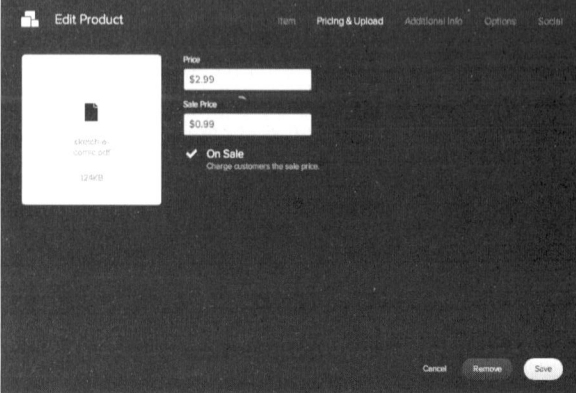

Figure 17-3:
Adding the
digital file
and price
for a digital
product.

The file size limit for digital files is 200MB.

Additional Info screen

If a simple paragraph or two of text in the description area of the Edit Product dialog box isn't sufficient for describing your product, use the Additional Info screen to build content with blocks. You have access to all the blocks available, as described in Chapter 10 and thoroughly explored in the chapters in Part IV.

Let's review how to add a block for the Additional Info screen:

1. **Click the plus sign in the lower-right corner, as shown in Figure 17-4.**

   The Add a Block dialog box appears.

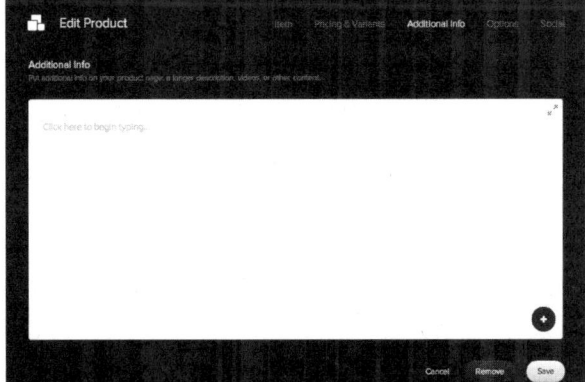

Figure 17-4:
The
Additional
Info screen.

2. **Click the block you want to add.**

   You can use the three links at the top of the Add a Block dialog box to choose blocks from three categories: Content, Structure, and Social.

   If you have multiple blocks already added, you can also click-and-drag a block to place it directly where you want it go in the Additional Info layout.

Looking for ideas for additional information you might want to include? Consider adding related or similar products (products block), including a video demo of the product (video block), or providing a slideshow of images of customers using the product (gallery block).

Options screen

Similar to blog posts, the Options screen (Figure 17-5) enables you to set your product's thumbnail image and custom URL. These settings are automatically created based on what you added in the image area and for product name of the Item settings in the Edit Products dialog box:

- ✔ **Thumbnail Image:** Add a thumbnail representing your product. The thumbnail is used to display the product and add the product to other areas of your site using content blocks, such as a summary block (see Chapter 13).

  For the thumbnail image, Squarespace automatically uses the first image from the Image area of the Item screen of the Edit Products dialog box.

- ✔ **Post URL:** The direct URL to the blog post's specific page on your site. Squarespace automatically generates this URL, but you can change it.

Figure 17-5:
The Options
screen.

Social

The Social configuration screen, shown in Figure 17-6, offers the same settings as the Social screen in blog and gallery page items.

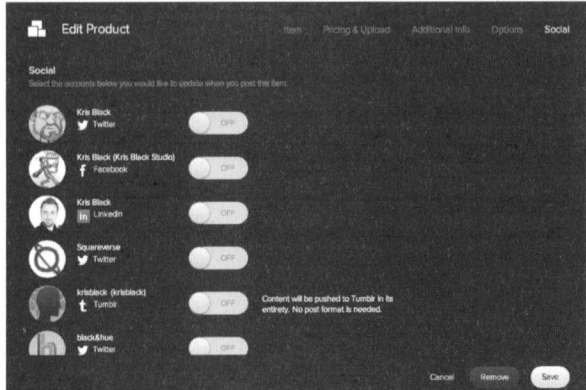

Figure 17-6:
The Social
screen.

You can read more about the Social screen in Chapter 10. To recap, the social area of an Edit Products dialog box displays the social accounts you add in Site Manager⟳Settings (see Chapter 15).

Removing a product

Removing a product from your store is easy. Just do the following:

1. **On the products page or from Site Manager⟳Commerce⟳Inventory, double-click the product to open it.**

2. **Click the Remove button.**

   A confirmation box appears, asking you to confirm the removal of the product.

3. **Click the Confirm button.**

   The product is deleted from your inventory and your site.

Rearranging products

You can rearrange the order of your products in Content Manager. Go to your products page and drag a product to move it. The other products will shift out of the way as you move the product.

Now that you know how to add products to your site, let's look at the settings for your store and how you get things up and running so you can begin accepting money for your wares.

Configuring Your Store

When you first go to Site Manager⟳Commerce, you'll see a Getting Started with Commerce screen, as shown in Figure 17-7. This screen walks you through the major steps for setting up your goods. You can dismiss this guide by clicking the Dismiss This Guide button in the upper right.

The seven areas of Commerce are

- **Orders:** Manage orders received on your site.
- **Inventory:** Track your products and how many you have in stock.

✔ **Shipping:** Create predefined, flat-rate shipping costs for physical products.

✔ **Coupons:** Create coupon codes to offer discounts.

✔ **Taxes:** Add the state tax and any other local taxes to be applied to orders.

✔ **Email Notifications:** Customize the e-mail notifications sent from your store.

✔ **Store Settings:** Configure settings that apply to all aspects of your store and orders.

Let's start at the end of the preceding list with Store Settings so you can configure some basic information and settings for your store.

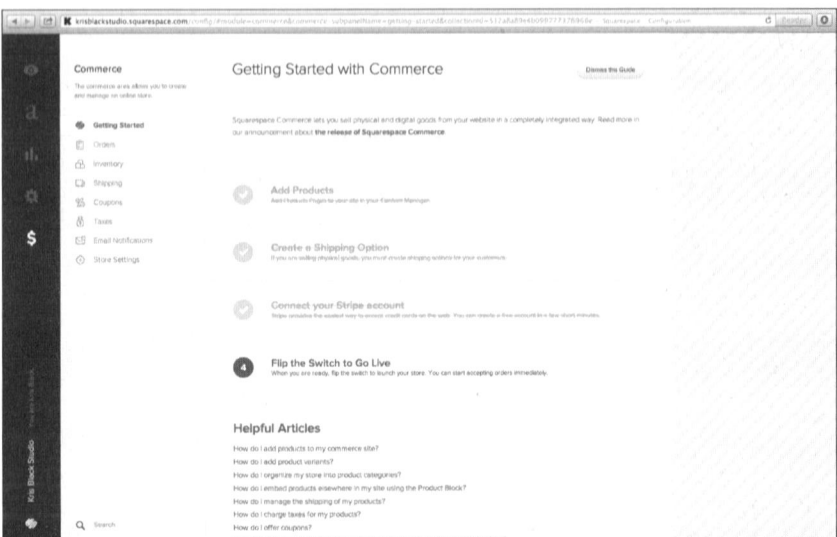

Figure 17-7:
Getting
started with
Commerce.

Store settings

The first thing you'll notice when you go to Site Manager➪Commerce➪Store Settings is the big yellow box at the top of the screen indicating that your store is not live, as shown in Figure 17-8. Before you can make your store live, you must connect your store to Stripe, the payment processing service used to accept payments on your site.

Start by clicking here

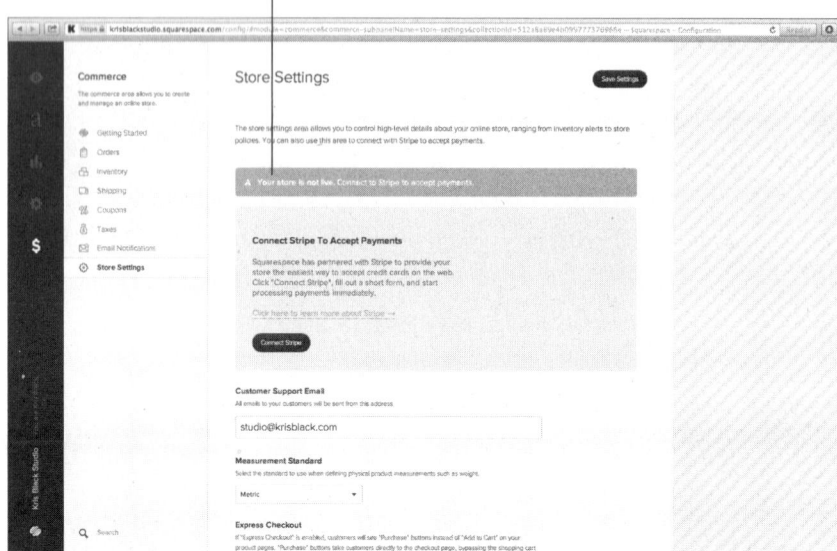

Figure 17-8:
The Store
Settings
screen.

You can read more about Stripe at www.stripe.com. Here's how you connect your site to Stripe:

1. **Click the Connect Stripe button.**

   A pop-up window appears, displaying the Stripe sign-up form.

2. **If you don't have a Stripe account, complete the sign-up form.**

3. **If you do have a Stripe account, log in to your account by clicking the login link at the top of the pop-up window.**

   After you are logged in to Stripe, the pop-up window will close and your Store Settings window will refresh. The Connect to Stripe box will now say Connected to Stripe, and you'll see a Store Live settings box, as shown in Figure 17-9.

   If you already have a Stripe account and are logged in, clicking the Connect Stripe button will instantly connect your site to Stripe without having to log in again.

   If you have more than one Squarespace site that will be using Commerce, you'll need a separate Stripe account for each site.

4. **If your store is ready to go live, you can click the switch in the Store Live box to start accepting orders and processing real payments.**

   Otherwise, leaving this switch off will allow you to process fake payments to credit cards to test your store.

You're connected   Store Live settings box

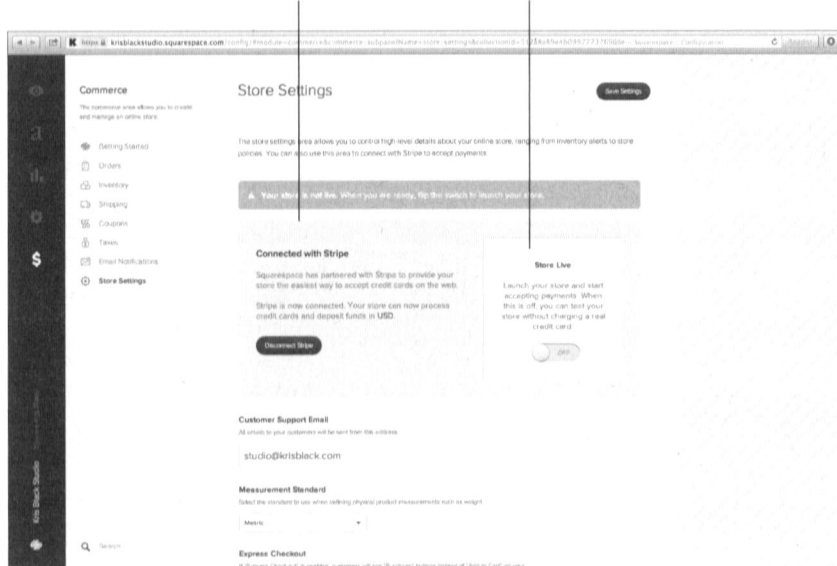

Figure 17-9:
Stripe con-
nected to
Commerce
in Store
Settings.

After you connect your site to Stripe and click the Store Live button to on, you will be ready to start accepting payments (assuming that you've added products and configured your store). Let's look at the remaining settings in Store Settings:

- ✓ **Customer Support Email:** Enter the e-mail address that you want to appear on all e-mails sent to your customers.

- ✓ **Measurement Standard:** Select between Imperial (pounds) or Metric (kilograms) standards for calculating measurements such as the weight of products and weight-based shipping charges.

- ✓ **Express Checkout:** Select this option if you want customers to skip the shopping cart and go directly to a checkout page. The Add to Cart button will change to a Purchase button. If your store sells a single item, you should select this option.

- ✓ **Shopping Cart Style:** Select this option if your site has a dark color scheme; this will apply a light color scheme for the shopping cart.

- ✓ **Newsletter:** Select this option to connect to your MailChimp account. You can select a mailing list you've set up to appear as an option during checkout, so that customers have an opportunity to join your mailing list.

- ✓ **Automatic Stock Level Alert Email:** Move the slider to indicate what stock level will trigger a restocking e-mail notification. You can select to never be notified or a number from 1–20.

✔ **Checkout Page's Store Policies:** Add your store policies to the fields available. You can add a return policy, terms of service, and a privacy policy. Links to store policies appear in the footer of the checkout page. If you don't add any policies, no links will be displayed.

Although a web search may yield boilerplate or template store policies that you can customize, I recommend consulting a lawyer with experience helping people establish their online businesses.

After adjusting any of these settings, make sure to click the Save Settings button at the top of the page to save your changes. The next area of Commerce we'll review is the Orders area.

Orders

When a customer places an order on your site, it will appear in the Orders area of Commerce. Orders are grouped into one of three status categories, accessible by the links at the top of the screen, as shown in Figure 17-10:

✔ **Pending:** Only orders for physical products appear here.

✔ **Completed:** All digital product orders will instantly appear as completed. Physical product orders will appear as completed after you've marked them as complete.

✔ **Cancelled:** Physical product orders will appear as cancelled if you mark them as such.

You'll need to process orders in all three status areas, depending on the requirements of the customer's order. Each status area presents a list of orders that display the following information:

✔ Invoice total

✔ Number of items ordered

✔ Order number

✔ Customer name and e-mail address

✔ Date and time the order was placed

✔ Order status

Status categories

Invoice total and number of items

Order number

Order status

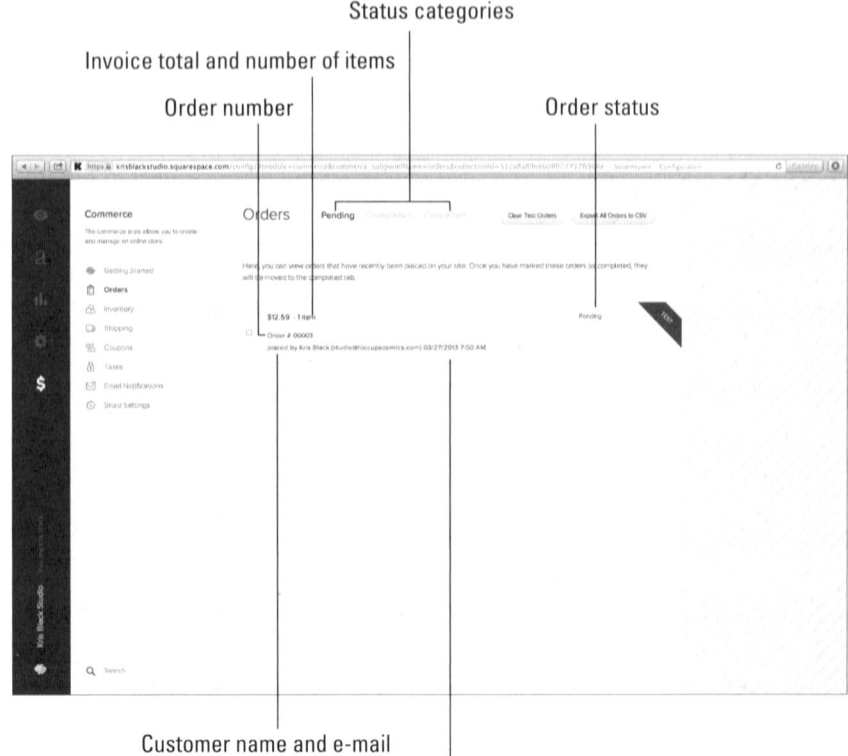

Figure 17-10:
Orders
screen in
Commerce.

Customer name and e-mail

Date and time of order

Here's how you manage orders individually or in bulk in all status areas:

✔ **Click the check box next to an order in the list to select it.**

When you click the check box for one or more orders, a toolbar appears at the bottom of the screen with the following options:

- **Mark Completed:** Pending orders only. Set the selected orders as complete to move them to the Completed Orders status category. A confirmation box appears where you can choose to send shipping confirmation e-mails after confirming the orders as complete.

- **Mark Pending:** Completed orders only: Set the selected orders as pending to move them to the Pending Orders status category.

- **Print:** Print invoices for the orders.

- **Clear Selection:** Deselects any orders selected in the list.

- **Select All:** Selects all the orders in the Pending status list.

✔ **Click an order (but don't click the check box).**

The order's Order Summary dialog box appears, as shown in Figure 17-11. Four processing areas are indicated by links at the top of the window:

- **Order:** View the entire order's information, including billing and shipping information, items and quantities ordered, subtotal, tax, shipping costs, and grand total.

- **History:** View a list of all the actions taken on an order. These actions might include when the order was shipped, marked completed, or cancelled.

- **Notes:** Add any private notes you need to record with the order. The customer won't see these notes.

- **Email Notifications:** Resend the order confirmation or shipping notice, as well as send a private message to the customer.

When a customer places an order on your site, he or she will receive an order confirmation e-mail. When you mark an order as complete, a shipping notice is automatically sent to the customer.

Processing areas

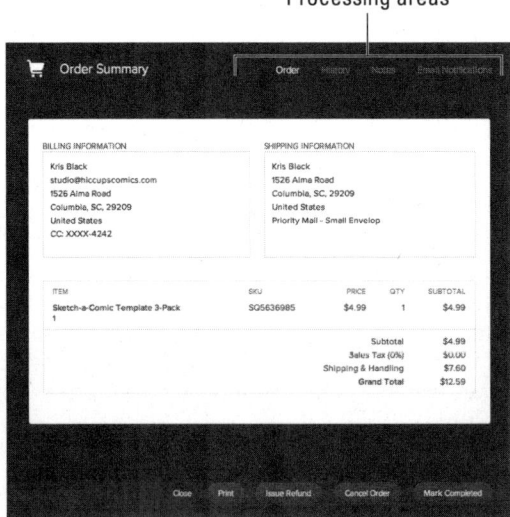

Figure 17-11: An Order Summary window.

At the bottom of the Order Summary window are the following options:

- **Print:** Print an invoice for the order.
- **Issue Refund:** Send the customer a partial refund.
- **Cancel Order:** Issue a full refund to the customer and move the order to the Cancelled status area.
- **Mark Completed:** Pending orders only. Set the selected orders as complete to move them to the Completed Orders Status category.
- **Mark Pending:** Completed orders only. Set the selected orders as pending to move them to the Pending Orders status category.

When a customer orders a physical product, it is added to the Pending area of Commerce⊅Orders. Digital orders are automatically added to the Completed area because your website will automatically send the customer a link to the digital file.

 At the top of the screen is a button to export all your orders from all three status categories. Export your orders to a spreadsheet, and you can open the spreadsheet in Microsoft Excel, Apple Numbers, or Google Docs and integrate the spreadsheet in a business application for accounting or other financial reasons.

Inventory

Earlier in the chapter, I mentioned that you could add multiple products pages to your site to organize products in your store. Whether you take this approach or just use a single products page, using the Inventory area of Commerce will allow you to centrally manage all products across your entire site.

The Inventory area displays your products in a list view with the following information about each product, as shown in Figure 17-12:

- **Product name:** The name of the product as it appears on your site.
- **Variants:** Physical products only. The variants of the product, if any.
- **Price:** The price of the product, and for physical products, the price of each variant. If your product is on sale, the sale price is displayed next to the original price.
- **Remaining stock:** The remaining stock of a product is calculated based on the number of units you indicate in a product's Edit Product dialog box in the Pricing and Variants options. Digital products display an infinity symbol because their stock is unlimited.

Product name

Price

Remaining stock

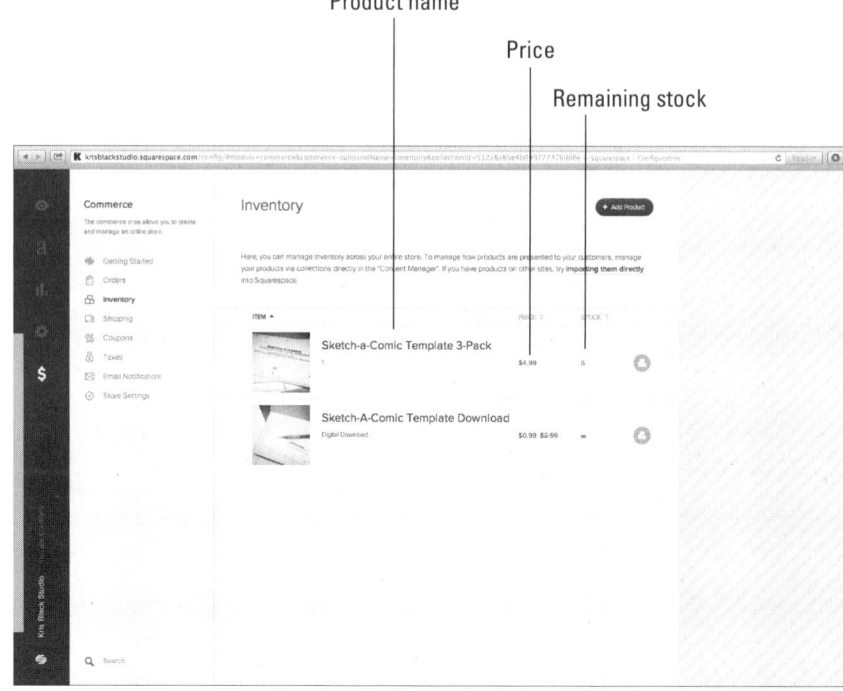

Earlier in the chapter, I showed you how to add a product to a products page in Site Settings➪Content Manager. You can add a product to your store also from Site Settings➪Commerce➪Inventory as follows:

1. **Click the Add Product button.**

   The Select a Page dialog box appears.

2. **Choose the products page.**

   If you only have one products page on your site, select the only page that appears. If you have more than one products page on your site, select the page from the list. After you select your page, the Select Product Type dialog box appears, as shown in Figure 17-13.

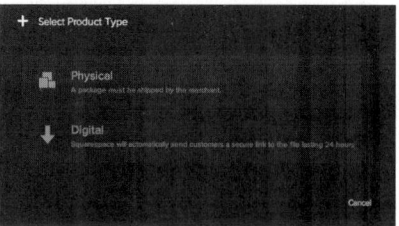

3. **Click the type of product you are adding: a physical product or a digital download.**

   Refer to the "Adding an item to a products page" section, earlier in the chapter, for details on configuring the products in your store.

4. **Add your product content.**

   Although you can save a product without any content in the Edit Product dialog box, I encourage you to add a title representing what the product is.

5. **Save your product.**

   If you want to finalize your product later, click the Save button to save it as a Not Listed item. To instantly publish the product on your site to sell, click Save & Publish.

You can open a product's Edit Product dialog box by clicking a product in the list.

Click the products icon on the far right of a product in the list (refer to Figure 17-12) to view the product page on your site.

Shipping

When you sell physical products in your store, those products must be shipped to your customers. You can create and configure multiple shipping methods in Site Manager⟳Commerce⟳Shipping.

To add a shipping method to your store, do the following:

1. **On the Shipping screen, click the Add Shipping Method button.**

   The Add Shipping Option dialog box appears.

2. **Choose a shipping option (see Figure 17-14):**

   • **Flat Rate:** Set a flat fee for each item in the order.

   • **Depending on Weight:** Determine shipping costs by the total weight of all the items in the order.

   After choosing your shipping option, an edit dialog box appears for you to configure.

Figure 17-14:
The dialog
boxes for
the Flat Rate
(left) and
Depending
on Weight
(right)
options.

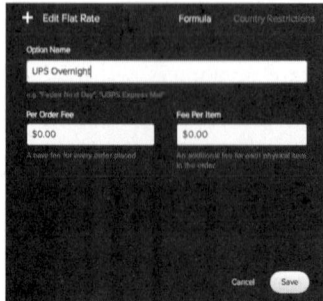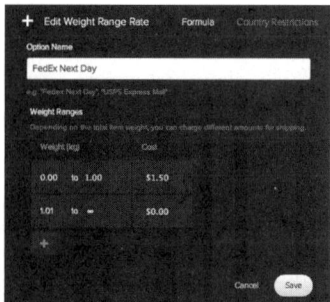

3. **Enter a description in the Option Name field.**

   Use a name that includes the carrier (UPS, FedEx, USPS, and so on) and the method (First Class, Next Day Air, 3-5 Day Delivery, and so on). For example, if you're setting up a shipping option for Priority Mail through the United States Post Office, you might name the shipping option USPS — Priority Mail.

4. **Set your shipping cost formula.**

   If you chose the Flat Fee option, fill in the following fields:

   - **Per order fee:** The flat fee applied to an order.

   - **Fee per item:** The cost applied for each item added to an order.

   If you chose the Depending on Weight option, you can modify the following criteria in the Weight Ranges area:

   - **Weight:** Change the ending weight, if desired. The weight you set here causes the beginning rate of the next range to be 0.01 pounds higher.

   - **Cost:** Determine the cost of the weight ranges based on the shipping method and carrier you will be using.

   The last weight range ends in infinity, so you can set a maximum shipping charge for orders that reach a certain weight and beyond. To add a new weight range, click the plus button below the last range. The new weight range is added between the last two ranges.

5. **Click the Country Restriction link and configure the following settings to control where your shipping option is available:**

   - **Ship to Rest of the World:** Use this setting to make the shipping option you're creating available to the rest of the world.

   - **Countries Allowed:** Set the countries where this shipping option is available. Click in the Countries Allowed field to reveal the Add

Countries pop-up box. Begin typing the country you want to add, and then select the country that appears, as shown in Figure 17-15. To remove a country in the list, hover your cursor over the country and click the x that appears next to the country name.

Click to view Country Restriction shipping settings

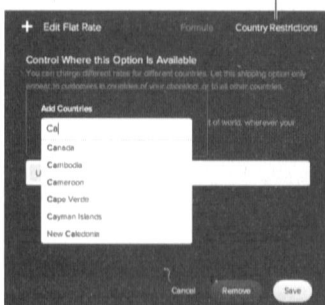

Figure 17-15: Adding a new country to a shipping option.

6. **Save your shipping option by clicking the Save button.**

   Your new shipping option is saved to the Shipping area of Commerce.

If you need to add more shipping options, click the Add Shipping Method button and repeat the preceding steps.

Coupons

If you want to offer customers an incentive for ordering from your site, you may want to offer coupon codes. To begin, go to Site Manager➪Commerce➪Coupons.

Then to create a coupon, do the following:

1. **Click the Add Coupon button.**

   The Create a Coupon dialog box appears.

2. **Choose the coupon type:**

   • **Any order:** Apply a discount to any order.

   • **Orders at least:** Apply a discount to orders over a specified subtotal.

- **Products by category:** Apply a discount to products in a certain category. See the "Adding an item to a products page" section, earlier in the chapter, for details on adding a product to a category.

- **Single product:** Apply a discount to a specific product.

After you choose the coupon type, the Select Discount Type dialog box appears.

3. **Choose the discount type.**

   You may be able to create three types of discounts, depending on the coupon type you selected in Step 2:

   - **Flat Discount:** The discount is a flat dollar amount.

   - **Percentage Discount:** The discount is a percentage of the cost.

   - Free Shipping (Any Order and Orders at Least only): The discount is free shipping on the entire order.

   After you select the discount type, the Edit Coupon dialog box appears.

4. **Configure your coupon.**

   The following configuration settings are available for all coupons:

   - **Coupon name:** Provide a name that describes the coupon.

   - **Promo code:** Create your own promo code, or let Squarespace generate a random code for you.

   The following configuration settings are available depending on the coupon type and discount type you choose in the preceding steps:

   - **Discount:** Provide a discount to be applied to an order.

   - **Minimum order total:** Provide the minimum subtotal to which a discount will be applied. This option is available only to discount types in the Orders at Least coupon category. Figure 17-16 shows the Edit Coupon dialog box with a flat discount that will be applied to orders over a minimum subtotal.

   - **Categories:** Select the category to apply a discount to when you create a Products by Category coupon.

   - **Find a product:** Select the product from your inventory to apply a discount to when you create a Single Product coupon type.

5. **Set the duration of the coupon.**

   At the top of the Edit Coupon dialog box, click the Duration link to view the duration settings. Set the beginning and end date and time the coupon will be active on your site.

6. **Save your coupon by clicking the Save and Publish button.**

Promo code

Coupon name

Duration

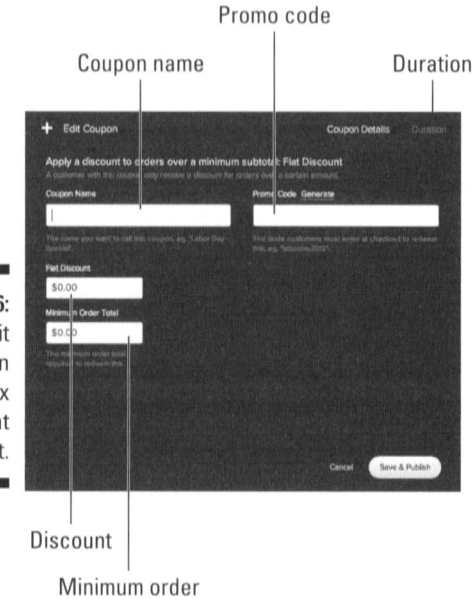

Figure 17-16:
The Edit
Coupon
dialog box
for a flat
discount.

Discount

Minimum order

Taxes

If you need to charge your customers tax for ordering on your site, you can create tax rules for the country, state, and even local area in which you are selling your products.

Check with the country, state, and local departments of revenue where you're selling your products to determine the tax rate you must charge for your products and shipping. If you're selling in the United States, check out the following website for information on determining tax rates: `www.bankrate.com/finance/taxes/check-taxes-in-your-state.aspx`.

Seek out professional advice from someone such as an accountant for assistance in figuring the ins and outs of charging taxes. If you're selling to a country other than the United States, check with that country's revenue department website for information on their tax rates.

To create a new tax rule, first go to Site Manager⇨Commerce⇨Taxes. Then follow these steps:

1. **On the Taxes screen, click the Add Country button.**

   The Create Country Tax Rate dialog box appears, as shown in Figure 17-17.

2. **Select the country.**

   Click Not Specified in the drop-down list and select the country for which you want to create a tax rule.

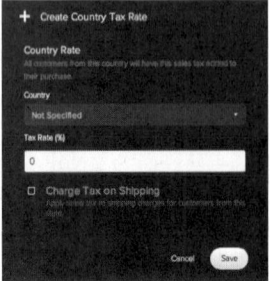

Figure 17-17:
The Create
Country Tax
Rate dialog
box.

3. **Set your tax rate.**

   In the Tax Rate field, set the percentage.

4. **If you need to charge tax on the shipping costs, select the Charge Tax on Shipping check box.**

5. **Click the Save button.**

You can create as many tax rules as you need in your store.

If you need to include state sales tax, do the following:

1. **Hover your cursor over the country you added in the preceding steps, and click the Add State link that appears.**

   The Create New State Rate dialog box appears.

2. **Click the State/Province setting and select the state from the list that appears.**

3. **Set your tax rate.**

   In the Tax Rate field, set the percentage.

4. **If you should charge tax on shipping costs, select the Charge Tax on Shipping check box.**

5. **Click the Save button.**

If the state you added displays an Add Local link when you hover your cursor over the name of the state, you can add local taxes to be charged to customers based on their zip code in one of two ways:

✔ **Single zip code:** Set a tax rate for a single zip code, as shown in Figure 17-18, left.

✔ **Zip code range:** Set a tax rate for a range of zip codes, as shown in Figure 17-18, right.

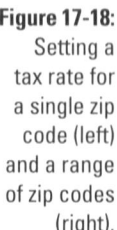

Figure 17-18:
Setting a
tax rate for
a single zip
code (left)
and a range
of zip codes
(right).

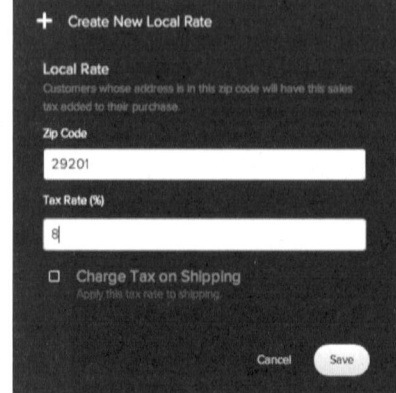
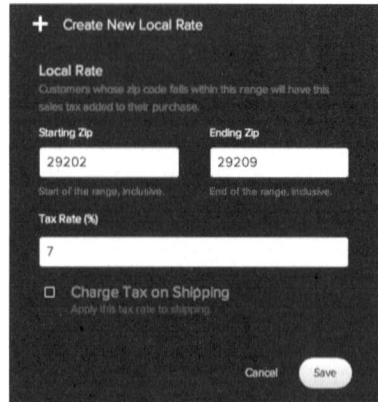

E-mail notifications

Your store will send e-mail notifications to customers when they place their
orders. You can customize these e-mails in Site Manager➪Commerce➪Email
Notifications, as shown in Figure 17-19.

Order confirmed message template

Figure 17-19:
Email
Notifications
area.

Order shipped message template

You can customize the following two e-mail templates:

- ✔ **Order Confirmed Message:** A message is sent immediately to a customer when they place an order.
- ✔ **Order Shipped Message:** An order summary and a message are sent to the customer when an order is marked as completed in the Order area of Commerce. (See the "Orders" section, earlier in the chapter, for details on marking an order as complete.)

Within these e-mail templates, you can customize the messages that are sent. You can also customize the header and footer of e-mail notifications sent to customers from your site.

If you decide to customize your messages, do not remove the template code within brackets. This code pulls information about the order to place in the e-mail messages.

If you have experience writing HTML and CSS, you can customize the formatting of the messages. Be sure to test the e-mails using the Send Test button below the Order Confirmed and Shipped messages. The Send Test button will send test e-mails to the e-mail address set for the Customer Support Email setting in Store Settings. See the "Store settings" section, earlier in this chapter, for details on configuring your store settings.

Chapter 18

Going Out with Squarespace

In This Chapter

▶ Adding a mobile account

▶ Posting to your blog from your mobile device

▶ Responding to and managing comments on the go

▶ Capturing notes and sending them to multiple accounts

▶ Showing off your images without an Internet connection

Sometimes, you'll need access to your website but you won't be near your computer. Fortunately, you can download the Squarespace app to your mobile device and use it to create and edit blog posts, reply to comments, and check your site's activity. Additionally, you can download two other apps by Squarespace, Note and Portfolio, to your iPhone, iPod touch, or iPad. (Sorry Android users, Note and Portfolio are not available for Android devices at the time of this writing.) In this chapter, you look at all three apps to see how you can interact with your Squarespace site on the go.

Accessing Your Site Anywhere, Anytime

Our mobile devices have become so integrated into our lives that not being able to update your site from your iPhone, iPod touch, iPad, or Android phone or tablet seems absurd. Fortunately, Squarespace has an app for all these devices.

Taking your site mobile

You can add as many Squarespace accounts as you want to your mobile app. If you don't have a Squarespace account, or want to start a new one, you can also sign up for an account from the mobile apps.

Have you added contributors to your site with permission to moderate comments, edit content, or help administer other updates on your site? If so, they can download and use the Squarespace app to help out on the go, too.

Adding an existing account

Do you already have a Squarespace account and want to add it to your iPhone, iPod touch, iPad, or Android device? Just do the following:

1. **Download the Squarespace app for your device.**

   - **iPhone and iPod touch:** `http://itunes.apple.com/ WebObjects/MZStore.woa/wa/viewSoftware?id= 318590874&mt=8`

   - **iPad:** `http://itunes.apple.com/us/app/squarespace- for-ipad/id408735801?mt=8`

   - **Android:** `https://market.android.com/details?id=com. squarespace.android`

   You can also go to your device's app store and search for Squarespace to locate the Squarespace app and download it to your device. On the iPhone, iPod touch, or iPad, tap the App Store icon on your device's home screen to open the App Store. On Android devices, tap the Google Play icon on your home screen to open the Google Play store.

2. **Open the Squarespace app.**

   The screen shown in Figure 18-1 shows the Squarespace app at the bottom of the screen on an iPhone.

Figure 18-1:
The Square-
space
app in my
iPhone's
dock.

3. **Tap the Add Account button.**

   The login form shown in Figure 18-2 appears.

Figure 18-2:
The account
login and
password
screen.

4. **Type your Squarespace login name and password.**

   Use the e-mail address and password that you used when signing into your Squarespace account in your computer's browser.

   If you're a contributor on this site, you can log in just like an owner under the Owner Login tab.

   The Editor Login tab is for the older version of Squarespace, version 5. At the time of this writing, the Editor Login tab is not used for logging into a Squarespace 6 account.

5. **If you have multiple Squarespace sites that use the same login and password, select the site to add to your account.**

   For example, Figure 18-3 shows my login screen.

6. **To add additional sites, repeat Steps 3–5.**

7. **Tap the Confirm button.**

   The account screen appears, displaying your newly added account.

Figure 18-3:
Select
which site
to add to the
Square-
space app.

Adding a new account

This section is for readers who want to sign up for a new Squarespace account. (If you want to add an existing account to your mobile device, see the preceding section.)

I don't recommend signing up for a new account using the Squarespace app because it's not optimized for a mobile experience. Instead, sign up using a desktop device if at all possible.

To sign up for a new Squarespace account, follow these steps:

1. **Download the Squarespace app for your device:**

   Use the links at the beginning of this section to download the app for your device. Or go to your device's app store and search for Squarespace to locate the Squarespace app and download it to your device. On the iPhone, iPod touch, or iPad, tap the App Store icon on your device's home screen to open the App Store. On Android devices, tap the Google Play icon on your home screen to open the Google Play store.

2. **Open the Squarespace app (refer to Figure 18-1) and tap the Get New Account button.**

   A template selection page from the main website appears. It's small but usable, as shown in Figure 18-4. For details on the sign-up process, see Chapter 3.

Figure 18-4:
Signing up
for a new
account.

3. **Select a template by clicking its thumbnail.**

   After selecting your template, you see further information about the template as well as customer sites that use that template.

4. **When you find a template you like, click the Start with This Design button.**

   The Create Your Website signup screen appears.

5. **In the Name fields, type your first and last names.**

   Your first and last names are used to create your Squarespace account name, which in turn is added to the beginning of your website's unique URL. If you want to use John Smith as your account name, for example, type John in the first name field and Smith in the last name field.

   If you want to create a custom domain, without `squarespace.com` (for example, `www.johnsmith.com`), see Chapter 12.

   Squarespace account names must begin with a letter and must be 3–25 characters. You can use letters, numbers, and hyphens within the account name.

6. **Provide a valid e-mail address.**

   Make sure that the e-mail address is one you use routinely because Squarespace uses your e-mail address to send important notifications about your account.

   If you're creating your second, third, or fortieth website with Squarespace, you can use the same e-mail address you used for another Squarespace account. Also, make sure to use the same password you used with the other Squarespace accounts, which leads us to Step 6.

7. **In the Password field, type a secure password.**

   When creating a password, don't use obvious options such as your account name or the words *square* or *space.* And don't share your password.

   Choosing a secure password is very important. Numerous articles online describe how to create a secure password. The best passwords are ones that are a combination of real words and numbers assembled in a phrase that can't be predicted or discerned. To check your password's security check out the How Secure Is My Password? site at `http://howsecureismypassword.net`.

8. **Click the Finish and Create Site button.**

   You have an official Squarespace account, and a website that's ready for you to customize and fill with content.

9. **Tap the Back button.**

   You return to the mobile app screen, where you can now add your new account by following the steps in the preceding section, "Adding an existing account."

Configuring your mobile account

After you add an account to the Squarespace app, you can configure it as you see fit. If you've added more than one account, you can configure each one differently.

To begin the configuration process, tap the app icon on your mobile device if the app isn't already open. If you don't see your account screen when the app opens, tap the Account (gear) icon to go to that screen (see Figure 18-5).

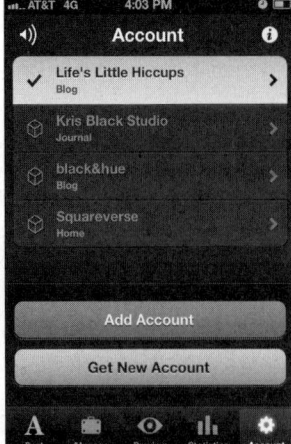

Figure 18-5:
An account screen with multiple Square-space accounts.

Tap your account name to load the configuration settings for your account, as shown in Figure 18-6.

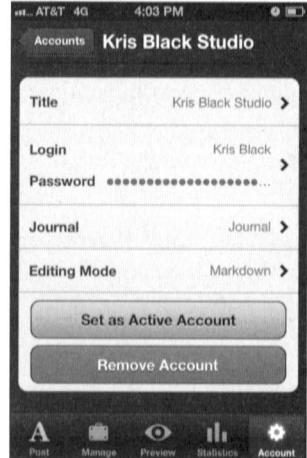

Figure 18-6:
Configur-
ation
settings
for your
account.

Following is a rundown of the settings on this screen:

- ✔ **Title:** By default, the title is set to the site title you added when signing up for the account. You can change the title.

  Try a shorter title that is more readable on the smaller screen of your mobile device.

- ✔ **Login and Password:** If you change your account name or password in your nonmobile account, you must make the same change to your mobile account. Otherwise, your Squarespace app can't stay connected to your site.

- ✔ **Journal:** If you have more than one blog page module on your site, make sure this setting is connecting to the blog page to which you want to post. To post to a different blog page later, simply change this setting.

- ✔ **Editing Mode:** The default editing mode is Text, which is the equivalent of WYSIWYG editing mode on your nonmobile site. Your other two options are HTML and Markdown. For details on the different editing modes, see Chapter 9.

  Editing modes can be changed on-the-fly when you're creating or modifying a blog post in the app. On the entry screen of your mobile device, choose your editing mode by tapping the A (text), <> (HTML), or # (markdown) icon.

✔ **Set as Active Account:** If you have more than one Squarespace account added to your app, you will see the Set as Active Account button at the bottom of the Account settings screen. Tap this button to set that account as the active account the app uses.

You can quickly see which account is the active account on your device because a check mark appears to the left of its name on the Account screen, and the account will be highlighted and displayed at the top of the list.

✔ **Remove Account:** Tap this button to remove the account from your device.

Because Squarespace is a hosted service on the Squarespace servers, removing your account from your device will not delete anything from your website. However, if you have any blog posts saved as drafts on your mobile device, those entries will be permanently deleted if you remove the account. See the section later in this chapter, "Adding a blog post," for more details on saving your entries as drafts on your mobile device or as drafts on your site.

Touring the Blog Post Screen

Adding blog posts with the Squarespace app is super easy. From almost any screen in your app, tap the Post icon in the lower-left corner. A blank entry window appears, ready for you to type a title and text in the message body, as shown in Figure 18-7.

Figure 18-7:
Blank blog post ready for content.

Following is a whirlwind tour of the screen:

✔ **Writing area:** Type a title and the text of the blog post at the top of the screen. If you want to save your entry so you can work on it later, tap the Save button at the top right. At the bottom of the writing area are three icons, described next.

✔ **Pencil icon:** Tap the pencil icon to display the Text window (refer to Figure 18-7).

✔ **Camera icon:** Add multiple photos to your blog post from your mobile device's photo app or camera. Begin the process by tapping the camera icon. When you publish your post, your photos will be uploaded to your Squarespace site.

✔ **Gear icon:** Tap the gear icon to set the publish date of your blog post and also apply categories and tags for organizing the post on your site. Tap in the category field to display the categories you're using in the blog. To add a new category, tap the plus icon on the far right. (Unlike in your desktop browser, tag names do not appear automatically as you type.)

✔ **A or <> or # icon:** The Squarespace mobile apps support the text (similar to WYSIWYG), HTML, and Markdown editing modes. (See Chapter 11 for information on using the text, Markdown, and code blocks to write content.) The actual icon you see depends on which editing mode is active. To set the default editing mode, change the Editing Mode setting on the Account screen. If you have more than one account, you can set each account to use a different default editing mode.

✔ **Keyboard icon:** Tap this icon to hide or show the keyboard.

Adding a blog post

You have several ways to add a blog post to your website. You can use your computer's browser (see Chapter 10), e-mail the entry from your computer (see Chapter 9) or mobile device, and use a mobile Squarespace app. In this section, you find out how to add a blog post using your mobile app:

1. **Tap the Post icon.**

   An empty blog post screen appears (refer to Figure 18-7).

2. **Add a title for your blog post.**

   This name appears as the title of the post on your site.

3. **Add your blog post text.**

   Tap in the area labeled *Description* and begin typing your post's content. If you need to hide the keyboard to enlarge the area for reading and reviewing your entry, you can do so by tapping the keyboard icon.

4. **To snap a photo and add it to your blog post:**

   a. **Tap the camera icon.**

      The screen shown in Figure 18-8 appears.

      You can snap or select only one image at a time, but you can add more photos by tapping either of the buttons again.

   b. **Tap the Take New Photo button.**

      Your camera opens so you can snap a picture and load it directly into the entry.

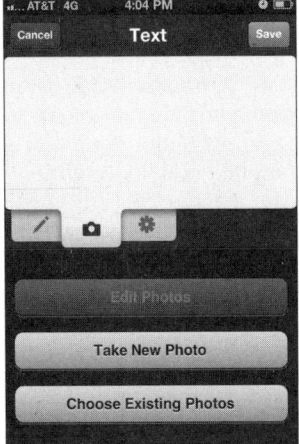

Figure 18-8:
Upload a photo for your entry.

5. **To add an existing photo to your blog post:**

   a. **Tap the camera icon.**

   b. **Tap the Choose Existing Photos button, and browse to select your photo.**

      You use this option to select a photo in your device's photo app.

6. **To remove an image:**

   a. **Tap the Edit Photos button.**

      This button appears only after you add your first photo. When you tap this button, the photos begin to jiggle.

   b. **To remove a single image, tap the remove icon (the *X*), which appears in the upper-left corner of the images.**

  c. To remove all images, tap the Delete All Photos button.

  d. Tap the Done Editing Photos button.

7. To move an image:

  a. Tap the Edit Photos button.

  b. Tap and hold down on the image to select it.

  You know the image is selected because it will fade slightly and become bigger.

  c. Drag the image to its new location.

  d. Tap the Done Editing Photos button.

8. To change the post date, tap the gear icon and enter a new date.

9. To assign a category to your entry:

  a. Tap in the blank area to reveal a list of previously used categories in your blog post.

  b. If you don't have any categories or you need to add a new one, tap the plus icon (shown in Figure 18-9) and type a new category.

  c. Tap as many categories as you want to apply to your post.

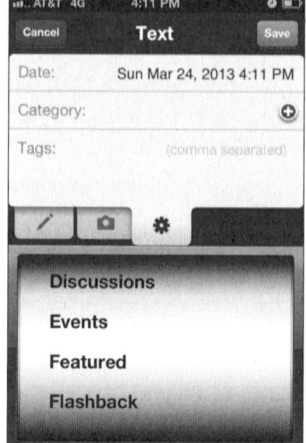

Figure 18-9: Adding categories to your entry.

10. To add a tag to your blog post:

  a. Tap in the Tags area.

  b. Type one or more tags that are relevant to your post, separating each tag with a comma.

11. **Save your blog post by tapping the Save button and choosing one of the options shown in Figure 18-10.**

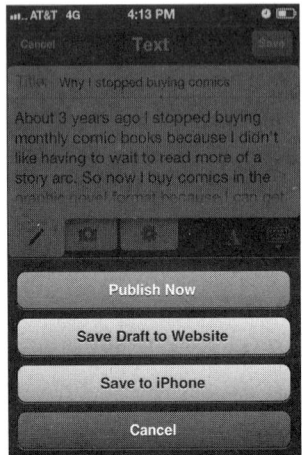

Figure 18-10:
Saving your
blog post.

You have the following choices:

- **Publish Now** saves your blog post to your site so your site visitors can read it.

- **Save Draft to Website** saves the blog post to your site as a draft. The draft appears on your mobile device in the Manage Post screen and also in the Content Manager area of your site (see Chapter 4) so you can access it later.

- **Save to *mobile device*** (where *mobile device* is your iPhone, iPod touch, iPad, or Android device) saves the blog post to your mobile device as a draft but will not save it to the site. This option is helpful if you have multiple editors on your site and don't want anyone to read the draft before it's ready.

Blog posts saved as drafts in the app and not to the site are not backed up. If your device is lost or you delete the Squarespace app, these entries will be gone forever.

- **Cancel:** Takes you back to the blog post so you can make further modifications or additions.

You can also e-mail blog posts to your site and have them published automatically to your blog. See Chapter 10 for more details.

Managing blog posts

You can delete, edit, publish, and view any blog post created on your mobile app in one central place: the Manage screen. To display the Manage screen, shown in Figure 18-11, tap the Manage icon at the bottom of the screen.

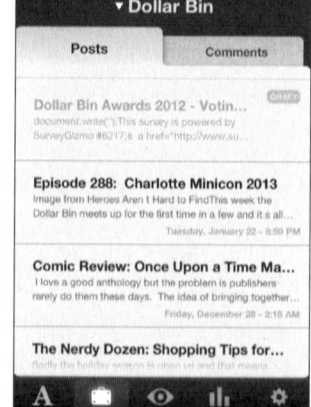

Figure 18-11: Manage post screen on the Squarespace iPhone app.

At the top of this screen are two tabs: Posts and Comments. To view all your blog posts, tap the Posts tab (refer to Figure 18-11).

To manage a particular post, tap it, and the screen shown in Figure 18-12 appears.

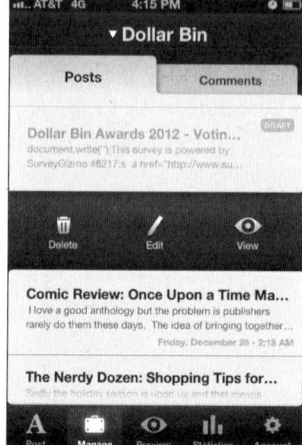

Figure 18-12: Tapping a blog post in the Manage post screen.

You have the following options:

- ✔ **Delete:** Remove the blog post from your mobile app and website. A confirmation message asks you to confirm the deletion.

  Deleting a blog post on your mobile device or in a browser is not reversible. After the post is deleted, it's gone forever.

- ✔ **Edit:** Open the blog post in a new screen, just as if you were creating a new blog post. You can then edit the post's content, add or remove photos, assign categories, add tags, and adjust the publishing date of the post. Save your changes when you have finished modifying the blog post.

  You may not be able to edit a blog post in the app that was previously created in your computer's browser if the post uses blocks that the app can't support. If this is the case, the app will notify you that the post is too complex to open on your mobile device.

- ✔ **Publish:** Publish your draft blog post. This option appears only if you've selected a draft post in the Manage Entries list.

- ✔ **View:** Display your blog post as it appears on your site.

The Manage screen displays all entries in a particular blog on your site. If you have multiple blog pages on your site, you can switch between them by tapping the Set as Active Account button on the Account screen.

Managing comments

You can view, reply, and manage your blog post's comments on the same Manage screen as your blog posts. Begin by tapping the Manage icon. The Manage screen appears (refer to Figure 18-11). Tap the Comments tab to display your blog post's comments, as shown in Figure 18-13.

On the Comments screen, you can mark all your comments as read by clicking the check mark icon in the upper-left corner of the screen.

To manage comments on your site, tap a comment in the list, and a screen like the one in Figure 18-14 appears.

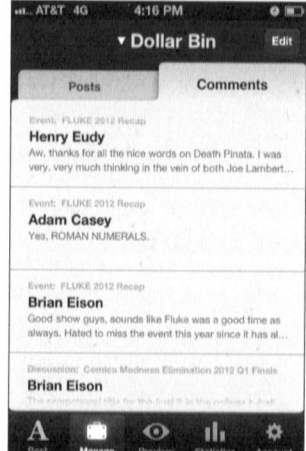

Figure 18-13:
Manage
Comments
screen.

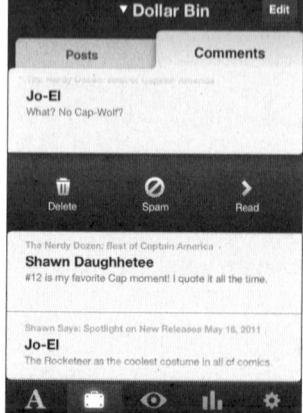

Figure 18-14:
Options
for a com-
ment on the
comment
screen.

The options on the Comments screen are as follows:

✔ **Delete:** Remove the comment from your mobile app and website. A confirmation message asks you to confirm the deletion.

After you delete a comment on your mobile device or in a browser, you
can't change your mind. When a comment is deleted, it's gone forever.

✔ **Spam:** Report the comment as spam and remove the comment from
your site. Reporting comments as spam, instead of simply deleting them,
helps Squarespace's spam filter prevent similar comments from slipping
through and posting to your site.

✔ **Read:** Read and respond to a comment. The Read screen displays the blog post title to which the comment was posted, the comment's author, and the comment itself, as shown in Figure 18-15.

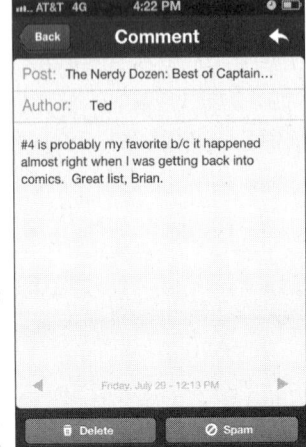

Figure 18-15:
A comment's Read screen.

When reading a comment, you have the following options:

- **Reply as a comment on your site:** Create a comment that responds to the comment you're reading by clicking the left-facing arrow in the upper-right corner of the Comment screen.

- **Reply via e-mail:** Reply to the comment by e-mail. If the commenter left an e-mail address as part of the comment information, the person's name appears in a button with an e-mail icon to the right. Tap the button to reply.

- **Delete:** Remove the comment from the entry and from your site by clicking the Delete button.

- **Spam:** Report the comment as spam by clicking the Spam button.

- **Comment navigation:** View a more recent comment by tapping the left arrow, or view an older comment by tapping the right arrow. These navigation arrows are on either side of the comment's date. (The arrows appear only if you have more than one comment in the blog.)

The Manage screen displays all the comments in a particular blog on your site. If you have multiple blog pages on your site, you can switch between them by tapping the Set as Active Account button on the Account screen.

Checking statistics

One of Squarespace's most useful features is the statistics and analytics information it collects about your site visitors. You can view data from the current day up to the last seven days.

Squarespace statistics are updated instantly in your account, making it fun to see how your site's traffic is shaping up, particularly if you've had a recent site update that might be pulling in a lot of hits from search results or if your site was featured on another site or an online publication.

The Squarespace mobile app provides you with four main areas of data about your site's traffic:

✔ **Visitor Information:** The top block of data shows statistics about your site visitors. Swiping left and right over the bar graphs switches between the following information:

   • **Page Views:** The default statistics shown in the visitor information block. The number of page views your site had each day for the last seven days, as shown in Figure 18-16. Tap a particular day to see that day's number of page views.

   • **Uniques:** The number of unique visitors your site had over a seven-day period. Tap a particular day to see that day's number of unique site visitors. You can also swipe the list to the left to see more information about your unique visitors.

   • **Robots:** The number of search engines that have visited your site to index your pages in their systems. You can also swipe the list to the left to see more information about the robots visiting your site.

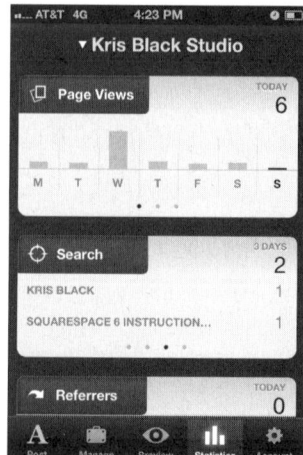

Figure 18-16:
Statistics for
Kris Black
Studio's
website.

✔ **Search** and **Referrers:** The last two blocks of data show the terms people used in search engines to get to your website and the referring websites that sent visitors to your site, respectively. Swiping left and right switches between the statistics across four time periods:

- **Today:** The default statistics shown in the Search and Referrers block. Search engine results from 12:00 a.m. to 11:59 p.m.

   Make sure you've set the correct time zone in your site. See Chapter 11 for details on setting the time zone in the Locale settings of Website Management.

- **2 Days:** Search engine results for the last 48 hours.

- **3 Days:** Search engine results from the last 72 hours.

- **Week:** Search engine results from the last seven days.

You can scroll the list of results. Tap and hold within either section and drag your finger up and down to see additional details. You can also swipe the list to the left to see more information about your referrers over a longer time span.

The Statistics section of the Squarespace mobile app gives you quick access to how your site is doing on the web. If you need more details about this information, log into the site and view all the statistics, as described in Chapter 16.

Capturing Ideas with Note

Note is Squarespace's minimalistic app for capturing notes quickly and sending them not only to your Squarespace site as a blog post but also to a list of third-party accounts. Note can be used for any purpose: to quickly capture ideas, to write down things you observe, or to send a message.

Connecting your Squarespace account

Before you can send your notes anywhere, you need to connect Note to your Squarespace site or configure it to send notes somewhere else. You don't need to have a Squarespace account to use Note, but because this book is about building your site using Squarespace 6, let's look at how you connect it to your Squarespace site.

Note is available only for Apple iOS devices. Although you can use the app on an iPad or an iPad mini, Note is optimized for use on an iPhone or iPod touch.

You can download Note to your Apple device at `https://itunes.apple.`
`com/us/app/squarespace-note/id561237934?mt=8`. Or go to the
App Store (tap the App Store icon) on your Apple device and search for
Squarespace Note. Click the Install button to download the app.

Tap the Note icon on your device to open the app. The screen shown in
Figure 18-17 shows the Note app at the bottom of an iPhone screen.

Figure 18-17:
Note
installed on
an Apple
device.

When you first open Note, an onscreen tutorial will walk you through the
basics of using Note. After the tutorial, the Note screen appears as shown in
Figure 18-18.

Figure 18-18:
The note
screen in
Note.

Do the following when viewing the Note screen:

1. **Swipe to the left.**

   The Note screen moves out of the way, revealing the list of accounts you can connect to Note.

2. **Tap Squarespace, at the top of the list.**

   A login screen appears for you to enter the e-mail address and password you use to log in to your site.

3. **Enter your e-mail address and password.**

4. **Tap the arrow button.**

5. **If you use the same e-mail address and password for multiple Squarespace sites, select the site that you want to connect to Note.**

   You can connect only one Squarespace account to Note.

6. **Configure your account settings.**

   The following is a list of the settings you can configure for sending notes to your Squarespace site, as shown in Figure 18-19:

   • **Default:** Set this to make your Squarespace account a default location to send your notes. You can make more than one destination a default. See the next section.

   • **Sync:** Back up your notes to your Squarespace account.

   • **Publish To:** Choose the blog page you want your notes sent.

   • **Post Type:** Send your notes as drafts for editing on your site later, or publish the notes immediately.

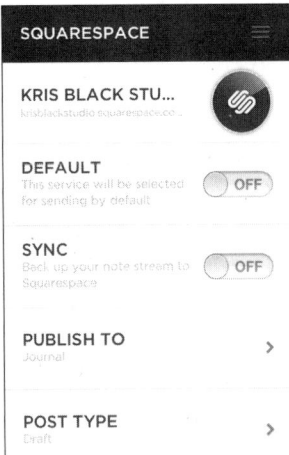

Figure 18-19: Configuration settings for connecting your Squarespace account.

7. **Tap the icon in the top right that looks like three lines.**

   You return to the list of accounts you can configure to connect with Note.

8. **Swipe to the right to return to the Note screen.**

You can connect Note to multiple accounts at once. Let's walk through the steps of sending a note to your site, and then we'll look at connecting to a third-party account for capturing your notes.

Sending a note

When you first launch the app, you see the Note screen (refer to Figure 18-18). To send a note from the Note screen, follow these simple steps:

1. **Type your note using the keyboard.**

   If your note is long, scroll the Note screen.

2. **Swipe your note up to send it.**

   By default, Note is set up to send your notes when you swipe a note toward the top of your screen. When you swipe your note up, you'll see a message at the bottom of the screen saying *Push to Send*. When the message changes to *Release to Send,* you can release the note and it will be sent.

   You'll see a brief confirmation below the note saying it was sent, and then the note and confirmation disappear from your screen. A blank note screen appears ready for you to send another note.

You can change the settings in Note to allow you to send a note by pulling (swiping down) or by clicking a Send button that appears at the top right of the screen. Let's look at how you can adjust the configuration settings for the app.

Changing Note settings

To change Note's settings, do the following:

1. **If Note is still open, exit it by pressing the Home button on your device.**

   You return to your device's home screen.

2. **Open the Settings app (gear icon) on your device.**

3. **Scroll down and tap Note's icon in the app list.**

   Individual app settings are located at the bottom of the main Settings screen, in alphabetical order.

4. **Modify Note's settings.**

   Note's settings screen appears, as shown in Figure 18-20, with the following options:

   - **Play Tutorial at Startup:** Play the Squarespace tutorial the next time you launch Note.

   - **Dark Theme:** Choose to use the dark theme all the time, never, or only after sunset.

   - **Push Up to Send:** Send notes by pushing (swiping) them up.

   - **Pull Down to Send:** Send notes by pulling (swiping) them down.

   - **Show Send Button:** Send notes by pressing the Send button.

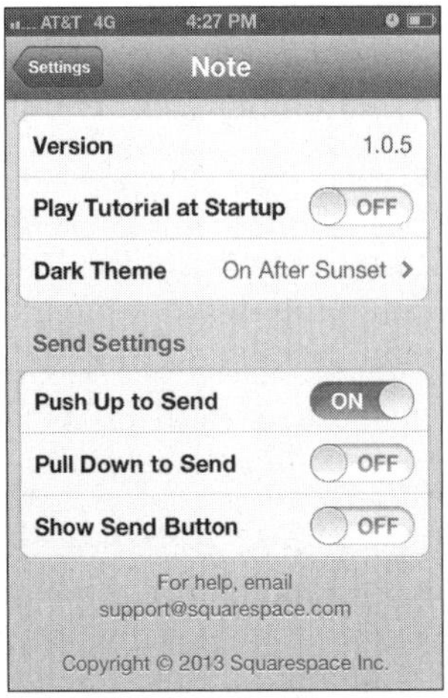

Figure 18-20:
App settings
for Note.

You can turn on all three options for sending your notes. If you turn off all three, Note will automatically turn Push Up to Send back on to send your notes.

Modifying the account list

In addition to connecting Note to your Squarespace account, you can also connect Note to multiple third-party accounts. To do this, you need to be viewing the account list. Open Note and, while viewing the Note screen, do the following to get to and work with the account list:

1. **Swipe to the left.**

   The Note screen moves out of view to the right, revealing a screen with the list of accounts already connected to Note. You may notice two types of circles next to your accounts:

   - **Solid circles:** The default accounts to which your notes are sent.

   - **Empty circles:** The accounts to which you can connect Note are not set as default accounts to receive your notes. (See the "Setting accounts as default destinations for your notes" section, later in this chapter, to find out how to set accounts as default accounts.)

2. **Swipe the list down.**

   Swipe the list of accounts down until the top of the list, above Squarespace, says _Pull Down to Edit_. Release when it says _Release to Edit_. The full list of accounts that can be connected to Note appears and the circles next to each account change as follows:

   - **Red circle with an x:** The account is connected to Note. You can tap the x to disconnect the account.

   - **Circle with a plus sign (+):** The account isn't connected with Note. See the next step for details on connecting the account.

3. **Tap the + next to an account to connect it.**

4. **If you connect with Facebook, Twitter, Evernote, Google Drive, or Dropbox, respond to the authentication screen that appears.**

   The account's configuration screen appears.

5. **Configure your account.**

   See the next section about the different settings available for each account.

6. **(Optional) To remove an account, tap the Remove Account option. Tap it again in the confirmation screen that appears.**

   The account is disconnected from Note and you return to the account list.

7. **Tap the three lines icon at the top of the screen.**

   You return to the list of accounts. Repeat Steps 3–5 to add another account.

8. **When you have finished adding and removing accounts, tap the x next to Edit Services (at the top of the screen).**

9. **Swipe to the right to return to the Note screen.**

Configuring accounts to receive notes

In addition to setting up your Squarespace site as an account to receive your notes (see "Connecting your Squarespace account," earlier in the chapter), you can also set up the following accounts:

✔ **Email:** Send a note to anyone's e-mail address.

  - **Send Location:** Include your location information as reported from your device.

  - **Subject Line:** Add a custom prefix or use an excerpt of text from the note.

✔ **Dropbox:** Save notes as text files to your Dropbox account.

  - **Send Location:** Include your location information as reported from your device.

  - **Separate Files:** Save your notes as separate files. Otherwise a single text file will be updated with each note.

  - **Filename Date:** Include in the filename the date when you sent the note. This option is available only if you have Separate Files turned on.

  - **Append Date:** Include the date in the file when you send the note.

✔ **Twitter:** Post Tweets to your Twitter account.

  - **Send Location:** Include your location information as reported from your device.

  - **140+ Character Limit:** Split your note into separate Tweets if your notes exceed Twitter's 140-character limit. Otherwise, Note will exclude notes that exceed 140 characters.

✔ **Facebook:** Post a status update to your Facebook profile.

✔ **Evernote:** Save notes to any notebook in your Evernote account.

  - **Notebook:** Select the notebook in your Evernote account for saving your notes.

✔ **Google Drive:** Save notes as documents to your Google Drive.

  - **Send Location:** Include your location information as reported from your device.

  - **Separate Files:** Save your notes as separate files. Otherwise a single text file will be updated with each note.

  - **Filename Date:** Include the date when you sent the note in the filename. This option is available only if you have turned on Separate Files.

  - **Append Date:** Include the date in the file when you send the note.

✔ **Add Service:** You can send notes to any service (account) that accepts e-mails.

- **Icon:** Represent your account as a triangle, check mark, dot, or diamond.

- **From Address:** Set the From address as either the default note's e-mail address (notes@squarespace.com) or a unique Notes e-mail address (such as notes-123456@squarespace.com).

- **Email Subject:** Send your note with an excerpt with a custom prefix, an excerpt without a custom prefix, the entire note, or no subject line.

- **Email Body:** Include the entire note in the e-mail body, or ignore the e-mail body.

Use the Add Service option to send notes to another Squarespace blog on your current site or another site by sending the note to the blog's secret e-mail address (located in the Post by Email Address setting of the Blog settings). See Chapter 9 for more details about using the Post by Email Address setting.

Setting accounts as default destinations for your notes

You can set one account or multiple accounts as the default accounts to receive the notes you send when you open Note. This feature is useful if you routinely send your notes to the same accounts.

To set an account as a default account to receive your notes, do the following:

1. **Swipe to the left.**

   The Note screen moves out of view to the right, revealing the accounts screen. If you need to add a new account, see the "Modifying the account list" section, earlier in this chapter.

2. **Long-tap an existing account.**

   Holding your finger down on a connected account will open that account's configuration screen.

3. **Tap the on/off switch for the Default setting.**

   Toggling the Default setting to on will set this account as a default account to receive notes anytime you open the app to send a note.

4. **Tap the three lines icon at the top of the screen.**

   You return to the list of accounts.

5. **To set another account as a default account, repeat Steps 2–4.**

6. **Swipe to the right to return to the Note screen.**

If you need to send a note to an account that is connected but not set as a default account, you can temporarily change which accounts will receive your note. Do the following:

1. **Open Note and swipe to the left to see the account list.**

2. **Tap the default accounts' solid circle to turn them off.**

3. **Tap the account with an empty circle to set it as the account to receive your note.**

4. **Swipe right to get back to the Note screen so you can send your note.**

After you send your note, the account list will automatically reset to your default accounts, switching off the account to which you just sent the note.

Reviewing previous notes

Note allows you to view past notes you've sent. You can edit, resend, remove, and even send notes to another account you've connected. To view the notes you've sent, get to the Note screen and then swipe to the right to reveal your notes.

You have the following options when viewing your previously sent notes:

- ✔ **Remove a note.** You can remove a note in two ways:

  - **Swipe to the right over a single note:** You see a red circle with an x next to the note. Tap the red circle to remove the note.

  - **Swipe down the list of notes to remove multiple notes:** Tap the circle next to each note you want to delete. (If you want to select all your notes, tap the circle next to Select All.) Tap Delete Selected at the bottom of the screen to remove the selected notes.

- ✔ **Edit a note.** Tapping a note will slide the list of notes out of the way, revealing the note full-screen with the following information (see Figure 18-21):

  - **Date and time:** The date and time you sent your note.

  - **Note:** Tap the note itself to reveal an edit screen. When you have finished editing the note, tap the three lines icon at the top of the screen and choose Save Changes, Discard Changes, or Cancel.

- **Icons of the accounts connected to Note:** Black icons are the accounts to which your note was sent. Tap any icon to reveal the name of the account and a Cancel option. Tap the name of the account to send your note to it, or tap Cancel to return to the edit note screen.

To get back to the list of notes, swipe to the left.

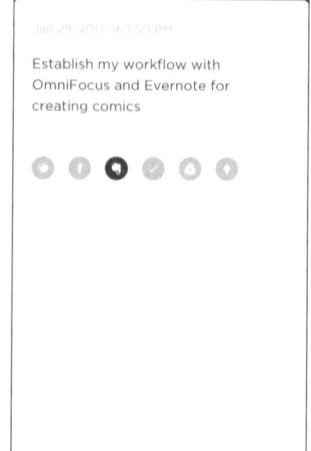

Figure 18-21:
Editing a
previous
note.

Showing Your Work with Portfolio

If you're a creative professional, you will appreciate Portfolio when you need to share your work with someone. Portfolio is a mobile app by Squarespace that allows you to store images you've added to galleries in your Squarespace site.

Because Portfolio downloads and stores the images directly in the app, you don't need to have Internet access to show off your work. Let's look at how you use Portfolio to show your work while on the go.

Before you can begin using Portfolio, you will need to have the following:

✔ Squarespace account

✔ Images in a gallery page

For details on adding a gallery page, see Chapter 9. To find out how to add items to that gallery page, see Chapter 10.

When your site has a gallery page with images, you're ready to download Portfolio to your iPhone, iPod touch, or iPad. Just do the following:

1. **Download the Portfolio app to your device.**

   Go to `https://itunes.apple.com/us/app/squarespace-portfolio/id569181277?mt=8`. Or go to the App Store (tap the App Store icon) on your Apple device and search for Squarespace Portfolio. Click the Install button to download the app.

2. **Open the Portfolio app.**

   Figure 18-22 shows the Portfolio app in the bottom row of an iPhone.

Figure 18-22: Portfolio on an iPhone.

When you first open Portfolio, you'll see a demo on how to use the app. You can swipe through the demo's screens, or click the red x in the upper left of the screen to close the demo.

Connecting your account

Portfolio will load some sample galleries, called collections, for you to use to see how to use the app. You can sync your own images from your Squarespace site to Portfolio, replacing the sample galleries.

Time to connect your account so you can use your own images with Portfolio:

1. **Open Portfolio**

2. **Swipe up from the bottom of the screen.**

   When viewing the Collection screen or an individual gallery of images, swiping up from the bottom of the screen reveals the settings panel. If you see the styling options, swipe left to slide the Sync settings into view as shown in Figure 18-23.

3. **Tap the Connect to Squarespace (circle) icon.**

   A login screen appears.

4. **Type the e-mail address and password for your Squarespace account.**

   Use the e-mail address and password you use to log in to your Squarespace site.

5. **Tap the arrow button.**

   The arrow button is to the right of the Demo Mode button.

6. **If you have multiple Squarespace sites associated with the login information you entered, select the site you want to use.**

   Next to each site is the number of gallery pages, or collections, available for syncing to Portfolio.

7. **Tap to select the collections you want to sync to Portfolio.**

   You can sync as few as one gallery page to as many as all your gallery pages. Next to each collection is the number of images it contains.

8. **Tap the Sync button.**

   The Sync button is at the bottom-right corner of the screen, as shown in Figure 18-23. When the syncing is completed, the Collection screen will appear.

Your site's gallery pages will be downloaded and synced to Portfolio, ready for you to show off your work. In the next section, you find out how to interact and view your images in Portfolio.

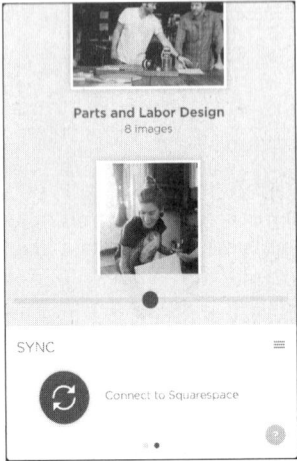

Figure 18-23:
Connect
Portfolio
to your
Square-
space site
to sync your
galleries.

Viewing your images

After you have added collections to Portfolio you will see them on the
Collection screen. Interacting with Portfolio is intuitive because it takes
advantage of the multitouch features of Apple's mobile devices.

If you have more than two collections synced to Portfolio, you may not see
them all initially when the Collection screen loads. Flick the screen up and
down to scroll through your collections until you find the collection you want
to view. Then do the following to view the images in that collection:

1. **Tap or unpinch the collection to view the gallery of images.**

   The images in the collection scatter out from behind the collection's
   thumbnail image.

2. **Tap or unpinch directly on top of an image.**

   The screen zooms in on the image.

3. **Swipe to view the next image.**

   Swipe left and right to scroll through your images in the gallery.

4. **To send an image as an e-mail attachment:**

   a. **Tap and hold down on the image.**

   b. **At the bottom of the screen, tap the arrow to open a new e-mail
      window with the image added as an attachment.**

      Tap the red circle to cancel and deselect the image.

5. **To view an image full-screen, double-tap or unpinch the image. To leave full-screen view, double-tap or pinch the image.**

   While view an image full-screen, you can

   - Rotate your device to landscape or portrait orientation for the best viewing experience.

   - Swipe left and right to view other images in full-screen mode.

   - Unpinch the image to zoom in. To view the image full-screen again, pinch it.

   - Swipe the image to move it.

6. **To return to the gallery of images, unpinch.**

7. **To return to your collections, unpinch.**

Customizing Portfolio settings

You can customize the look of the Collection screen and the Gallery screen. Simply follow these steps:

1. **Swipe up from the bottom of the Collection or Gallery screen.**

   Position your finger at the very edge of your screen and swipe up to reveal the settings panel shown in Figure 18-24.

   The settings panel of the Collection screen is titled Collection Styling. The settings panel on the Gallery screen is labeled Gallery Styling.

   Adjusting the styling of one gallery screen will adjust the styling for all of them.

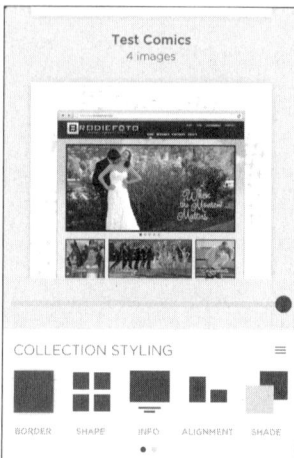

Figure 18-24: The settings panel in Portfolio.

2. **Tap on a styling icon to change to its options.**

   The different style settings follow:

   - **Border:** Display a border around your thumbnail images.

   - **Shape:** Switch between square thumbnail images or thumbnails shaped like the images' original aspect ratio.

   - **Info:** Configure thumbnails in the Collection screen to display the gallery title and number of images in the gallery.

   - **Alignment:** Position your thumbnail images at the top, center, or bottom when thumbnails are sized so that they are next to each other.

   - **Shade:** Choose a light or dark background for your thumbnails.

   - **Image size:** Adjust the slider above the settings panel to resize your thumbnail images.

3. **Swipe the settings panel to the left to reveal the Sync panel.**

4. **If you've updated the galleries on your site, sync them again to update Portfolio.**

   Tap the sync icon to resync Portfolio.

5. **Swipe down to hide the settings panel.**

That's it. Portfolio is a simple mobile app you can use to show anyone your gallery images on the go.

Part VI
The Part of Tens

the
part of
tens

In this part . . .

- ✔ Getting a custom e-mail address
- ✔ Discovering the importance of regularly updating your website
- ✔ Tips for promoting your website to attract new visitors
- ✔ Comparing popular e-mail marketing solutions
- ✔ Making money with your website

Chapter 19

Ten Features of a Good Website

In This Chapter

▶ Organized content

▶ Content optimized for search engines

▶ About page

▶ Contact page

▶ Custom domain

▶ Custom e-mail address

▶ Branding

▶ Design related to content

▶ Social media integration

▶ Regular updates and maintenance

*T*his chapter describes the top ten features of a good website, Squarespace or otherwise. Before you launch your website, review this chapter for tips on making your site even better.

Organized Content

The single most important aspect of any website is its content. A blogger should have blog posts, a painter should have images of paintings, and a real estate agent should have information and photos of houses. In addition to this basic information, every website should have content about who you are and what you do.

So that readers can find all this information, you need to organize it into sections and parts as well as guide visitors through your site. A well-organized site can do wonders for your online success. For more on the details of organizing your content, see Chapter 2.

What's great about Squarespace is that you have options when it comes to putting organized content on your site. Do you want to upload photos? Use a blog page to organize your images in individual gallery blocks in different blog posts. With this type of photo-blog, your site visitors can interact with you through the blog's commenting feature. Chapter 12 has detailed information about using the gallery block, and Chapter 10 goes into detail about adding and using the blog page.

If you blog and want to expand your site into a more robust news source, add multiple blog pages to organize your articles into defined site sections. You could also invite other writers to join your site as contributors and write articles and edit content. See Chapter 15 for details on adding contributors with editor permissions.

However you organize your content, remember that the organization must make sense to your site visitors. They should be able to understand how to move from page to page on your site. And don't forget to make the look of your text more interesting by styling the major text elements in Style Editor, as shown in Figure 19-1. Chapter 7 discusses how to use Style Editor to design your site, including styling text.

Format menu

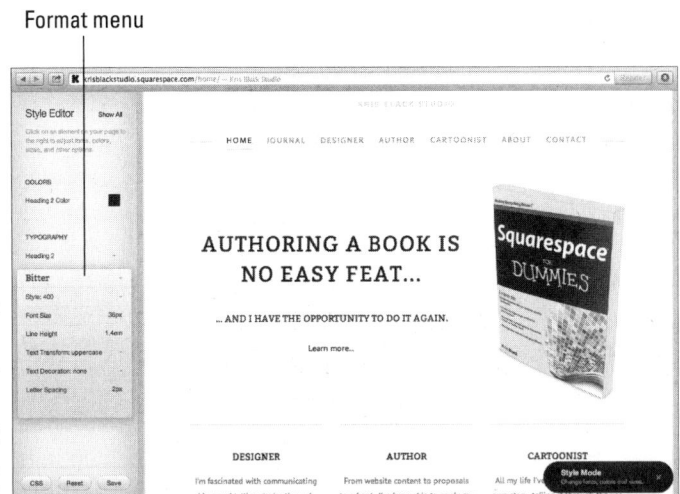

Figure 19-1: Style your text with the Format menu.

Content Optimized for Search Engines

The most important site visitor you will ever have is the almighty search engine, be it Google, Bing, Yahoo!, or AOL Search. The search engine helps drive traffic to your site. If you organize your content so that humans can read and understand it (as described in the preceding section), you will be well on your way to providing optimized content for search engines.

Squarespace sites are already optimized for search engine optimization (SEO). (Search engine optimization in Squarespace 6 is significantly improved.) Squarespace generates the appropriate meta tags and data for your pages, including Facebook's Open Graph tags for improved Facebook sharing. For an in-depth article on SEO, visit `http://answers.squarespace.com/questions/620/what-does-squarespace-do-for-seo`.

However, you still need to do some work to ensure that your site stays optimized with the content you add:

- ✔ Add a relevant site title, description, and meta description (choose Site Manager➪ Settings➪Site).

- ✔ Adjust the format of your site's home page title, collection titles, and item titles to suit your site's needs (choose Site Manager➪ Settings➪General).

- ✔ For each page on your site, add a relevant page title and description (choose Site Manager➪ Content Manager➪Page Settings).

- ✔ Add a descriptive caption to each image. The caption helps explain the image to search engines. You can set the caption to not be displayed on the site; Squarespace still adds the caption as alternative descriptive text in the site's code. See Chapter 9 for detailed help on adding images to your site.

If you are ambitious and want to see how Google is indexing your site, get a free Google Webmasters Account at `www.google.com/webmasters`. Then start tweaking some settings to see whether you can improve your ranking in search results.

About Page

Have you ever been to a website that didn't have an About page? You had no way to find background information about the person or company maintaining the site.

It's always a good idea to include a page or section dedicated to information about you or your company. Depending on the type of website you're creating, your About page might be called

✔ **About, About Me, About Us:** Every site visitor knows what to expect when clicking one of these common titles. This type of About page typically includes a brief bio answering the who, what, where, when, and why questions that someone might have. Anyone from bloggers to corporations might use one of these titles. Figure 19-2 is a great example of an About page. The page, at `http://thedollarbin.net/about/`, provides photos and bios of the site owners and contributors.

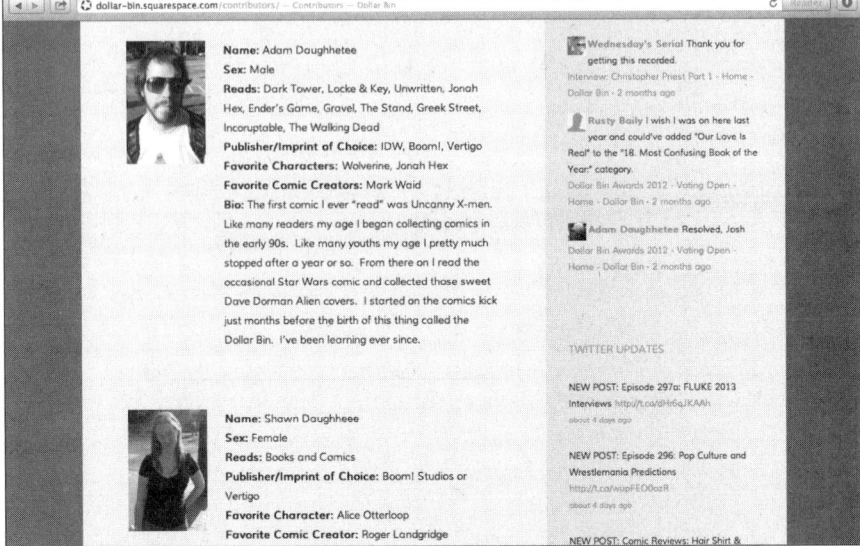

Figure 19-2:
Dollar Bin has a great example of an About page.

✔ **Colophon:** This publishing term refers to the pages in a book that provide information about printing and publication. Web creators have adopted this term to refer to their About page. A Colophon page provides technical (and usually geeky) information about how the site was created and maybe the software applications used to create the site. A good example of a Colophon page is on my studio site, Kris Black Studio (see Figure 19-3) at `http://krisblack.com/colophon/`.

✔ **Company Info, About *Company Name*:** These titles can be used when information about your company or institution can't fit on one page, such as bios of board members and top-ranking officials, information on stock options, a press kit, and job opportunities. For an example, see the footer area on the Wiley site, at `www.wiley.com`, the company behind the For Dummies brand, which features a careers page, a locations page, the privacy policy, a press center, and more.

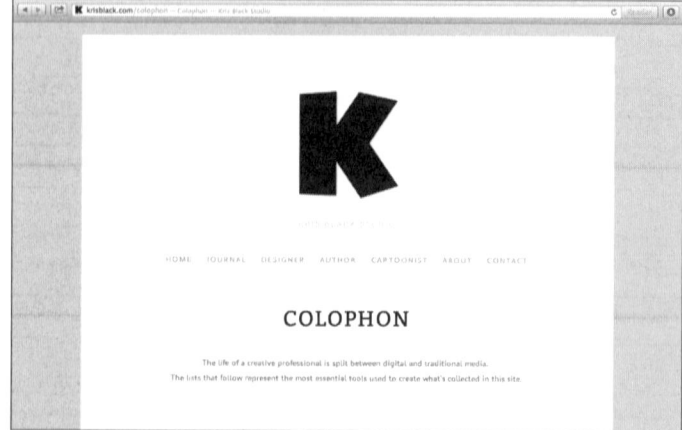

Figure 19-3:
The
Colophon
page on my
studio site.

Contact Page

It goes without saying that most people who have a website don't mind being contacted. Setting up a Contact page on Squarespace is simple: Add the form block to your page. (See Chapter 10 for more on adding blocks to your site.) The form block's default features are the exact fields you need for a contact form:

✔ Name

✔ Email

✔ Subject

✔ Message

If you need to collect more specific information in an initial contact with someone, add additional fields to the form block. (If you want to use more than the basic four fields just listed, you must sign up for the Unlimited or Business plan.) Perhaps you need to collect a potential client's budget range. Add a radio field with different pricing options. See Chapter 11 for more on customizing the form block on your site.

You may be thinking, "But I have a blog and visitors can just comment on a blog entry." Although this is true, what if someone wanted to advertise on your site or wanted to offer you an opportunity to expand your site's reach? What if someone wants to contact you in a less public way? These are all good reasons for including a Contact page on your website.

Following are two examples of a Contact page as shown in Site Manager⇨Content Manager:

- ✔ black & hue (`www.blackandhue.com/new-client-signup-form`) uses the Squarespace form block to create a robust New Client Signup Form page, as shown in Figure 19-4.

- ✔ Immaculate Consumption (`www.immaculate-consumption.com/contact/`) uses the default form block features for their Contact page, as shown in Figure 19-5.

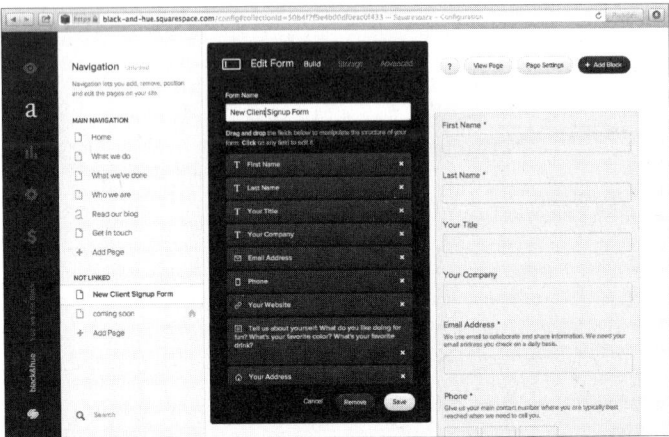

Figure 19-4:
black &
hue's
Contact
page.

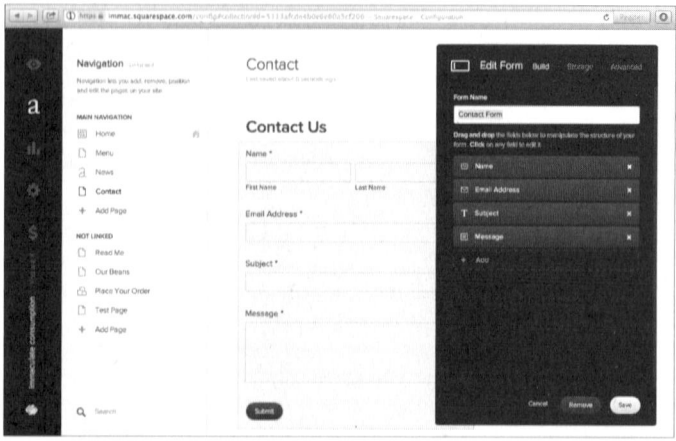

Figure 19-5:
Immaculate
Consump-
tion's
Contact
page.

Custom Domain

Squarespace provides you with a Squarespace URL for your site when you sign up. If you're serious about creating a site with unique content and style, however, you should invest in a custom domain name.

Choose a custom domain that people will remember. Make the name short and easy to spell and avoid hyphens. If your domain name contains a word that can be spelled different ways, consider purchasing the variations. For example, if your business name is 2design, you may want to purchase 2design.com, todesign.com, twodesign.com, and toodesign.com. (I realize that you would never use this crazy name for a business.) Don't forget all the extensions. You may want to also buy variations of your main domain, including .net, .org, and .me.

Squarespace allows you to map more than one domain to your Squarespace site while setting one as the primary domain. For more information on mapping a custom domain, see Chapter 15.

Custom E-Mail Address

A custom e-mail address is a great way to increase the branding on your site and enhance your professionalism. If you purchase your own custom domain (see the preceding section), you might as well go ahead and set up a custom e-mail address. For example, if your primary domain were 2design.com, the e-mail address would be *yourname*@2design.com. Your domain provider should have instructions on how to set up a custom e-mail address.

If you're running a business with multiple employees, another solution to getting e-mail addresses with your domain is to use Google Apps (`www.google.com/apps/`). Google Apps is Google's answer to using its Gmail e-mail service (along with the Google Calendar and Google Docs services) with your own domain. Google Apps, which is a paid service (approximately $5.00 per month per user) provides ample amounts of storage space, as well as e-mail and phone support.

Branding

Your website's name should be uniquely styled and consistent with any other material you use to promote your site. The addition of a logo lends credibility to your site.

If you want to design a logo yourself, stay away from common, instantly identifiable fonts. For example, avoid the Arial, Comic Sans, Curlz, Impact, and Papyrus fonts. You might consider using Helvetica, Times, or Lucida. Although these fonts are common, they are classic and blend well. Search for *logo design* in your favorite search engine to find tons of resources, services, and designers.

Design Related to Content

Creating a site design that is relevant to your content and brand should be high on your list of priorities when creating your website. You don't want a site that looks similar to other sites — unless you want visitors to think that you aren't creative enough to come up with a unique style.

Squarespace provides many different templates that you can use as-is or as the foundation for your own design. Whichever route you choose, be sure to add a logo and branding, as described in the preceding section.

For more on creating a custom design, see Chapters 6 and 7.

Social Media Integration

Many people have both a Facebook account and a Twitter account, which means you should as well, to provide a way to connect with more people. After all, one of your goals is to get as many people to your site as possible.

You can also have more than one account in a particular social media service, such as a personal Twitter account and a business Twitter account. Perhaps you have a Facebook profile for connecting with family and friends, but add a Facebook page for your site or business to separate the personal you from the business you. Maintaining all these social profiles and accounts can be a pain. Several solutions are available:

- ✔ **HootSuite** (http://hootsuite.com) is an online solution that helps you maintain multiple social service sites, including Facebook, Twitter, LinkedIn, and Foursquare. You can also add members to help with maintenance, which is beneficial if an employee or a partner is involved in promotion or connecting with others online.

- ✔ **Sprout Social** (http://sproutsocial.com) is an alternative to HootSuite that lets you maintain multiple Twitter accounts, Facebook profiles and pages, and your LinkedIn profile. Whereas HootSuite keeps updates separated into different streams on one screen, Sprout Social provides a single stream of updates from across all your profiles.

You can have only one Twitter account per e-mail address. If you have a custom e-mail address for your website (as described earlier in the chapter), tie that to a business Twitter account. Then use your personal e-mail address for your personal Twitter account.

I know what you're thinking: "How do I let site visitors share my information on their social networks?" For the answer, see the discussion in Chapter 15 on promoting through social media.

Regular Updates and Maintenance

Your site must offer some indication that a living, breathing person is behind it. Otherwise, people will turn elsewhere.

You can update and maintain your site in several ways, depending on the nature of your business and the direction of your marketing and promotion. For example, you can

- ✔ **Use the Squarespace social blocks.** Add the Twitter, Flickr, Instagram, or Foursquare block to automatically pull information from your social accounts for display on your website pages. Even if your site content is static or doesn't change a lot, a social block on your site at least shows that you are around and available. Make sure to update the social media service regularly.

- ✔ **Add a blog and update it regularly.** Your blog doesn't necessarily require long articles or entries. You can use the journal page to announce upcoming events, site changes, or any other snippets of information.

Squarespace makes it easy to add pages and content, modify your site design, upload images to a gallery, and facilitate connecting with your site visitors. In addition, the mobile apps (see Chapter 18) enable you to manage your site on the go, so you don't have to be at your desk to make site updates. Take advantage of Squarespace and make sure you are putting forth the best site you can.

Chapter 20

Ten Ways to Attract Attention to Your Site

In This Chapter

▶ Promote through social media

▶ Take advantage of e-mail marketing

▶ Write an elevator pitch

▶ Try word of mouth

▶ Use stationery

▶ Include an e-mail signature

▶ Advertise

▶ Comment on other sites

▶ Write for other sites

▶ Use an easy-to-remember custom domain name

*P*romoting your site and maintaining a steady stream of traffic requires dedication and consistent work. In this chapter, I present what I think are the most effective and rewarding methods for driving traffic to your site.

Promote through Social Media

Before the existence of Facebook, Twitter, and other social network sites, the web was not very social. Interactions were with people who already knew about the site and involved exchanging e-mail messages, chatting in forums, and commenting on blog posts. With the advent of social sites, you can put the power of marketing in the hands of your family, friends, and followers to help send traffic to your website.

Social promotion can take as much dedication and time as maintaining your website. To make the task easier, update your profile or status automatically. In this section, I show you how to automate updates on two of the behemoth social giants: Facebook and Twitter.

Connecting your site to your social accounts

Squarespace allows you to connect your site to your social profiles (choose Site Manager⇨Settings⇨Connected Accounts). You can add as many accounts as you have, and doing so will allow you to selectively choose which to notify when you publish new posts in your blog page (see the next section).

Additionally, you can connect your site directly to your Facebook page (choose Site Manager⇨Settings⇨Facebook Page). If you don't have a Facebook page, you can get one for free (`www.facebook.com/pages/create.php`). See Chapter 14 for more about connecting your site to a Facebook page.

Updating your social profiles

When you're ready to publish a new blog post, you can toggle on or off which social profiles to publish to. You choose these options in the Social settings areas of the Edit Post dialog box (choose Site Manager⇨Content Manager⇨your blog page). See Chapter 10 for details on the Edit Post dialog box options.

Post updates to your social accounts for the gallery, events, and products pages. In their respective Edit dialog boxes, toggle the on/off switches to post to your social media accounts just like you post to your blog.

If you want to have more control over updating your social profiles, check out Twitterfeed (`www.twitterfeed.com`).With Twitterfeed, you can update your Twitter profile with the title and link to your newly published entry. Twitterfeed can also publish updates to profiles on Facebook and LinkedIn.

Twitterfeed has advanced configurations that enable you to add or modify what is published along with your entry title and link, as shown in Figure 20-1. You can add a prefix or suffix to your updates, determine how often Twitterfeed looks for updates, and decide which URL shortening service to use, such as bitly.com or TinyURL.

Figure 20-1:
The
advanced
Twitterfeed
settings.

Helping others share your content

One popular way of enabling others to promote your site's updates and content is to add a social sharing link, such as the Facebook Like button, to your site. You can add similar links to Twitter, Google+, LinkedIn, and many more.

You can share your content in several ways:

✔ **Squarespace Share buttons:** Blog posts have a Share link that site visitors can click to share an article on their favorite social network, as shown in Figure 20-2. You turn on the buttons you want to display by choosing Site Manager⇨Settings⇨Share Buttons.

Figure 20-2:
Some
Square-
space Share
buttons.

Share buttons

✔ **Third-party social sharing:** If the Squarespace Share button feature is not your cup of tea, you can use an alternative service that replicates this feature on your site but offers more control. AddThis (`www.addthis.com`), shown in Figure 20-3, and ShareThis (`www.sharethis.com`) offer similar features, such as analytics, customization of the sharing drop-down menu, and the addition of the big Share buttons of popular social networks such as Twitter, Facebook, and Google+.

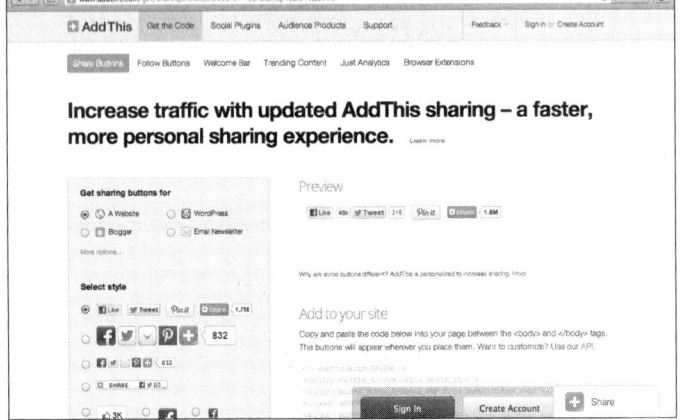

Figure 20-3: AddThis social sharing buttons.

✔ **Add Twitter's Tweet button and Facebook's Like button:** Twitter and Facebook have their own buttons that you can add to your blog posts through the Blog Post Item Code Injection feature in the blog page's configuration settings. Following are the links to download these buttons:

- **Twitter button:** `https://twitter.com/about/resources/buttons`

- **Facebook Like button:** `https://developers.facebook.com/docs/reference/plugins/like/`

See Chapter 9 for more information on configuring your blog settings.

✔ **Use Disqus for commenting:** Replace Squarespace's blog commenting with the commenting service from Disqus. With Disqus, commenters can post comments not only to your site but also to their own social networks. Disqus also allows people to log in to the Disqus commenting system on your site using their favorite social profile or a Disqus profile, as shown in Figure 20-4. You can find out more at `www.disqus.com`. Chapter 12 shows you how easy it is to implement Disqus commenting on your site with nothing but your Disqus user name.

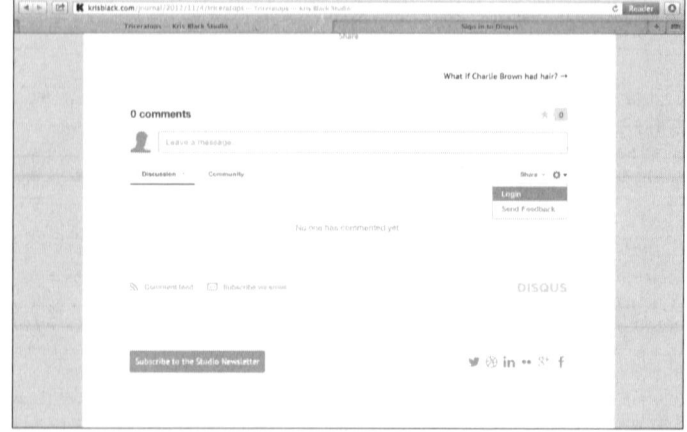

Figure 20-4:
Disqus
commenting
login
window.

You can allow people to subscribe to an RSS (Really Simple Syndication) feed, an automated announcement feature of a blog's posts and updates. RSS feeds are used by programs and services to notify you of updates to a site. Squarespace doesn't provide an easy way to display your blog's RSS feed on your site. You have to do a little bit of manual work, as explained in a helpful article in their knowledge base (`http://help.squarespace.com/customer/portal/articles/668493-how-do-i-find-my-rss-feed-url-`).

Take Advantage of E-Mail Marketing

The old-school way of keeping people up-to-date is called "e-mail." Remember when people used to e-mail each other? Sorry for the sarcasm.

E-mail is still a powerful promotional tool. You can't be sure that everyone has a Facebook or Twitter account, but almost everyone who surfs the web has an e-mail account. You need a way to collect these e-mail accounts into a system that will enable you to send e-mail newsletters.

With the Squarespace form block, you can create a form to collect e-mail addresses and add them to a MailChimp e-mail list. (See Chapter 11 for more information about connecting a form block to a MailChimp account.) Most, if not all, e-mail marketing solutions provide you with code to embed a sign-up form on your site. You can add this code in a code block on your site, as shown in Figure 20-5.

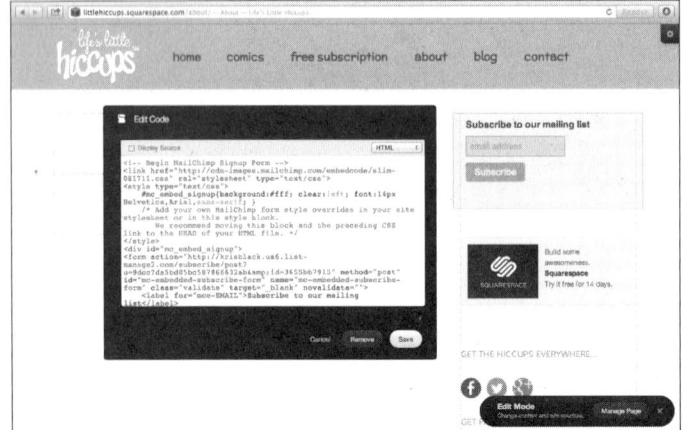

Figure 20-5:
Where to
paste sign-
up code.

Following are some e-mail newsletter services that you might want to check out:

- ✔ **AWeber** (www.aweber.com), a solid solution that is a favorite of many bloggers, provides social integration and sign-up forms that match pre-made e-mail templates.

- ✔ **Campaign Monitor** (www.campaignmonitor.com) targets its service to allow web designers and agencies to resell Campaign Monitor as a white label to their business customers. This means you can remove all Campaign Monitor branding, add your own branding (logo and design style), and set your own pricing for sending e-mail campaigns — essentially passing off Campaign Monitor as your own custom e-mail campaign software that customers buy from you.

- ✔ **Constant Contact** (www.constantcontact.com) is a long-time contender in the e-mail newsletter service and also provides event marketing and online survey solutions.

- ✔ **MailChimp** (www.mailchimp.com) provides professionally designed templates by world-class designers plus an easy-to-use template builder to design your own free e-mail marketing resources, social integration, and logo.

Write an Elevator Pitch

An *elevator pitch* is a short description about a product or service. I'm guessing that this name came from the desire to be able to briefly explain your product or service in a short elevator ride. As goofy as this sounds, crafting and memorizing a descriptive phrase about your website is a good idea.

You'll be able to quickly explain your site to someone when the topic comes up in conversation.

Your elevator pitch can also double as the description you add to your profile at Facebook, Twitter, and other social sites and online accounts.

You might be able to use your elevator pitch as the basis for a slogan. This short phrase can be used where space is too limited to accommodate the elevator pitch.

I would also recommend to think beyond the elevator pitch idea and make sure you have rehearsed more in-depth explanations and answers to questions, should the person you're talking to want more information about your site.

Try Word of Mouth

Speaking of conversations, get up off your chair, head out to a public place, and start telling people about your website. Believe it or not, word of mouth can be an effective promotional weapon in your arsenal.

When you're engaged in conversation, let the person know that you have a website. Ask friends and family members to promote your site to people they meet. If you run a local business site, using word of mouth to promote your business can be just as effective as all the online solutions.

Tying word of mouth with an elevator pitch is a good idea too. Imagine having an elevator pitch that is simple and clearly worded that anyone can remember it. Now imagine you worked with a client or customer who loved your product or service, and loved it so much that they tell a colleague about what you did for them. If they can have a clear understanding of what you do, they can be more effective in helping spread the word about you. It's worked for me numerous times, and I can tell you that personal recommendations by customers and clients are more effective than anything I can say to someone.

Use Stationery

Adding your site's URL to all your stationery is an effective promotional tool. Stationery products can include

- Business cards
- Letterhead

✔ Envelopes

✔ Labels

✔ Notepads

✔ Flyers

Probably the most important stationery of all is your business card. You can print your own or find an inexpensive online print service by typing *business card printing* in your favorite search engine. One easy-to-use service for making your own business cards that look good is Moo (www.moo.com).

Include an E-Mail Signature

All e-mail programs and applications have a *signature* feature. This little bit of information at the end of a person's e-mail message typically contains the person's full name and e-mail address.

It's time to tap this resource. Add your website's URL to your signature. Remember the elevator pitch mentioned earlier? Add it to your e-mail signature as well. You might even consider adding links to your social media profiles.

I think keeping your signatures simple is the best way to go. When you engage in a lengthy e-mail conversation with someone, nothing is more annoying than an obnoxious e-mail signature in multiple colors and large images. I recommend plain text signatures. Following is an example of how I like to format my e-mail signature for black&hue:

Kris Black

partner

kris@blackandhue.com

black&hue, LLC

www.blackandhue.com

Advertise

One way to target a specific audience and location is to go where the people are. Sites with large amounts of traffic typically have an advertising system implemented on their site, with a page describing how to advertise with them. (If they don't, use their Contact page to inquire about advertising on their site.)

You can also sign up with an advertising service. Let that service distribute its own advertising campaign — or one you develop — over its advertising channels. Check out the following ad services:

- ✔ Chitika (`http://chitika.com`)
- ✔ Kontera (`http://kontera.com`)
- ✔ TextLinkAds (`http://text-link-ads.com`)

And don't overlook Google's AdWords (`https://adwords.google.com`), one of the most popular advertising tools. AdWords are displayed in the Google AdSense network, so your ads can appear in search results as well as on other websites that display AdSense. Use the AdWords keyword tool to figure out which keywords are popular to help determine which searches you want your ads to display. If you have a small or targeted niche, Google AdWords could push a lot of traffic to your site.

Comment on Other Sites

Commenting on other sites can be a great indirect way to promote your website and drive more traffic. Actively engage in commenting and conversations on sites you regularly frequent. Target sites in your industry or sites where your unique knowledge can help further your online success.

People hate spam comments even more than spam e-mail. Make sure that your comments on other people's blog posts do more than simply promote your site. Your comments should be relevant to the conversation of other commenters or in direct response to the message of the original blog post.

Use commenting as a form of passive advertising. Build up your reputation on blog sites as a valued commenter. If you visit and comment on a site enough times with valued input, you can gain trust with the site owner and commenters.

Write for Other Sites

Writing for someone else's site can be a successful advertising and marketing method for your site. While you wait for your site to become a popular destination on the Internet, why not write some guest posts for sites that are already a go-to destination? The worst that can happen is that you drive a few new people to your site.

Being a guest writer is like being a guest speaker at a conference or local meet-up — except you don't even have to change out of your pajamas for the former!

Finding guest writing gigs will take some work at first. Make sure your site has plenty of examples of your best writing. Then start e-mailing contacts. If you're already commenting on another site, perhaps the site owner would be willing to let you write a guest post. On the flip side, you can also drive traffic to your site by offering guest writing spots to other bloggers and writers.

Use an Easy-to-Remember Custom Domain

When you sign up for your Squarespace account, you get a URL in the following format: `http://youraccountname.squarespace.com`. That URL is hard to remember, though, so think about investing in your own domain name, one more relevant to your site. Check out Chapter 15 for information on getting a domain name and applying it to your Squarespace account.

Increase your SEO (bonus tip)

Make sure that your site is optimized for search engines. You want them to index your site so it can be seen by as many people as possible through Internet searches.

Squarespace sites are already optimized for maximum efficiency when it comes to SEO (search engine optimization), but you still need to make sure that you properly fill in all the blanks for the SEO features you can set on Squarespace. See Chapter 15 for information about adding a site title and description. Make sure to add page descriptions in each page's settings, as described in Chapter 9.

Also make sure that your site content is formatted and written to take full advantage of SEO techniques. Following are two of my favorite books on SEO and writing for the web:

✔ *Search Engine Optimization For Dummies,* 5th edition, by Peter Kent (Wiley), is an easy-to-understand book on how search engines index your site.

✔ *The Yahoo! Style Guide: The Ultimate Sourcebook for Writing, Editing, and Creating Content for the Digital World,* by Yahoo! and Chris Barr, provides tips, tricks, and techniques for making sure that your writing targets your web audience as well as search engines. Although it's cowritten by Yahoo!, the information is relevant for other search engines too.

The Squarespace help site has an entire section dedicated to SEO and how it relates to your Squarespace site. Make sure you're properly using and understanding all the SEO features in Squarespace.

And finally, if you're looking for ideas and tips, check out Josh Braaten's website, Big Picture Web (`www.bigpictureweb.com`). Josh is a dedicated Squarespace user, like me, and has tons of helpful articles about SEO and marketing.

Chapter 21

Ten Ways to Make or Save Money

In This Chapter

▶ Getting a Squarespace discount

▶ Finding a coupon code

▶ Starting a conversation

▶ Selling out

▶ Starting shopping

▶ Selling yourself

▶ Creating a portfolio

▶ Developing a brochure site

▶ Providing exclusive content

▶ Blogging for dollars

*M*aking money. Most people have this topic in mind when creating a website these days.

In this chapter, I present ten possible methods for saving and earning money with your Squarespace site. How much money you earn depends on several factors, the most important of which is your determination. Other key ingredients are what your site is about, the work you put into your site, and luck.

Get a Squarespace Discount

Squarespace offers a number of ways to save money on your site. You can choose from three billing plans: monthly, yearly, and every two years. The one-year plan offers a 20 percent discount, and the two-year plan offers a 25 percent discount. See Chapter 3 for more information about pricing and choosing which plan is right for you.

If you're a web designer or own a company that offers website creation services, you can save money while developing your client's site if you use a Developer account to create the Squarespace site. The trial sites you create with a Developer account don't expire. Moreover, you don't have to start paying until the client's site is launched publicly. See Chapter 1 for more information about Developer accounts.

So how do you make money from the client's site? Simple, you pay for it, and bill your clients for a little bit more. Just make sure you offer more in return to your client than just being a middleman. For example, you might help them with simple support issues on a continuous basis.

Find a Coupon Code

Squarespace, like most services on the web, offers the chance to save some cash if you have a coupon code. The discount for these codes is usually 10 percent off your billing. You can combine a coupon code with a plan discount, resulting in a total of 30 percent off the yearly plan and 35 percent off the two-year plan!

To find a coupon code for Squarespace, you'll have to search the web. In addition to a text search in your favorite search engine, also search podcasts and online video content creators that Squarespace sponsors.

Start a Conversation

For a great way to engage with your site visitors, use the Squarespace form block. If you're selling a service, every person visiting your site is a potential customer. Being able to easily capture data from your visitors could be a key factor in the growth of your business.

To help turn prospects into leads, you can use the form block to provide an easy way for them to contact you. You can configure the form block to ask specific questions using a variety of form elements: drop-downs, check boxes, radio buttons, and free-form text fields. Standard universal form elements are also available for collecting preformatted data such as phone numbers, snail-mail addresses, e-mail addresses, and names.

If you use an address book, collecting specific information can help you get a jump on getting your prospects into your management system to track and measure your progress in converting these people to customers.

Sell Out

When people think about making money online, the first method that comes to mind is adding advertisements to their site.

The most popular advertising solution is Google AdSense. Just get an account, pop some code on your site, and — bam — you have ads. AdSense reads your site's content and (theoretically) displays ads that are relevant to your site and your audience.

Although AdSense is easy to implement, it's not a powerful money-maker unless your site sees thousands of hits daily. Several other options for putting ads on your site follow:

- Amazon Associate Program (`https://affiliate-program.amazon.com`)
- Chitika (`http://chitika.com`)
- Fusion Ads (`http://fusionads.net`)
- Kontera (`http://kontera.com`)
- TextLinkAds (`www.text-link-ads.com/`)

Make sure that the ads are relevant to your audience and don't overpower your site's content. After all, your content should be the reason your visitors are coming to your site.

Start Shopping

T-shirts, books, baby clothes, or car parts: We all have something we could sell online. You could use eBay or Amazon Marketplace to sell these items, but why do that when you can create a custom store on Squarespace to peddle your goods to the masses?

If you want to use something other than Squarespace Commerce baked right into your site (see Chapter 17), consider signing up for a PayPal account so you can add their Buy Now, Donation, and Subscription buttons to your site. In addition, check out these third-party shopping cart solutions:

- E-Junkie (`www.e-junkie.com`)
- FoxyCart (`www.foxycart.com`)
- Pulley (`www.pulleyapp.com`)
- Ecwid (`www.ecwid.com`)

All these solutions enable you to embed code on your site and sell real or digital products through their payment system. Each solution has pros and cons, so weigh all the options to see which would work best for you.

Sell Yourself

Don't forget to promote yourself. For instance, if you're a freelance writer, you may want to maintain a blog to show that you're actively engaged in writing. Let people know that writing is your passion. Or use your blog to promote other work that makes you money and to engage with fans.

You can use social sites such as Facebook and Twitter to broaden your reach, but always point people back to your site, where you can control how you are represented. See Chapters 14 and 15 for more on using social sites to promote your Squarespace site.

Sites with few updates or little new material appear dead and no longer worth visiting. If you don't have the time to maintain a blog on a routine basis, make sure that the blog page of your site is not the front page.

Create a Portfolio

All artists and designers — from dancers to painters to architects — need a way to present their work. After all, if you're trying to promote yourself and your art, you need a way to show off what you've done. You probably already have an offline portfolio of work, so why not create an online version as well?

Use the gallery block or a gallery page to create your digital portfolio galleries. Offering instant gratification to fans or potential clients who want to see your work is a sure-fire way to land some leads to new jobs.

Combine the gallery block with the form block to jump-start a conversation that may lead to new opportunities.

Develop a Brochure Site

You may find that maintaining an active blog is too much to handle. If you want to sell a service rather than a product, consider creating a simple brochure website.

A brochure site basically provides clear information about who you are, what you do, and how you do it. The site can consist of one page or several pages. The Squarespace Standard plan is perfect for sites like this.

Make it easy for people to contact you. Use the default fields when you create a form block so that visitors can send an e-mail message. If you've signed up for the Unlimited or Business plan, you might also create a form customized for your business to collect more specific data from your site visitors.

Provide Exclusive Content

Squarespace doesn't natively support a way to collect recurring dues for paid memberships, but with a little creativity and the use of PayPal, you can create a process to collect subscription money to enable membership access to exclusive content on your site.

The process is fairly simple:

1. **Add an access password to a page on your site.**

    Refer to Chapter 9 for information on adding a password to a page's settings on your site.

2. **If you don't already have a PayPal account, sign up for one.**

    Visit www.paypal.com, click the Sign Up link, and follow the onscreen instructions.

3. **Add a PayPal Subscription button to your website. Log in to the PayPal site and then**

    a. **Click the Merchant Services tab.**

    b. **Click Create Payment Buttons for Your Website, as shown in Figure 21-1.**

    c. **Follow the onscreen instructions.**

    Switch the Choose a Button Type pop-up menu to Subscriptions, and fill in all the relevant and required information about your subscription in Steps 1 and 2. In Step 3, Customize Advanced Features, add the URL to a hidden Squarespace page in the Take Customers to This URL When They Finish Checkout field, as shown in Figure 21-2. This link will take your new subscribers to the hidden page on your site that shares the password and link to the page on your site with the protected content.

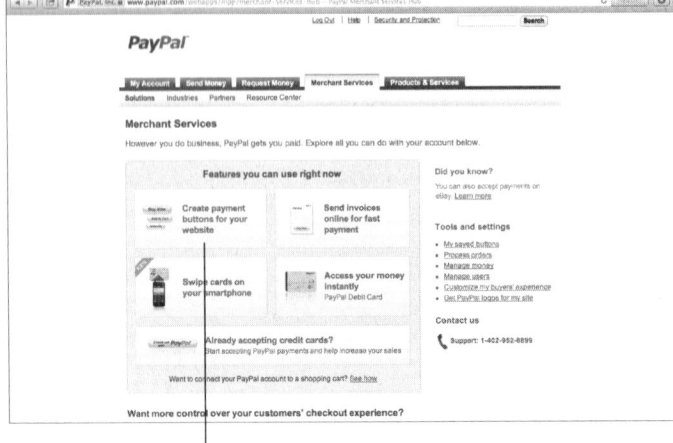

Figure 21-1:
The PayPal
Website
Payments
Standard
option.

Click here

Figure 21-2:
Add your
Registration
page URL
to the
Subscription
button.

> **d. Click Create Button.**
>
> **e. Copy the embed code for your newly created Subscription button and paste it in your site.**
>
> You can add this code to your site using the code block.

Placing a password on a page on your site, even on a hidden page, is not secure. You'll need to weigh the benefits of offering paid access in this manner versus the lack of control you have over the security of your content's password. Should you feel that your password has been compromised and shared with more people than you believe are subscribers, I suggest changing the password and notifying your subscribers of the new password.

If you want a more secure way of controlling access to subscription content, check out the e-mail subscription service from MailChimp at `http://mailchimp.com/features/paid-newsletter-subscriptions/`.

Blog for Dollars

You might want to try to make extra cash by providing reviews and information about products in your blog posts. You can take a direct or an indirect approach:

- ✔ **Direct approach:** Write a blog post about a product you have tested and used. For this approach, the review can be unsolicited or sponsored by a manufacturer, meaning the manufacturer will pay you to write about its product. A sponsored review doesn't mean you have to compromise your integrity and the trust your readers have for your opinion. Manufacturers should expect an honest review. Your payment for a sponsored review might be a paycheck, the product itself, or both.

  If the manufacturer lets you keep the product, you might want to offer it as a giveaway on your site. Contests such as this can increase your readership and help promote the manufacturer's product.

- ✔ **Indirect approach:** You can link to products mentioned in your content. For example, suppose you write a blog about severe weather and decide to create an entry about essential survival gear in case of evacuation. You could mention specific products that can be easily purchased on Amazon or another shopping site that offers an affiliate program. Add an affiliate link to the product, and you can earn a percentage of the sale of that product if your visitors click the link and buy the product immediately.

If you use either of these options, consider mentioning in the blog post that the review is a sponsored review or that links you provide to a product on another site help support your site using the affiliate network. Just be honest about what you're doing. It's the right thing to do.

Index

• Numerics •

301 redirects, 223
302 redirects, 223
404 page errors, 201
500px, account configuration, 205
500px blocks, 188, 190

• A •

About page, 303–305
Activity area
  comment management, 50, 236–239
  Detailed Activity statistics, 50, 234–235
  overview, 44, 49–50, 229–230
  Popular Content statistics, 49, 233–234
  Referrers statistics, 49, 232–233
  Search Queries statistics, 50, 234
  Traffic Overview statistics, 49, 230–232
AddThis, 314
Adobe Dreamweaver, 10
Adobe Typekit, 75
Advanced settings
  defined, 198
  redirecting URLs, 222–223
advertising, 318–319, 323
Amazon Associate Program, 201, 323
Amazon item blocks, 152, 161–162
analytics
  checking, 25
  detailed activity statistics, 50, 234–235
  popular content, 49, 233–234
  referrers, 49, 232–233
  search queries, 50, 234
  traffic statistics, 49, 230–232
audio blocks
  defined, 166
  determining file size, 175
  embedding audio, 174
  external links, 175
  file types, 175
  podcast settings, 175
  settings for, 174
author index blocks
  defined, 180
  numbers in parentheses, 185
  overview, 185
Avenue template, 106
Aviary photo editor
  closing, 59
  features of, 57
  mobile app, 59
  resuming edits, 59
  saving changes, 59
  steps for using, 57–59
AWeber, 316

• B •

Big Cartel, 40, 219
Big Picture Web, 320
Billing settings
  defined, 199
  updating billing information, 226–227
  upgrading trial accounts, 225–226
black & hue, 32, 306
blocks. See also Content blocks; Social blocks; Structure blocks
  adding, 141–142
  floating, 144, 147
  inserting, 144–147
  moving, 143–144
  overview, 130
  placing in columns, 144–145
  removing, 143
  separating into rows, 144–145
  types of, 141

blog pages. *See also* blogging
  attributes of, 100–101
  author information, 139
  categories, 133–134
  comments, 133–134
  defined, 100
  excerpts, 139
  featured posts, 139
  location information, 139
  post titles, 133–134
  posting via e-mail, 121–122
  posts per page, 119–121
  Quickpost bookmarklet, 123
  setting status of items, 133–134
  Simple Liking feature, 202
  social media status updates, 139–140
  tagging, 133–134
  thumbnails, 138
  URLs, 138–139
  uses for, 101
Blog post page view, 120
Blogger, 219
blogging. *See also* blog pages
  adding posts, 275–278
  blog width, 91
  frequency of posts, 121
  guest writing, 319–320
  image management, 276–277
  as item-based content, 26–27
  limiting images in posts, 121
  making money through, 327
  managing posts, 279–280
  organized content, 302
  as part of business site, 29, 31
  posting images via e-mail, 122
  posting via e-mail, 121–122
  previewing excerpts, 121
  as primary functionality of site, 28–29
  Quickpost bookmarklet, 123
  serialized content, 121
  with Squarespace app, 273, 275–280
  tagging, 27, 277
bold text
  markdown blocks, 155
  Style Editor, 87–88
  text blocks, 153

Braate, Josh, 320
branding, 308
brochure sites, 324–325
browsers
  icons, 200
  tracking those used by visitors, 232
business cards, 317–318
Business pricing plan, 40, 241
business sites. *See also* Commerce area
  blogging as part of, 29
  as primary functionality of site, 29, 31–33

• *C* •

calendar blocks
  defined, 180
  overview, 182
  settings for, 183
Campaign Monitor, 173, 316
canvas
  defined, 91
  padding, 91
captions for images, 167
Casalena, Anthony, 10
case changes, 85, 89
categories
  blog pages, 133–134
  events pages, 134–135
  images, 135–136
  summary blocks, 184
  tag cloud blocks, 184–185
  videos, 136–137
category index blocks
  defined, 180
  lists, 185
  numbers in parentheses, 186
chat technical support, 13
Chitika, 319, 323
Chrome browser, 74
clickthrough URLs, 139
CMS (content management systems; online
      website construction solutions)
  offline solutions versus, 10–11
  types of, 11
code blocks, 152, 157

Code Injection settings, 198, 220–221
collection link blocks, 180, 181
collections. *See also* blog pages; events
    pages; gallery pages; products pages
  folders, 100, 104–105
  index pages, 106
  links, 100, 105–106
  overview, 100
  pages, 99, 103–104
  title format, 201
  types of, 99–100
Colophon page, 304–305
color
  color pickers, 73
  hex color method, 73, 83
  mood boards, 72
  RGB color method, 73, 83–84
  RGBa color method, 83–84
  selecting, 82–83
  selecting color schemes, 72–73
  transparency, 83–84
  underlying code, 74
  value, 83
color pickers, 73
ColorSchemer, 73
ColorSchemerColorPix, 73
ColorZilla, 73
columns
  placing blocks in, 144–145
  placing horizontal rules at bottom of, 164
comments
  anonymous, 202
  approving, 236, 237–239
  avatar visibility, 202
  deleting, 237
  Disqus, 201, 314–315
  enabling likes, 202
  enabling/disabling, 133–134, 202, 236
  flagged, 202–203, 236, 239
  on other sites, 319
  overview, 25
  providing guidelines, 239
  replying to, 236
  settings for, 202–203
  sorting, 203
  Squarespace app, 280–282
  threading, 202

Commerce area
  Business pricing plan, 241
  Coupons area, 251, 261–263
  digital products, 243–245, 247–248, 257
  Email Notifications area, 251, 265–266
  images, 242
  Inventory area, 243, 250, 257–259
  Orders area, 250, 254–257
  overview, 44, 50–51, 241
  physical products, 243–247, 257
  product status, 244–245
  products pages, adding, 242
  products pages, adding items to, 243
  rearranging products, 250
  removing products, 250
  Shipping area, 251, 259–261
  shipping costs, 242
  Store Settings area, 251–254
  Taxes area, 251, 263–265
Connected Accounts settings
  connecting accounts, 204
  defined, 198
  disconnecting accounts, 206
  overview, 203–204
  supported websites, 205–206
Constant Contact, 173, 316
Contact page, 305–307
content
  adding and updating, 24–25
  considering when planning social media
    integration, 28
  design related to, 308–309
  exclusive, 325–327
  optimized for search engines, 302–303
  organized, 301–302
Content blocks
  adding, 152
  Amazon item blocks, 152, 161–162
  audio blocks, 166, 174–175
  code blocks, 152, 157
  defined, 141
  embed blocks, 166, 172–173
  external link blocks, 152, 161
  form blocks, 152, 158–160
  gallery blocks, 165, 167–171
  horizontal rule blocks, 152, 164
  image blocks, 165–167

Content blocks *(continued)*
  map blocks, 166, 176–177
  markdown blocks, 152, 154–156
  overview, 48, 151
  product blocks, 152, 162–163
  quote blocks, 152, 156
  space blocks, 152, 163–164
  text blocks, 152–154
  video blocks, 165, 171–172
content management systems (CMS; online
    website construction solutions)
  offline solutions versus, 10–11
  types of, 11
Content Manager
  accessing, 107
  block management, 130, 141–147, 152
  blog pages, 119–123
  disabling pages, 118–119
  Edit... dialog boxes, 132–140
  enabling pages, 119
  folder collections, modifying, 125–126
  link collection items, modifying settings,
    126–127
  navigation areas, 108–113, 123–124
  navigation title, 114
  opening Configure dialog box, 113
  overview, 44, 48
  page descriptions, 114–115
  page items, 129–132, 140
  page title, 114
  passwords, 116
  sections of, 107–108
  setting page as home page, 118
  thumbnails, 117
  URLs, 115
Contributors settings
  adding contributors, 209–210
  defined, 198
  modifying invitations, 211
  modifying permissions, 211–212
  permissions, 209
  removing contributors, 211
Coupons area, Commerce
  creating coupons, 261–263
  defined, 251

cropping images
  avoiding automatic cropping of image
    focus, 56–57
  Slideshow display option, gallery
    blocks, 170
CSS, 81

• D •

Daring Fireball, 154, 156
Daughhetee, Adam, 29
deleting
  comments, 237
  folder collections, 125–126
  links, 127
  pages from navigation areas, 110–112
  text blocks, 154
desktop (offline) website construction
    applications, 10–11
Detailed Activity statistics, 50, 234–235
Developer accounts, 14, 224
Developer Center, 14
Developer settings, 223–224
  defined, 198
digital products
  defined, 243
  order processing, 257
  pricing and uploading, 244–245, 247–248
Disqus, 201, 314–315
DNS settings, 215
Dollar Bin Comics, 22–23, 29, 303
Domains settings
  defined, 198
  overview, 212–213
  pointing existing domains to
    Squarespace, 215–216
  registering free domains from
    Squarespace, 214
  transferring Squarespace-managed
    domains, 213–214
Dovetail template, 115
Dribbble, 205
Dropbox, 206, 289–290

• E •

Ecwid, 323
Edit... dialog boxes
  Edit Amazon Item dialog box, 161–162
  Edit Audio dialog box, 174–175
  Edit Calendar dialog box, 183
  Edit Code dialog box, 157
  Edit Collection Link dialog box, 181, 182
  Edit Coupon dialog box, 262–263
  Edit Embed dialog box, 172–173
  Edit Event dialog box, 134–135
  Edit Foursquare Block dialog box, 189–190
  Edit Gallery dialog box, 167–169
  Edit Horizontal Rule dialog box, 164
  Edit Image dialog box, 135–136, 166–167
  Edit Instagram Block dialog box, 191
  Edit Map dialog box, 176–177
  Edit Post dialog box, 133–134
  Edit Product dialog box, 163, 243–249
  Edit Quote dialog box, 156
  Edit Social Links dialog box, 193–194
  Edit Summary dialog box, 184
  Edit Tag Cloud dialog box, 184–185
  Edit Twitter Block dialog box, 191–192
  Edit Video dialog box, 136–137, 171–172
  Item section, 132–137
  Location section, 133, 139
  Options section, 132, 137–139
  overview, 132–133
  Social section, 133, 139–140
E-Junkie, 323
element width, 77–78
elevator pitches, 316–317
e-mail
  automatic stock level alert, 253
  Connected Accounts settings, 206
  connecting Note app to, 290–291
  custom addresses, 308
  customer notification, 265–266
  customer support, 253
  marketing through, 315–316
  newsletter services, 173, 253, 316, 326
  order processing, 256

posting via, 121–122
sending form submissions via, 160
sending images as attachments, 296
signatures, 318
technical support, 12–13
Email Notifications area, Commerce
  customizing messages, 265–266
  defined, 251
  testing messages, 266
embed blocks
  defined, 166
  digital file services, 173
  e-mail newsletter services, 173
  form-building services, 173
  overview, 172
Esc key
  accessing personal website via, 41
  disabling login page display, 202
events pages
  attributes of, 102
  author information, 139
  categories, 134–135
  end date, 134–135
  event titles, 134–135
  excerpts, 139
  layout formats, 101
  location information, 139
  start date, 134–135
  tagging, 134–135
  URLs, 138–139
Evernote, 72, 289–290
express checkout, 253
external link blocks
  defined, 152
  settings for, 161

• F •

Facebook
  Connected Accounts settings, 205
  connecting Note app to, 289–290
  Like button, 314
  search engine optimization, 303
  Share Buttons settings, 208
  signing up for, 312

Facebook Page settings, 198, 206–207
FedEx, 242
Filtered page view, 120
Firefox browser, 74
Five template
    overview, 22–23
    previewing, 64
    Read Me page, 64–65
    thumbnails, 117
500px, account configuration, 205
500px blocks, 188, 190
Flatiron template, 106
Flickr, 188, 205
Flickr blocks, 188, 190
focus ring, 56–57
folder collections
    adding, 125
    deleting, 125–126
    disabling, 126
    modifying settings, 125
    overview, 100, 104–105
fonts. *See also* text
    body, 76
    bold, 87–88
    font style, 85, 87–88
    font weight, 87–88
    font-family, 85
    headlines, 76
    italics, 87
    letter spacing, 85
    line height, 85
    overview, 84–85
    previewing, 85–86
    selecting, 76
    selecting fonts, 85–86
    supported, 74–75
    text decoration, 85
    text size, 77–78, 85–87
    text transform, 85
    titles, 76
footers
    injecting code into, 221
    in outline (sitemap), 21
    padding, 91

form blocks
    advanced settings, 160
    changing storage options, 160
    creating and following business leads, 322
    customizing elements, 159
    default elements, 158
    defined, 152
    moving elements, 159
    storing form submissions, 160
    Unlimited and Business plan elements,
        158–159
Formstack, 173
404 page errors, 201
Foursquare, 188, 206
Foursquare blocks, 188, 192–193
FoxyCart, 323
Fusion Ads, 323

• *G* •

gallery blocks
    defined, 165
    Grid display option, 170–171
    overview, 30, 167–168
    pulling images from gallery pages, 168
    Slider display option, 170
    Slideshow display option, 169–170
    Stacked display option, 171
    uploading images to, 168
gallery pages
    author information, 139
    categories, image, 135–136
    categories, video, 136–137
    descriptions, 135–136
    embedding videos, 136–137
    excerpts, 139
    image overlay for videos, 136–137
    location information, 139
    overview, 102
    Portfolio app, 293–298
    social media status updates, 139–140
    tagging, images, 135–136
    tagging, videos, 136–137

thumbnails for videos, 136–137
titles, image, 135–136
titles, video, 136–137
uploading images, 135–136
URLs, 138–139
General settings
  comment settings, 202–203
  defined, 198
  overall site configurations, 201–202
  third-party services, 200–201
GitHub, 206
Go Daddy, 215
goal setting, 17–18
Google AdSense, 323
Google AdWords, 319
Google Analytics, 200–201
Google Apps, 308
Google Docs, 160
Google Drive, 289–290
Google Maps, 139
Google web fonts, 75
Google Webmasters Account, 303
Google+, 13, 205, 208
Grid display option, gallery blocks, 170–171
Gruber, John, 154, 156
guest writing, 319–320

• *H* •

headers
  images, 76–77
  injecting code into, 221
  logos, 77
heading styles, 153, 155
Help & Support settings, 199, 227–228
help resources
  Developer Center, 14
  e-mail technical support, 12–13
  Google+ Hangout, 13
  Help & Support settings, 227–228
  knowledge base, 12
  live chat, 13
  Squarespace Answers community help, 14
  video tutorials, 13
  workshops, 13

hex (hexadecimal) color method, 73, 83
hidden content
  allowing users to find, 124
  uses for, 124
home page
  setting page as, 118
  title format, 201
HootSuite, 309
horizontal rule blocks, 152, 164
How Secure Is My Password? site, 38, 272
Hudson template, 78, 106

• *I* •

image blocks
  defined, 165
  options for, 166–167
  overview, 166–167
image galleries
  as item-based content, 27
  as part of portfolio sites, 30
image overlay for videos, 136–137, 172
images
  author information, 139
  background, 77
  categories, 135–136
  descriptions, 135–136
  editing, 55, 57–59
  header, 76–77
  limiting in posts, 121
  location information, 139
  Portfolio app, 293–297
  posting via e-mail, 122
  product, 242, 244, 249
  removing, 55
  setting focus of, 56–57
  Squarespace app, 276–277
  tagging, 135–136
  thumbnails, 91, 117, 136–137, 170–172, 182, 249
  titles, 135–136
  uploading, 52–53, 135–136
  URLs, 138–139
Immaculate Consumption, 31, 306–307

Import/Export settings
  defined, 198
  exporting content from Squarespace,
    219–220
  importing content from other websites, 219
  overview, 218–219
index pages, 106, 108
Instagram, 188, 206
Instagram blocks, 188, 190
Internet Explorer browser, 74
Inventory area, Commerce
  adding products via, 243, 258–259
  defined, 250
  product information, 257–258
Invite Contributor dialog box, 209–210
Issuu, 173
italic text
  markdown blocks, 155
  Style Editor, 87
item-based pages, 26–27, 100. *See also* blog
    pages; events pages; gallery pages;
    products pages
iTunes, 175

• J •

Jenson template, 106
Jirick template, 106
JotForm, 173

• K •

Kaikkonen, Tommi, 76
kerning (letter spacing), 85, 88
knowledge base, 12
Kontera, 319, 323
Kris Black Studio, 304–305

• L •

language settings, 203
LayoutEngine
  arranging content in rows, 32
  floating blocks, 144, 147

inserting blocks, 144–147
location of, 48, 107–108
moving blocks, 143–144
placing blocks in columns, 144–145
separating blocks into rows, 144–145
letter spacing (kerning), 85, 88
Life's Little Hiccups, 27
Lightbox mode
  gallery blocks, 171, 191
  image blocks, 167
Likert form element, 158
line height, 88–89
link collections
  adding items, 126–127
  deleting links, 127
  overview, 100
  uses for, 105–106
LinkedIn, 206, 208
links
  Clickthrough URL setting, 54
  to content, 54
  creating from images, 167–168
  creating from text, 153, 155
  external, 54, 139
  external link blocks, 152, 161
  to files, 54
  to hosted audio, 175
  Link icon, 53
  overview, 53–55
Lock page, 221
logos
  branding, 308
  header images and, 77
  Site settings, 200
  sizing, 91

• M •

MailChimp, 40, 160, 173, 253, 316, 326
map blocks
  defined, 166
  Map and Satellite views, 177
  overview, 176
  settings for, 177
  sizing maps, 177

markdown blocks
  defined, 152
  formatting strip, 143
  overview, 154–156
  replacing text blocks with, 202
  styling options, 155
media-based blocks
  audio blocks, 166, 174–175
  embed blocks, 166, 172–173
  gallery blocks, 30, 165, 167–171
  image blocks, 165–167
  map blocks, 166, 176–177
  video blocks, 165, 171–172
message
  considering when planning social media
    integration, 28
  focusing, 18
Microsoft Expression, 10
Minsk template, 106
Mobile Apps settings, 198
mobile device integration
  Note app, 284–293
  Portfolio app, 293–298
  Squarespace app, 267–284
Modify Invitation dialog box, 211
Modify Permissions dialog box, 211–212
Montauk template, 106
month index blocks
  defined, 180
  lists, 185
  numbers in parentheses, 186
mood boards, 72

• *N* •

Native template, 65
navigation areas, Content Manager
  adding pages to, 112–113
  deleting pages from, 110–112
  effect of changing templates, 109
  Footer, 108–109
  Index, 108–109

Main/Top, 108–109
Not Linked, 108–110, 112, 123–124
positioning pages in, 109–110
restoring deleted pages, 111
Secondary, 108–109
too many pages, 109–110
navigation title, 114
Nelson, Nikole, 30
Nettica, 215
Network Solutions, 215
Nikole Nelson, 30
Note app
  configuring accounts to receive notes,
    290–291
  connecting to accounts, 284–287
  default destinations, 291–292
  editing notes, 292–293
  modifying account list, 288–289
  removing notes, 292
  sending notes, 287
  settings for, 287–288
numbered lists
  markdown blocks, 155
  text blocks, 153

• *O* •

online website construction solutions
    (content management systems [CMS])
  offline solutions versus, 10–11
  types of, 11
operating systems, tracking those used by
    visitors, 232
Orders area, Commerce
  defined, 250
  exporting orders to spreadsheets, 257
  order management, 255–257
  status categories, 254
outlines (sitemaps)
  footer and social networking links, 21
  main navigation, 20–21
  overview, 19–20

• P •

padding
  elements, 91
  Grid display thumbnails, gallery blocks, 170–171
page items
  adding, 130–131
  adding content to, 140
  overview, 129–130
  removing, 132
  setting status of, 132
page pages
  overview, 99
  uses for, 103–104
page title, 114
page views
  tracking, 231
  tracking with Squarespace app, 283
pages. *See also* blog pages; events pages; gallery pages; products pages
  folders, 100, 104–105
  index pages, 106
  links, 100, 105–106
  overview, 100
  pages, 99, 103–104
  title format, 201
  types of, 99–100
passwords
  to access exclusive content by subscription, 325–326
  adding to pages, 116
  changing, 116, 273
  creating secure, 38, 272
  forgotten, 42
  Lock page, 221
  removing, 116
  site-wide, 201
patterns as backgrounds, 77
PayPal, 323, 325–326
Peak template, 117
physical products
  defined, 243

order processing, 257
pricing and variants, 244–247
Pinterest, 72, 205, 208
placeholder text, 159
podcast settings, audio blocks, 175
Popular Content statistics, 49, 233–234
Portfolio app
  Collection screen, 297
  connecting to accounts, 294–296
  Gallery screen, 297
  overview, 293–294
  settings for, 297–298
  viewing images, 296–297
portfolios
  blogging as part of, 29, 31
  creating, 324
  image galleries, 30
  as item-based content, 27
  as primary functionality of site, 29–31
Preview area
  Content mode, 46
  moving toolbar, 47
  overview, 44–45
  Style mode, 47
Preview Editor toolbar, 80
pricing plans
  Business plan, 40, 241
  coupon codes, 322
  discounts, 321–322
  Standard plan, 39
  Unlimited plan, 39–40
printed materials, promotion through, 317–318
product blocks
  defined, 152
  overview, 162–163
  product pages versus, 163
products pages
  adding, 242
  adding items to, 243
  overview, 102–103
  product blocks versus, 163
promotion codes, 262
Pulley, 323

• Q •

Qubert template, 78, 106
Quickpost bookmarklet, 123
quote blocks, 152, 156
quote styling
  markdown blocks, 155
  text blocks, 153

• R •

Read Me page, 64–65
Really Simple Syndication (RSS) feeds, 315
Reddit, 208
Referrers statistics, 49, 232–233
refunds, 257
RGB color method, 73, 83–84
RGBa color method, 83–84
robot hits, tracking, 232, 234, 283
RSS (Really Simple Syndication) feeds, 315

• S •

Safari browser, 74
sale prices, 246–247
Scribd, 173
search blocks, 180, 181
search engine optimization (SEO)
  dashes in URL, 115
  meta description, 200
  overview, 302–303
  page descriptions, 114
  resources for, 320
  robot hits, tracking, 232, 234
  routinely adding content, 25
  site title, 200
  text style, 90
Search Queries statistics, 50, 234
Select Product Type dialog box, 258–259
SEO. *See* search engine optimization
Sessions settings
  active login session tracking, 224–225
  defined, 198

Share Buttons settings
  defined, 198
  helping others share content, 313
  overview, 207–208
  supported websites, 208
Shipping area, Commerce
  adding shipping methods, 259–261
  country restrictions, 260–261
  defined, 251
  shipping costs, 260
Shopify, 40, 219
shopping carts
  styles, 253
  third-party solutions, 323–324
Site Manager. *See also* Activity area;
    Commerce area; Content Manager;
    Preview area; Site Settings
  accessing, 46–47
  switching between websites, 49
Site Settings
  accessing, 198
  Advanced settings, 198, 222–223
  Billing settings, 199, 225–227
  Code Injection settings, 198, 220–221
  Connected Accounts settings, 198,
    203–206
  Contributors settings, 198, 209–212
  defined, 198
  Developer settings, 198, 223–224
  Domains settings, 198, 212–216
  Facebook Page settings, 198, 206–207
  General settings, 198, 200–203
  Help & Support settings, 199, 227–228
  Import/Export settings, 198, 218–220
  Mobile Apps settings, 198
  overview, 44, 50, 199–200
  Sessions settings, 198, 224–225
  Share Buttons settings, 198, 207–208, 313
  Site settings, 198–200
  Templates settings, 198, 216–218
  Time/Geography settings, 198, 203
sitemaps (outlines)
  footer and social networking links, 21
  main navigation, 20–21
  overview, 19–20
site-relative URLs, 216

sizing
  blog width, 91
  elements, 90–91
  images, 167
  logos, 91
  maps, 177
  padding, 91
  page width, 91
  site width, 91
  social media icons, 91
  space blocks, 163–164
  text, 77–78, 85–87
  thumbnails, 91
  using space blocks, 163–164
SKU (stock-keeping unit), 246
Slider display option, gallery blocks, 170
Slideshare, 173
Slideshow display option, gallery blocks,
    169–170
SmugMug, 206
Social blocks
  500px blocks, 188, 190
  connecting social accounts to, 188–190
  defined, 141
  Flickr blocks, 188, 190
  Foursquare blocks, 188, 192–193
  Instagram blocks, 188, 190
  listing social accounts, 193–194
  overview, 48, 187
  social links blocks, 193–194
  supported websites, 188
  Twitter blocks, 188, 191–192
social links blocks, 193–194
social media icons
  displaying, 205
  sizing, 91
  styles, 92
social media integration
  Connected Accounts settings, 203–206
  as item-based content, 28
  links in outline (sitemap), 21
  notification of new items, 245, 249–250
  overview, 28, 309
  website promotion, 311–315
source URLs, 139
space blocks, 152, 163–164

spam, 209, 237, 281–282
Sprout Social, 309
Squarespace
  accessing personal website, 41–42
  history of, 10
  home page, 36
  image management, 52–53, 55—59
  link management, 53–55
  pricing plans, 38–40, 321–322
  signing up for, 11, 35–38
  support services, 12–14, 227–228
  supported browsers, 74
  switching between websites, 49
  template selection page, 36
  versatility of, 14–16
  website hosting via, 11–12
Squarespace Answers community help, 14
Squarespace app
  adding existing accounts, 268–270
  blogging, 274–280
  comment management, 280–282
  configuring accounts, 272–274
  creating accounts, 270–272
  overview, 267
  removing accounts, 274
  statistics and analytics, 283–284
Squarespace Google+ Hangout, 13
Squarespace knowledge base, 12
Squarespace videos, 13
Squareverse, 22
Stacked display option, gallery blocks, 171
Standard pricing plan, 39
static content, examples of, 26
statistics
  checking, 25
  detailed activity statistics, 50, 234–235
  popular content, 49, 233–234
  referrers, 49, 232–233
  search queries, 50, 234
  traffic statistics, 49, 230–232
stock-keeping unit (SKU), 246
Store Settings area, Commerce
  automatic stock level alert e-mail, 253
  connecting to Stripe, 251–253
  customer support e-mail, 253
  defined, 251

express checkout, 253
measurement standard, 253
newsletter, 253
shopping cart style, 253
store policies, 254
Stripe payment-processing service
Business plan, 40
connecting site to, 251–253
Structure blocks
adding and setting up, 180–181
author index blocks, 180, 185
calendar blocks, 180, 182–183
category index blocks, 180, 185–186
collection link blocks, 180–181
defined, 141
month index blocks, 180, 185–186
overview, 48, 179–180
search blocks, 180–181
summary blocks, 180, 183–184
tag cloud blocks, 180, 184–185
tag index blocks, 180, 185–186
StumbleUpon, 208
Style Editor
accessing, 47, 79–80
aligning elements, 92
case changes, 89
color, 82–83
element resizing, 90–91
exiting, 80–81
font customization, 84–88
hiding/revealing elements, 84, 92
letter spacing, 88
line height, 88–89
mobile-specific settings, 92
moving elements, 92
overview, 79
resetting changes, 94–95
saving changes, 92–93
sections of, 81
selecting elements, 81–82
social media icons, 92
testing changes, 93–94
transparency, 83–84
style selection, 22–24
Subtle Patterns, 77

summary blocks
defined, 180
overview, 183
settings for, 184
support services
Developer Center, 14
e-mail technical support, 12–13
Google+ Hangout, 13
Help & Support settings, 227–228
knowledge base, 12
live chat, 13
Squarespace Answers community help, 14
video tutorials, 13
workshops, 13

• *T* •

tag cloud blocks
defined, 180
overview, 184
settings for, 185
tag index blocks
defined, 180
lists, 185
numbers in parentheses, 186
tags
blog pages, 133–134
defining, 27
events pages, 134–135
images, 135–136
Squarespace app, 277
summary blocks, 184
videos, 136–137
target audience
considering when planning social media
integration, 28
defining, 18
focusing message based on, 18
Taxes area, Commerce
country tax rules, 263–264
defined, 251
state tax rules, 264–265
tax rate information, 263
templates. *See also* Style Editor
changing, 67–69, 216–217
customizing, 22–23

templates *(continued)*
effects of changing, 67, 69, 109
enabling, 217–218
mobile styles, 201
overview, 11, 63
for portfolio sites, 30
previewing, 64, 67–68, 216–217
promoted blocks, 201
Read Me page, 64–65
resetting customizations, 93–94
saving changes to, 92–93
selecting, 22, 37, 66
testing customized, 93–94
versatility of, 66–67
viewing customer sites using chosen
    template, 66–67
Templates settings
changing templates, 216–217
defined, 198
enabling templates, 217–218
previewing templates, 216–217
text
alignment, 153
body, 76
bold, 87–88, 153, 155
case changes, 85, 89
dividing with blocks, 146
floating blocks next to, 147
font style, 85, 87–88
font weight, 87–88
font-family, 85
heading styles, 153, 155
headlines, 76
italics, 87, 155
letter spacing, 85, 88
line height, 85, 88–89
link styling, 153, 155
numbered lists, 153, 155
overview, 84–85
previewing fonts, 85–86
quote styling, 153, 155
selecting fonts, 76, 85–86
size, 77–78, 85–87
supported, 74–75
text decoration, 85, 87–88

text transform, 85, 89
titles, 76
unordered lists, 153, 155
wrapping, 147
text blocks
defined, 152
deleting, 154
formatting strip, 143
overview, 152–154
replacing with markdown blocks, 202
styling options, 153
TextLinkAds, 319, 323
textures as backgrounds, 77
301 redirects, 223
302 redirects, 223
thumbnails
blog posts, 138
collection link blocks, 182
Grid display option, gallery blocks,
    170–171
padding, 91
product, 249
sizing, 91
Slideshow display option, gallery
    blocks, 170
uploading for pages, 117
video blocks, 172
for videos, 136–137
Time/Geography settings, 198, 203
timelines, establishing for project, 24
Traffic Overview statistics, 49, 230–232
transparency, 83–84
trial accounts, upgrading, 225–226
Tumblr
Connected Accounts settings, 206
importing content from, 219
Share Buttons settings, 208
Twitter
Connected Accounts settings, 206
connecting Note app to, 289–290
embedding Tweets, 172
Share Buttons settings, 208
Tweet button, 314
Twitter blocks, 188, 191–192
Twitter form element, 158

Twitterfeed, 312–313
Typekit, 200–201
typography, 76. *See also* fonts

• *U* •

unique visitors, 231, 283
United States Postal Service (USPS), 242
Unlimited pricing plan, 39–40
unordered lists
  markdown blocks, 155
  text blocks, 153
UPS, 242
URLs
  changing, 115, 138
  clickthrough, 138
  custom domains, 307–308, 320
  Domains settings, 212–216
  redirecting, 222–223
  shortening services, 312
  site-relative, 216
  source, 138
USPS (United States Postal Service), 242

• *V* •

video blocks
  defined, 165
  overview, 171
  settings for, 171–172
video tutorials, 13
videos
  author information, 139
  categories, 136–137
  embedding, 136–137
  excerpts, 139
  image overlay, 136–137, 172
  location information, 139
  tagging, 136–137
  thumbnails, 136–137
  titles, 136–137
  URLs, 138–139
Vimeo, 171, 205

visitors
  browsers used by, 232
  operating systems used by, 232
  page views, 231
  popular content, 233–234
  referrers, 232–233, 284
  search queries made by, 234, 284
  tracking, 230–232
  tracking with Squarespace app, 283
  unique, 231, 283

• *W* •

web forms
  advanced settings, 160
  for business sites, 33
  changing storage options, 160
  creating and following business leads, 322
  customizing elements, 159
  default elements, 158
  defined, 152
  form blocks, 158–159
  form-building services, 173
  as item-based content, 28
  moving elements, 159
  overview, 28
  storing form submissions, 160
  submission maintenance, 25
  Unlimited and Business plan elements,
    158–159
web typography, 76
website construction
  accessing Content Manager, 107
  block management, 130, 141–147
  blog pages, 119–123
  collections, 99–106
  disabling pages, 118–119
  Edit... dialog boxes, 132–140
  enabling pages, 119
  folder collections, modifying, 125–126
  link collection items, modifying settings,
    126–127
  navigation areas, 108–113, 123–124
  navigation title, 114
  opening Configure dialog box, 113

website construction *(continued)*
    page descriptions, 114–115
    page items, 129–132, 140
    page title, 114
    passwords, 116
    setting page as home page, 118
    thumbnails, 117
    URLs, 115
    via coding, 9
    via desktop applications, 10
    via online solutions, 10–11
website design
    accessing Style Editor, 79–80
    aligning elements, 92
    case changes, 89
    color, 72–74, 82–84
    element resizing, 90–91
    element width, 77–78
    exiting, 81
    features of good websites, 301–310
    font customization, 84–88
    fonts, 74–76
    hiding/revealing elements, 84, 92
    images, 76–77
    letter spacing, 88
    line height, 88–89
    mobile-specific settings, 92
    moving elements, 92
    overview, 71–72, 79
    resetting changes, 94–95
    saving changes, 92–93
    selecting elements, 81–82
    social media icons, 92
    templates, 63–69
    testing changes, 93–94
    text size, 77–78
website hosting via Squarespace, 11–12
website maintenance
    comments, 25
    form submissions, 25
    regular, 309–310
website management
    activity statistics, 50, 234–235
    checking statistics, 25
    popular content, 49, 233–234
    referrers, 49, 232–233
    search queries, 50, 234
    traffic statistics, 49, 230–232

website planning
    adding and updating content, 24–25
    defining target audience, 18
    focusing message, 18
    goal setting, 17–18
    item-based content, 26–27
    outline, 19–21
    primary functionality, 28–33
    project timeline, 24
    social media integration, 28
    static content, 26
    style selection, 22–24
    web forms, 28
website promotion
    overview, 324
    through advertising, 318–319
    through commenting, 319
    through custom domains, 320
    through elevator pitches, 316–317
    through e-mail marketing, 315–316
    through e-mail signatures, 318
    through guest writing, 319–320
    through social media, 311–315
    through word of mouth, 317
    through written word, 317–318
Wikipedia article on web color, 73
Wiley, 304
Wistia, 171
word-of-mouth promotion, 317
WordPress
    exporting content to, 219–220
    importing content from, 219
workshops, 13
Wufoo, 173

xScope, 73

YouTube, 171, 205